AN

EARNEST MINISTRY

THE

WANT OF THE TIMES.

BY

JOHN ANGELL JAMES.

WITH AN

INTRODUCTION.

BY

Rev. JONATHAN B. CONDIT, D. D.,

Professor of Sacred Rhetoric and Pastoral Theology in Auburn Theological Seminary, N. Y.

PHILADELPHIA:
PRESBYTERIAN BOARD OF PUBLICATION,
No. 821 Chestnut Street.

NOTICE.

THIS work was republished a number of years ago in the city of New York, and had at that time an extensive circulation. But it gradually disappeared from the market, and for some years has been out of print or not procurable, although often inquired for.

A generous friend of the Board of Publication recently found an opportunity to purchase the stereotype plates, which he did wholly at his own cost, and presented them to the Board, which is thus enabled, advantageously to the Church and to itself, to reproduce this valuable book.

There are some references in the volume to persons and to local circumstances peculiar to Great Britain which, some may suppose, could have been omitted with advantage from this new issue. But after a careful examination and much reflection and counsel, it has been deemed best, to avoid any possible charge of injustice to the author, who has within a few years gone up to his reward, to reissue it without alteration or abridgment. Let it, however, be borne in mind that it was originally intended more especially for British readers.

The volume is now sent forth afresh, with the earnest hope of all concerned that it may carry new life and a blessing from on high to the ministry of our American Presbyterian Church, and especially to our more youthful ministers.

EDITOR OF THE BOARD.

Philadelphia, A. D. 1868.

INTRODUCTION.

By the Rev. JONATHAN B. CONDIT, D.D.

The Christian ministry, in its character and work, is a subject of growing interest in this country. During the last twenty-five years it has been the object of much effort to furnish a sufficient number of men to meet the demand. The claims of the office have been set forth strongly in view of our extending and destitute population. Institutions have been multiplied for the purpose of educating men for the work. So deeply has this necessity been felt, and so many were the agencies to be organized and sustained to supply it, that we have been in danger of thinking too little of the *character* of the ministry. While the efforts to increase its numbers ought not to be diminished, it must not be forgotten that a numerous ministry may not be an efficient one.

Many, it is believed, will rejoice in the appearance of this work by Mr. James, who has presented the subject, in one of its departments, in a most impressive manner, If the respected author had written for American readers, doubtless some things would have been omitted. But nothing will be found in the book to hinder its usefulness.

It is obvious that the subject has deeply interested the mind of the writer. An earnest heart guides his able pen. No minister, or candidate for the ministry, can read the book without receiving a deep impression of the greatness of the trust and some valuable aid in the discharge of it.

It is generally acknowledged, that we must rely on the living ministry as the principal agency for the extension of the Gospel in this land, not simply in view of the prominence which Christ has given it in his word, and in the progress of the church, but because of its adaptation to the condition and character of the people.

The mind of this nation presents some remarkable features in its present character and position, deeply interesting to the Christian as well as the philosopher and statesman. It is an intellectual life which is not marked by the quiet pursuit of its object, but by an incessant and hurried movement. It is not the intellectual action of a few, concentrating in one constellation the light of the age, but it involves the entire people. It is pre-eminently a diffused mental activity. The superiority of mental energy is acknowledged from the town-hall of the country village, to the chamber of the senate. If this action is somewhat superficial, and if it is often sustained by unhealthy means, yet it is everywhere discernible.

This mind is not of one common type, not having been educated under the same political institutions, nor taken the impress of any one system of religious faith. Many old erroneous opinions, as well as new, have their adherents, and are struggling for prevalence over the truth. We have a mixture of intellectual and moral elements, strikingly diverse. Tributaries from every quarter of the globe are finding their way into our stream, and must ultimately impart to it their different hues. We wonder not that the wisest are unable to foretell what is to be the result in respect to the strength and permanence of government or the religious character of coming generations. We wonder not that we witness the conflict of thought and feeling; or that we are sometimes shaken with a sudden and violent concussion. These cross-currents of mind will be likely to keep up a deep agitation.

We must have a religious agency which is fitted to meet this posture of things. It must be that which will powerfully arrest mind, in the midst of its warm conflicts, and bring the Gospel in its full power to the sympathies and hearts of the people. It must be that which will come in where worldliness, ignorance, and corruption reign, with resources adapted to overcome prejudice, supplant error, and lay broad and permanent foundations for the reign of truth and righteouness. It must possess the wisdom, energy, and facility in action to meet character and opinion of every type, and with the divine blessing to mould them according to the truth and law of God.

To what agency do such qualifications belong, if not to the Christian ministry? It comes with the power of a living character, visibly illustrating and practically enforcing the truth. By its ever-living presence it encompasses mind with an attracting and moulding influence. To this, it adds the wondrous influence of oral delivery. We impute no magic charm to the human voice and countenance. Yet that voice is made to speak the truth in tones which move the heart. In the human face there is a strange power of speech. It is the language of the soul kindling into sympathy with it the souls of the hearers. Reason about it as we may, the fact is as wonderful now as it ever was. There is no example of influence over mind more simple and sublime than that of a man of God in the earnest delivery of the gospel message. He does not exert it by means of unholy stratagem or mere novelties in style and action, but by the exhibition of truth on old, familiar themes, with old and familiar tones. But he exhibits that truth with a heart all glowing under its power. He separates his hearers from the associations of worldly business, and gathers them into the presence of Jehovah. He charges their sins against them, arraigns them at the bar of God, and pronounces their doom as impenitent men. Now he collects over them the clouds of Divine wrath, and then he draws them around the cross and makes them hear the winning voice of the Redeemer. He does it with the strength and courage imparted by confidence in God, but with the humility and love of a man and a sinner. They love to hear the tones of such a voice; to feel the power of that speaking eye, as that voice and that eye utter the gushing thoughts of a spirit intensely moved in sympathy with them. What reader of Edwards' sermon, entitled "Sinners in the hands of an angry God," is impressed as they were who heard him utter it in the solemn earnestness of the pulpit? We read the sermons of Whitfield without the realization of the power which accompanied his preaching. We by no means attribute the astonishing effects of his preaching only to his look, tone, and action as a speaker. We forget not that these were the expression of a soul, into the depths of which the truth had come with a penetrating, awakening influence, and that the power of God attended him. Yet, in his ready speech, so as never "to stumble at a word, and never to stop for the want of one;" in his natural gracefulness and inimitable power of action; in his ability "to paint with all the effect of real scenery," and to make sinners tremble, as if about to sink into perdition, and even believe themselves doomed as in the tone and air of a judge he pronounced the sentence, "Depart!"—we have those qualities which constitute the peculiar advantage of the preacher in gaining attention to the truth, and which are worthy of being diligently cultivated.

Now we affirm that in view of the genius and habits of our people, we must look to the living ministry to do a great work in this nation. Such an agency will accord with the method of awakening and guiding mind in other departments of thought and action among all classes. If this is true of the older sections of the country, it is even more characteristic of communities less enlightened, and less disciplined to the patient study of truth. The people are accustomed to instruction and persuasion by the earnest speaker. So the voice of the living preacher must obtain the ear of the people, as, with the Bible in his hand, he unfolds its doctrines, if these glorious truths find a lodgment, and mould the mind and character of successive generations. We tremble to think of the amazing responsibility resting on the gospel ministry in its relation to our country's salvation. In view of its intrusted work, what importance belongs to its spirit and character. How shall it execute its trust without a large endowment of the graces of the Spirit, and a Christ-like devotion and self-denial?

In view of the work which it is called to perform, the Christian ministry in this land must be eminently *spiritual* and *practical* in its character. The importance of a complete intellectual furniture is not disputed. The point is settled that the men who are to occupy the sacred office must have the opportunity for making thorough literary and theological attainments. The demand for learning in the ministry is too loud to be disregarded. Wherever the preacher finds his field of action, he will have occasion for the most skilful use of the best weapons. Let him not venture forth into the field of battle without full armor. But if the result of that intellectual training is to appear in abstract, philosophical preaching, the American pulpit will never accomplish its appropriate work. Far off be the day when the ministers of Christ shall exalt metaphysical subtleties above the doctrine of the cross; when they shall seek to attain skill in frigid argumentation, rather than a holy facility in the spiritual and practical work of guiding souls to Christ and to heaven; when intellectual gratification shall be more thought of than the edification of the humble Christian; in their mode of exhibiting truth, overlooking the spiritual wants and difficulties of the common mind. Such ministers will make the pulpit jejune and powerless in respect to its most essential objects. Their cold light will shine without touching the hearts of men. They will defeat the mission of truth from the throne to this world of sin and darkness. They cannot compass the mighty work which God puts into their hands.

We need a ministry whose intellectual furniture and energy have come under the influence of a spiritual piety, nurtured in communion with Christ. Then it will be "strong and do exploits." The preacher must not only know what conscience is, but how to reach it with the truth. He must know what is the hungering of a soul after the bread of life, and how to divide and distribute the word so as to satisfy the hungry. It must be the "living bread," and not the speculations of the theorist, however expert he may be; that which will be the element of vigor and life to the spiritual man. To show unto men the way of salvation, he must regard as the object worthy of his most select and untiring efforts. The practical rules of

Christian living, must be his familiar themes of discourse. Hence scholastic learning is not enough, lest he be a mere scholastic preacher. Rhetorical rules, however thoroughly mastered, are not enough, lest he be a mere orator. His investigations of truth, though pursued with enthusiasm, and presented in elaborate discussion, will affect no human heart, if they are not made to bear directly on the repentance, faith, and sanctification of men. If his commission as minister of the gospel is executed in a manner appropriate to its high designs, he must be a man skilled in the workings of the human soul, interested in all the relations of common life, and apt in the inculcation of truth with regard to all the difficulties and duties of those relations; while he is absorbed in the one great object for which Christ died.

This characteristic of the ministry is worthy to be greatly exalted above the observance of any one law in the structure of sermons. Yet this is not a point of little moment. We should much regret if the American pulpit should ever become chiefly hortatory. Examples have proved that the pulpit has lost power when the hortatory style has been habitually adopted. Earnestness in the pulpit is entirely consistent with a discriminating and instructive exhibition of truth. It is by no means supposed that this can only be done with written discourses. Yet, while some are eminent for such a style of preaching, who seldom write, we believe if this practice should become universal, the instances would be multiplied in which the permanent interest and power of the pulpit would not be sustained. It is admitted that the *immediate* effects of Payson's preaching were often most striking in connection with some of his unwritten discourses. But this might not have been, if he had not preached one written sermon every Sab bath. This, his practice, was doubtless indispensable to make his ministry what it was, and to perpetuate its remarkable influence.

The quality of the ministry to which allusion has been made, would naturally tend to give it a more scriptural character. And what improvement is more desirable than a richer infusion into the discourses of the pulpit of the pure word of God? Not only make the text penetrate the sermon, but let other parts of the Scriptures be made to gather around it, to shed light upon it and receive light from it. Occasional American hearers of some ministers in England and Scotland have marked this characteristic with great pleasure. If it should diminish the brilliancy of the pulpit it would add to its richness. Fewer orations will be delivered, but many better sermons. A prevalent unhealthy taste may not be so well satisfied for a time, but a better taste will soon be formed. It will furnish the best opportunity for awakening emotion and affecting the conscience, as well as imparting instruction. Thus obtaining vivid impressions of truth, the preacher will possess one element of true earnestness in the pulpit; for he will speak not only with all the authority of truth, but with a soul deeply imbued with the spirit of it. Then he will have a holy unction, and will give forth both light and heat. A spiritual, practical, scriptural, as well as learned ministry will be earnest; and that is the ministry God will bless for the enlightenment and salvation of our country.

TO THE

PROFESSORS AND COMMITTEE

OF CHESHUNT COLLEGE,

THE FOLLOWING TREATISE,

BEING THE EXPANSION OF A SERMON

PREACHED

BEFORE THEM AT THEIR LAST ANNIVERSARY,

IS INSCRIBED

WITH SENTIMENTS OF AFFECTIONATE RESPECT,

AND WITH EARNEST PRAYERS

FOR THE PROSPERITY

OF THEIR VALUABLE INSTITUTION,

BY

THE AUTHOR.

CONTENTS.

PREFACE

Has the modern evangelical pulpit lost, and is it still losing, any of its power? This is a question far too momentous to be asked in the spirit of mere curiosity, or to be answered in unreflecting and ignorant haste. An affirmative reply involves consequences so deeply and so painfully affecting the eternal welfare of mankind, as well as the cause of orthodox doctrine, that it should not be given but upon indubitable evidence; while on the other hand, a negative answer will only perpetuate the evil, if it really exists, by preventing all measures which might be taken to correct it. In settling this question, it is necessary to define what is meant by the loss of the power of the pulpit. If by this it is intended only to ask whether evangelical ministrations have lost their attractiveness in drawing the people together to hear them, it may be unhesitatingly affirmed that they have not, for perhaps there was never anything approaching the numbers which now are found listening to the glad tidings of salvation. The true intent of the inquiry then is this: Has the modern pulpit lost any of its efficacy as regards the great end for which the Gospel is preached, that is, the conversion of sinners, and the spiritual advancement of believers? In coming to a right conclusion upon this matter, another inquiry still must be proposed, which is this: With what past period of history is the present compared? If we go back to the time of BAXTER, HOWE, OWEN, BATES, MANTON, and CHARNOCK, there can be little reason to believe, it may be presumed, that the moderns preach with the same results that these men did. As little can it be questioned whether WHITFIELD and WESLEY, with the men called up by their labors, proclaimed the gospel of the grace of God, with more power and success than the preachers of the present day. It is better, therefore, to limit the range of inquiry to the last quarter of a century, and to state the matter thus: Does the preaching of the gospel now, taking all evangelical denominations into the investigation, appear to be followed with the same saving and sanctifying results, as it was then; and if not, does there appear to be a progressive diminution of effect still going on?

This, it must be obvious, is a question which cannot be settled by very accurate statistics, and for the solution of which we must depend pretty much upon general reports, and concurrent testimony. It may be asked, then, whether the want of efficiency is not matter of acknowledgment and lamentation by all evangelical bodies? True it is that to a certain extent similar acknowledgments and lamentations have been made in every age, and by ministers of all denominations. But the inquiry now supposed is made chiefly by those who compare themselves with themselves; and their success at the present time, with their own success in the past time. The confession from the United States, made by Presbyterians, Congregationalists, Baptists and Methodists, is concurrent, that there is a flatness over the churches, that revivals are rare, and conversions few, while the power of godliness among professing Christians is low. The Methodist body in these United Kingdoms, reported last year but an increase of about seven hundred members. The evangelical clergy of the Church of England lament the want of conversions by their preaching, and confess that the power of VENN, and ROMAINE, and CECIL, and NEWTON, seems wanting to their successors. The Baptists and Independents have no better report to make. Dr. CHALMERS, in a late article in the North British Review, in speaking of Scotland, and that at a time when the disruption of the Presbyterian Establishment might have been supposed to have given new activity to the Free Church at least, uses the following mournful language: "As things stand at present, our creeds and confessions have become effete, and the Bible a dead letter; and the orthodoxy which was at one time the glory, by withering into the inert and lifeless, is now the shame and reproach of all our churches." This is strong language, and a startling opinion. But the most melancholy thing connected with it is its truth.

Assuming then the fact that the modern evangelical pulpit *has* lost, and is losing, something of its power, in the way of converting sinners, and carrying forward the spiritual life of believers, it surely becomes us all to reflect upon the painful fact with the deepest seriousness, and the most intense anxiety, and at the same time to inquire after the cause. It would ill become us, in a spirit of antinomian indolence or fanaticism, to resolve this whole matter into Divine sovereignty, and to say, "God wills it." With the same reason, and on as good ground, might the impenitent sinner be satisfied with his condition, and trace it up to a withholding of the influence necessary for his conversion. That there is a suspension of Divine influence must be admitted, if there be a diminished saving result; but as the Spirit uses appropriate means, may not this very suspension itself be traced up to some fault of the preachers themselves? Would not a different order of means lead to a removal of this suspension of the Spirit's power? The question for us to ask in all seriousness and prayerful examination, is this: Does the diminished power of the pulpit arise from a diminished adaptation of the pulpit, or is the deficiency which is lamented to be traced up exclusively to the circumstances of the times that are now passing over us? Something may be set down to both these causes.

This is a matter that concerns all, and deeply concerns them too, for the tendency of decline is always downward; what is weak will become weaker, if not stopped.

There is another consideration which may account for the diminished effect of the pulpit, and that is an increased power of the press and of the school. At one time the preacher had the public mind almost to himself. There were indeed Bibles, and schools, and tracts, but how few and uninfluential, compared with what they are in the present day! Evangelical truth now comes before the million in every possible variety of form, and in every variable quantity: the child learns its lessons from the Sunday school teacher, and the poorest adult reads it at home in the tract and the penny magazine; and though this is a help in one respect to the preacher, it takes from him all the advantage which novelty of representation can give him, for he has been already forestalled by the living voice of the teacher, and the silent invitations of the tract. These auxiliary means of conversion will never supersede the pulpit, if the pulpit does not allow itself *to be* superseded; but it is evident that such competitors with it as these for the public mind, should increase its labors to be, what God ever intended it to be, his power to the salvation of men. That the pulpit has nothing to fear from the increase of religious knowledge by the school and the press, is evident from the fact that as science multiplies its treatises, and cheapens them down to the poorest pocket, it multiplies in equal proportion its public lecturers.

The views thus set forth in this preface will account for the subject of the volume which they introduce. We live in an earnest age, and nothing but an earnest ministry may hope to succeed in it. With this conviction, when honored with an invitation to preach last year the anniversary sermon for Cheshunt College, the author found his subject in his own views and convictions. The publication of the discourse then preached was solicited at the time of its delivery; but as it was given to the world pretty fully in the pages of the Patriot newspaper, he abandoned all thoughts of complying with a request so kindly preferred.

His attention was, however, called again to the subject, and his resolution changed by the solicitation of that distinguished man who presides over the collegiate institution at Cheshunt with so much wisdom and dignity; and who to all his other works, so rich in practical piety, has added another of a very different kind, which, while it lays the world under deep obligations to its author, will associate the name of Dr. Harris with the most profound religious philosophers of any age or any country. May his valuable life be spared to complete that magnificent series of treatises, which, with such adventurous but well-balanced intellect, he has projected, and of which the volume lately issued is but the commencement!

When revising the manuscript for publication, the author of this work found it admitted of more expansion of thought and more extended amplification than at first struck him; and he resolved as soon as time should be found for it, to prepare a small treatise which should have a better chance of living than an ephemeral pamphlet. The subject grew under his hand, and has at length swelled into this volume. In undertaking to become, especially at such length, the counsellor of his brethren, he can scarcely acquit himself of the charge of presumption. He feels that he has little claim upon the attention of his fellow laborers in the ministry, even the youngest of them, and very little right to ask it. True it is that he is now arrived at an age whe he takes his place among the fathers; but then years d not always teach wisdom. It is no less true that he has now labored two and forty years in the ministry of the Word, and has had no very limited opportunity of observing and of knowing, experimentally, what contributes to ministerial acceptableness and usefulness; still he can truly say, without a grain of vanity concealed under a simulated modesty, he offers the present treatise to the notice of his brethren, with fear and trembling. He knows that what is offered to them should, both as to matter and manner, be worthy of their attention; and had he a literary reputation to sustain, over which he was jealous even to fastidiousness, he would feel still more solicitude about the reception of his work; but as he aims at nothing but usefulness, without making any pretensions to a finished style, he can ask them to accept it as an affectionate endeavor, made in his own way, to aid their usefulness. God has helped him to do something for His cause, and knowing how it has been done, he is anxious to draw others in the same way. And now while his shadows lengthen the plain, and his eye is on the declining sun, he feels tha in the review of life, the thought of having done something to save souls from death is more precious, than could have been his consciousness of having made the largest acquirements of learning and science. There is a time coming in every man's history when the knowledge of having been the instrument to pluck a single brand from the eternal burning, will yield more real satisfaction than the certainty of having accomplished the loftiest objects of literary ambition.

The author anticipates a remark which will be made by many of the readers of this volume, that it is a book of extracts. They will, however, have no cause to complain of this, since what he has given from the stores of other men's thoughts is so much better than what he could have brought from his own. Besides, in so important a matter as advice to the ministry, he was anxious to be sustained in what he advanced, by the authority of men, whose names and counsels would carry far more weight than his own. Be it so, then, that the book will present the appearance of a literary mosaic,—the author is quite content, for the sake of such precious stones, that his own part of the volume should perform no higher office than to be the framework in which they are set.

There will be found some repetitions of sentiment, and even of expression, in the work; and this was hardly to be avoided from the nature of the subject. It is a poor excuse for imperfections, to plead the want of time for correcting them; and yet it is the best excuse the author has to make for the many that will be found in his little volume. His situation exposes him to a thousand vexatious interruptions, which many in more retired nooks know nothing about. These pages have been written amidst such abounding and various occupations, that they could be composed only during snatches of time redeemed from other duties, and from the intervals of busy activities.

If this work should do nothing more than draw the attention of writers in our Reviews and Magazines, as well as of our more talented authors, to a renewed consideration of that *most vital point*, OUR MINISTRY, it will, however humble are its pretensions and low its merits, have accomplished a high and holy vocation.

CHAPTER I.

THE APOSTOLIC MINISTRY.

"Now then we are ambassadors for Christ, as though God did beseech you by us; we pray you in Christ's stead, be ye reconciled to God."—2 Cor. v. 20.

In this truly wonderful passage, viewed in connection with its context, are set before us with beautiful simplicity, yet with surpassing grandeur, the theme, the design, and the method of the Christian ministry: the *theme* is God reconciling the world to himself, a subject compared with which the negotiations of hostile nations and the treaties which put an end to the horrors of war, and bind in concord the fiercest passions of humanity, are matters of only momentary and limited importance: the *design* of the ministry, which is strictly in harmony with its theme, is to bring sinful men into actual reconciliation with God on the ground of that system of mediation through Christ, which God himself has devised and proclaimed: and its *method* is the earnestness of persuasion addressed to the rebel heart of man, to induce him to lay aside his enmity against his offended Sovereign, and to accept the offer of a gracious amnesty. The union and the harmony of these three views of the ministry are singularly impressive: he who leaves out the great scheme of Christian reconciliation from his habitual ministration, omits the divinely appointed theme: he who does not supremely aim to bring sinners into a state of actual friendship with God, falls short of the design of the sacred office; while he who does not employ all the arts and efforts of persuasion, mistakes the method of fulfilling its duties.

As the apostle is writing to a Christian church, it is perhaps a matter of surprise to some that he should entreat *them* to be reconciled to God, who by their very profession of religion must have been supposed to be already in that state. Upon looking attentively at the passage the reader will perceive that the pronouns of the second person are in italics, intimating that they are not in the original Greek, but are supplied in our English translation to complete the sense; consequently any other term that would accomplish this better may be substituted for them. If therefore we put the substantive "men," instead of the pronoun "you" in the first clause of the verse, and the third personal pronoun "them" for the second personal pronoun "you" in the latter clause, we shall avoid the improbability of his calling upon professing Christians to come into a state to which they must be supposed to have already attained, and shall bring out what the apostle intended to set forth, the usual manner in which he discharged the functions of his momentous office; and with the alterations it would read thus: "As ambassadors for Christ, as though God did beseech *men* by us, we pray *them* in Christ's stead to be reconciled to God." It was as if he had said, "Wherever we go, we find men in unprovoked hostility, inveterate enmity, and mad rebellion against God's holy nature, law, and government. We carry with us, as his ambassadors, the proclamation of mercy through the mediation of our Lord Jesus Christ. We tell them that we are appointed by the God whom they have offended, and who could overwhelm them with the terrors of his justice, to call upon them to lay down their arms and accept the offer of eternal pardon and peace: but we find them everywhere so bent upon their sins and the enjoyment of their worldly occupations and possessions, that we are compelled to use the language of the most vehement entreaty, and to beseech and implore them, in God's name, and in Christ's stead, to come into a state of reconciliation."

The apostle not only used the most intense earnestness of entreaty as an expression of his own concern, but he told the objects of his imploring anxiety that *his* importunity for their welfare was but an imitation of, and a substitute for, that of God himself—that his beseeching solicitation to them, on behalf of their own salvation, was uttered in Christ's stead. This is the most wonderful scene that the universe will ever witness—a beseeching God, and an imploring Saviour, standing at the door of the sinner's heart with eternal salvation in his hand, knocking for entrance, and begging to be let in; the insulted Omnipotent Creator of the universe, beseeching a worm, whom a volition of his will could sink in a moment to perdition, and whose justice would be glorified in the act, to accept his pardoning mercy; and waiting, year after year, in all long-suffering, for the sinner's reconsideration of his obstinate refusals. Be astonished, O heavens! at God's unutterable mercy, and be horribly afraid, O earth! at man's indescribable wickedness! Here is the climax of God's divine love, and man's desperate depravity. Infinite benevolence did not reach its uttermost when Jesus Christ was nailed to the cross; that was reserved for the scene before us.

I might, with ineffable delight, expatiate at length on this scene of matchless mercy; but I pass on to other applications of the passage appropriate to the subject before us; and what a view does it give us of the Christian ministry. It is *an embassy from God to man*, and therefore how *dignified* and *honorable!* I admit that it is only in a qualified sense that the title and office of an "ambassador" for Christ can be applied to the ordinary ministers of the gospel: but in such a sense it may be applied to them, since they are ordained to do what he would do were he personally present: they are to propose the same blessings, to lay down the same terms of peace, as he would, were he again on earth, and are, therefore, so far, his ambassadors: and if the honor of an ambassador be in proportion to the power and glory of the sovereign that employs him, what *is* the dignity of him who is the ambassador of the King of kings, and Lord of lords; and, at the same time, what *ought to be* the sanctity of his conduct, and the elevation of his character? If nothing unworthy of the monarch who sends him, and the nation which he represents, should be done by him who is dispatched on an embassy to a foreign court and people, how vigilant and solicitous to do nothing unworthy of God and his Christ, should he be whose business it is to negotiate with man the weighty affairs of judgment and of mercy from Heaven. If he bears the dignity of office, let him couple with it a corresponding dignity of character. How natural, how just, how necessary the reflection, "I am an ambassador for Christ: what manner of person ought I to be in all holy conversation and godliness? What should *I* be who represent, so far as my office is concerned, the Majesty of heaven and earth?"

The ministry of the gospel is shown in this passage to be an embassy of *peace:* this is its very designation, "THE MINISTRY OF RECONCILIATION." Never was anything more beautiful expressed or conceived: nothing could be devised to throw over the ministry a charm of greater loveliness. If in one hand the preacher of the gospel carry the sword of the Spirit, it is only to slay the sin; while he holds forth the olive branch in the other, as the token of peace and life to the sinner. He enters the scene of strife and discord to harmonize the jarring elements, and goes to the field of conflict to reconcile the contending parties. It is his to proclaim the treaty of man's peace with God, to explain its terms, to urge its acceptance, and to bring the sinner into friendship with his offended Lawgiver; to carry peace into man's troubled bosom, and reconcile him to his own conscience; to cast out the enmities and prejudices of his selfish and depraved heart, and to unite him by charity to his fellows; to calm down the violence of his temper, and give him peace at home; and then to conduct him to the realms of undisturbed tranquillity in the celestial world. This is his business. Angels hover over him in his course, and chant over his labors their ancient song, "Glory to God in the highest, and on earth peace and good will to men;" redeemed men and women saved by his instrumentality from the wrath of God, the stings of conscience, and the turbulence of passion, hail him in the language of the prophet, "How beautiful upon the mountains are the feet of him that bringeth good tidings, that publisheth peace;" while the Saviour himself pronounceth upon him the beatitude, "Blessed are the peace-makers; for they shall be called the children of God." Honored and happy man, where thy labors are faithful and successful: minister of reconciliation, friend and promoter of peace, the world knoweth thee not, because it knew not Christ; nor, perhaps, does even the church duly appreciate or adequately reward thy services; but even now thy work is its own reward: peace attends upon thy steps, and its blessings spring up in thy path.

But still it is an embassy of *difficulty*. It is to treat with those who are unwilling to be saved, and to persuade the sinful, proud, and stubborn hearts of men to capitulate to holiness and grace. The minister carries the offer of infinite and ineffable blessedness, but it is to men who have no taste for that species of felicity. His were an easy office did he find men everywhere predisposed to close in with the proposals of infinite benevolence; but he meets, wherever he goes, with hearts, not only indifferent, but hostile, to his message. The parable which represents the excuses made for not coming to the marriage feast, is still applicable to the children of men in referenee to the invitations of the gospel: men are, as they ever were, too busy, or too well satisfied with their enjoyments and possessions, to care about salvation. They are madly set upon the objects of the present world; they are asleep, and need to be roused; careless, and need to be interested; indolent, and need to be stimulated; and it is with the greatest difficulty we can engage their attention to the invisible realities of eternity. No one can form a true estimate of the nature, design, and difficulties of the ministerial office, who leaves out of view the desperate wickedness of the human heart: and the reason why there is so little of that hard labor, and intense earnestness, and beseeching entreaty in the ministers of the gospel is, that there is the want of that deep conviction or proper consideration of the resistance to their endeavors which is perpetually meeting them from the sinner's heart.

This brings me to the subject of my present discourse, and that is the necessity of AN EARNEST MINISTRY. Nothing less than earnestness can succeed in any cases of great difficulty; and the earnestness must of course be in proportion to the difficulty to be surmounted. Great obstacles cannot be overcome without intense application of the mind. How then can the work of the ministry be accomplished? Every view we can take of it replies, "Only by earnestness." Every syllable of the apostle's language replies, "Only by earnestness." Every survey we can take of human nature replies, "Only by earnestness." Every recollection of our own experience, as well as every observation we can make of the experience of others, replies, "Only by earnestness." This, this is what we want, and must have, if the ends of the gospel are ever to be extensively accomplished—*an* EARNEST *ministry.*

We have heard much of late about a *learned* ministry, and God forbid we should ever be afflicted by so great an evil as an unlearned one. We have been often reminded of the necessity of an *educated* ministry; and in this case, as in every other, men must be educated for their vocation; but then that education must be strictly appropriate and specific. We are very properly told from many quarters, we can do nothing without a *pious* ministry. Nothing can be more true, nor can any truth bearing upon this subject be more momentous; for of all the curses which God ever pours from the vials of his wrath upon a nation which he intends to scourge, there is not one so fearful as giving them up to an *unholy* ministry. I trust our churches will ever consider piety as the first and most essential qualification in their pastors, for which talents, genius, learning, and eloquence, would and could be no substitutes. It will be a dark and evil day when personal godliness shall be placed second to anything else in those who serve at the altar of God. But still there is something else wanted in addition to natural talent, to academic training, and even to the most fervent, evangelical piety, and that is, *intense devotedness.*

It appears to me that this is the *one thing* more than any, or all other things, that is wanting in the modern pulpit, and that has been wanting in most ages of the Christian church. In a valuable article in a late number of the British Quarterly Review occurs the following sentence: "No ministry will be really effective, whatever may be its intelligence, which is not a ministry of strong faith, true spirituality, and deep earnestness." I wish this golden sentence could be inscribed in characters of light, over every professor's chair, over every student's desk, and over every preacher's pulpit. Condensed into that one short paragraph is everything that needs be said on this subject. I feel as though every syllable I have to write were superfluous, if all our pastors, students, and tutors would let that one sentence take full occupation of their hearts, possess their whole souls, and regulate all their conduct.

CHAPTER II.

THE NATURE OF EARNESTNESS.

PERHAPS there is scarcely one single phrase more frequently employed in the sphere of human activity, or better understood, than this—BE IN EARNEST. What distinctness of aim, what fixedness of purpose, what resoluteness of will, what diligence, patience, and perseverance of action, are implied or expressed in these three words. He who would stimulate indolence, quicken activity, and inspire hope; he who would breathe his own soul into the soul of another, and kindle the enthusiasm which glows in his own bosom, says to his fellow, "Be in earnest:" and that short sentence, uttered by his lips, has often been like a scintillation flying off from his own ardent soul, which, lighting upon the spirit of the individual whom he was anxious to move to some great enterprise, has kindled the flames of enthusiasm there also. And what else, or what less, does Jesus Christ say to every one whom he sends into the work of the Christian ministry than "Be in earnest?"

There is something in the aspect and power of earnestness, whatever be its object, that is impressive and commanding. To see a man selecting some one object of pursuit, and then yielding up his soul to the desire of its attainment, with a surrender which admits of no reserve, a steadiness of aim which allows of no diversion, and a diligence which consents neither to rest nor intermission; which is so uppermost in his heart as to fill his conversation, and so entirely and constantly before his mind as to throw into its broad shadow every other subject of consideration; and which borrows from the intensity of his own feeling, a strange fascination to engage the feelings of others—such an instance of decision, amounting to a ruling passion, exerts over us, while witnessing it, an influence which we feel to be contagious. We involuntarily, to a certain extent, sympathize with the individual who is thus carried away by his own fervor; and if at the same time all this be an earnestness for promoting our own interests, its effect is absolutely irresistible. That man must be a stone, and destitute of the ordinary feelings of humanity, who can see another interested, active, and zealous for his welfare, while he himself remains inert and indifferent. Even the apathetic and indolent have sometimes been kindled into ardor, and led to make efforts for themselves, by the solicitude which others have manifested for their welfare.

How strictly does this apply to the ministry of the Word, which relates to the most momentous matters that can engage the attention of the human understanding. Sympathy is a law of our mental economy which has never been sufficiently taken into the account in estimating the influences which God employs for the salvation of men. There is a silent and almost unperceived process of thought often going on in the mind of those who are listening to the sermons of a preacher really laboring for the conversion of souls, of this kind: "Is he so earnest about my salvation, and shall I care nothing about the matter? Is my eternal happiness so much in his account, and shall it be nothing in mine? I can meet cold logic with counter-arguments, or at any rate, I can raise up difficulties against evidence. I can smile at the artifices of rhetoric, and be pleased with the displays of eloquence. I can sit unmoved under sermons which seem intended by the preacher to raise my estimate of himself, but I cannot stand this earnestness about *me*. The man is evidently intent upon saving my soul. I feel the grasp of his hand laying hold of my arm as if he would pluck me out of the fire. He has not only made me think, but he has made me *feel*. His earnestness has subdued me."

But it will be necessary now to meet and answer the question, What is meant by an earnest ministry?

I remark, in the first place, that earnestness implies, *The selection of some one object of pursuit, and a vivid perception of its value and importance.* It is next to impossible for the mind to be intently employed, or the heart very deeply engaged, on a multiplicity of objects at once. We have not energy enough to be so divided and distributed. Our feelings, to run with force, must flow pretty much in one channel: the attention must be concentrated, the purpose settled, the action expended, upon one thing, or there can be no efficiency. The earnest man is a man of one idea, and that one idea occupies, possesses, and fills his soul. To every other claimant upon his time, and regard, and labor, he says, "Stand by; I am engaged, I cannot attend to you; there is something else waiting for me." To that *one* thing he is committed. There may be many subordinate matters, amidst which he divides what may be called the surplus water, but the main current flows through one channel, and turns one great wheel. This "one thing I do," is his plan and resolution. Many wonder at his choice, many condemn it: no matter, *he* understands it, approves it, and pursues it amidst the ignorance which cannot comprehend it, or the peculiarity of taste which cannot admire it. He is no double-minded man, unstable in all his ways, whose preference and purpose are shaken by every cross-current of opinion. It is nothing to him what others do, or what they say of *his* doing: he must do that, whatever else he leaves undone. No one can be in earnest who has not thus made up his mind, and he who has, and is resolutely bent upon it, keeps the object constantly before his mind; his attention is so strongly and tenaciously fixed upon it, that even at the greatest distance, "as the Egyptian pyramids to travellers, it appears to him with a luminous distinctness, as if it were nigh, and beguiles the toilsome length of labor and enterprise by which he must reach it." It is so conspicuous before him that he does not deviate a step from the right direction, and every movement and every day is an approximation. Break in upon him at any moment, you know where you shall find him, and how employed.

There is the first part of the description of an earnest minister: he too has selected his object, and made up his mind concerning it, and insulating it from all others, sets it clearly and distinctly before his mind. And what is it? What should it be? Not science, nor literature, nor philosophy; not a life spent in the acquisition of knowledge, nor the gratification of taste; not the power of adding to the treasures of national elegance in the department of letters, nor to the ornaments which embellish our civilized existence, and give amenity to our social intercourse. The man who has entered the sacred office merely to luxuriate in the haunts of the muses, has mistaken his errand to the pulpit, and is no less guilty, though somewhat less sordid, than he that says, "Put me in the priest's office that I may eat a morsel of bread." That a minister may to a certain extent indulge a literary or scientific taste, and could even make it subservient to a higher and more sacred object, is admitted. The pulpit has done, and is doing, much service in all the departments of learning and philosophy. It is in Christian countries that the valuable remains of Eastern, Greek, and Roman wisdom and eloquence have been preserved, studied, imitated, and sometimes even excelled. Christian nations have conducted philosophical inquiries with the best success, and improved them for the most useful and benevolent purposes. "If these things are good and profitable unto society, a large portion of the honor of such usefulness belongs to men set for the defence of the gospel, desirous by sound reasoning to convince gainsayers, and conscious what arms human literature furnishes for this holy war. And then in addition to all this, consider the effect of the pulpit upon what might be called the popular mind. To thousands who have comparatively little leisure or opportunity to form their taste, and cultivate their rational powers, by conversation with the wise and enlightened, or by reading their works, a school is thus open, established indeed for higher purposes, where men of sound understandings, though low in rank, may, without expense, and almost without intending it, learn from example to distinguish or connect ideas, to infer one truth from another, to examine the force of an argument, and so to arrange and express their sentiments as deeply to impress themselves and others. As in a few years the child gradually acquires the faculty of speaking his mother-tongue with a considerable degree of ease and fluency, without any formal lessons, merely by hearing it spoken, so there is a natural logic and rhetoric which some acquire without designing it, who go to church for nobler ends, whereby they are enabled to detect the cunning craftiness with which the enemies of religion or of public tranquility lie in wait to deceive. Indeed, the culture of the talents and improvements of that respectable class of men who earn their bread by the sweat of their brow, generally rises or falls in proportion to the character and genius of their religious instructors."

This is as true as it is beautiful, and should remind all ministers of the gospel of the necessity and importance, at all times, but especially in such times as these, of keeping in mind the collateral and secondary objects of pulpit instruction, and of preparing themselves for conducting it with power and efficiency. There is not a temporal interest of man as an individual, or of society, on which the sermons and general influence of the ministry may not be made to bear; but then it must never be forgotten that these things which have just been enumerated, are at best only the incidental, secondary, and collateral benefits of the ministry of the Word: they are among the many things that may be touched, but are not *the one thing* that must be grasped: they are, as I have already said, like the little lateral rills which may be led off from the main stream for the purpose of irrigation, but are not the great body of water that rolls onward in its channel for the purpose of commerce and national wealth.

Nor is it the great object of our ministry merely to preside with dignity over the solemnities of public worship; to content ourselves and please our people with preparing and delivering two well-studied discourses on the Sabbath; to keep all quiet and orderly in the church; to maintain a kind of religious respectability and intellectuality in the congregation; and to infuse into them much of the element of political power. The end and aim of the ministry are to be gathered from the apostle's solemn and comprehensive language, "THEY WATCH FOR YOUR SOULS AS THEY THAT MUST GIVE ACCOUNT." There, in that short, but sublime and awful sentence, *the* end of the pastoral office is set before us. The design of the pulpit is in harmony with that of the cross; and the preacher is to carry out the design of the Saviour in coming to seek and to save that which was lost. Preaching and teaching are the very agency which Jesus Christ employs to save those souls for which he died upon Calvary. If souls are not saved, whatever other designs are accomplished, the great purpose of the ministry is defeated.

We are now prepared to understand what is the nature of real earnestness in a minister. I mean a distinct, explicit, practical recognition of his duty to labor for the salvation of souls as the end of his office. Such a man has settled with himself that this is *his* vocation and his business. He has looked at everything which could be presented to his mind, has weighed the claims of all, and with intelligence and firmness has said, and is prepared to stand by his affirmation, "I watch for souls." He thus understands his errand; he is under no mistake, no uncertainty, no confusion. He has entered into fellowship with God the Father in his eternal purpose of the salvation of the human race; with the Son in the end of his incarnation and death; and with the Holy Spirit in his coming down upon our desolate world. Of this salvation, which is the object of his ministry, the prophets inquired; to accomplish it apostles preached, and angels ministered; and thus justified in his choice by the Triune God and the noblest of his creatures in the universe, he leaves far below him, in the aspirations and the soarings of his ambition, the scholar, the philosopher and the poet. He has taken up an object in reference to which, if he succeed but in a single instance, he will have achieved a triumph which will endure infinite ages after the proudest monuments of human genius have perished like a garland in the conflagration of the world.

I have spoken of the salvation of souls as the great object of the ministerial office; this is a generic phrase, including as its species the awakening of the unconcerned; the guidance of the inquiring; the instruction of the uninformed; and the sanctification, comfort, and progress of those who through grace have believed—in short, the whole work of grace in the soul. But I now direct the attention of my readers to the first of these particulars as the most commanding object of ministerial solicitude, I mean the conversion of the unregenerate; and if without an offence of the law of modesty I may refer to my own history, labor, and success, I would observe that I began my ministry, even as a student, with a strong desire after this object; and long before this, while yet a youth engaged in secular concerns, I had been deeply susceptible of the power of an awakening style of preaching, which was strengthened by the perusal of the rousing sermons of Dr. DAVIES,* of New Jersey. From that time to the present I have made the conversion of the impenitent *the* great end of my ministry, and I have had my reward. I have been sustained in this course by the remarks of BAXTER in

---

* I wish these discourses were better known and more imitated by our young ministers. They are admirable specimens, formed upon the model of BAXTER, of persuasive, hortatory and impressive preaching. It is *such* preaching we want. In these striking discourses may be seen what I mean by *earnest* preaching. They are by no means scarce, and I would advise my younger brethren to buy and read them.

his "Reformed Pastor," a long extract from which I will now furnish.

"We must labor in a special manner for the conversion of the unconverted.

"The work of conversion is the great thing we must drive at; after this we must labor with all our might. Alas! the misery of the unconverted is so great that it calleth loudest to us for compassion. If a truly converted sinner do fall, it will be but into sin which will be pardoned, and he is not in that hazard of damnation by it as others are. Not but that God hateth their sins as well as others, or that he will bring them to heaven, let them live ever so wickedly; but the spirit that is within them will not suffer them to live wickedly, nor to sin as the ungodly do. But with the unconverted it is far otherwise. They 'are in the gall of bitterness, and in the bond of iniquity,' and have yet no part nor fellowship in the pardon of their sins, or the hope of glory. We have therefore a work of greater necessity to do for them, even 'to open their eyes, and to turn them from darkness to light, and from the power of Satan unto God; that they may receive forgiveness of sins, and an inheritance among them which are sanctified.' He that seeth one man sick of a mortal disease, and another only pained with the tooth-ache, will be moved more to compassionate the former than the latter; and will surely make more haste to help him, though he were a stranger and the other a brother or a son. It is so sad a case to see men in a state of damnation, wherein, if they should die, they are lost forever, that methinks we should not be able to let them alone, either in public or private, whatever other work we have to do. I confess I am frequently forced to neglect that which should tend to the further increase of knowledge in the godly, because of the lamentable necessity of the unconverted. Who is able to talk of controversies or of nice, unnecessary points, or even of truths of a lower degree of necessity, how excellent soever, while he seeth a company of ignorant, carnal, miserable sinners before his eyes, who must be changed or damned? Methinks I even see them entering upon their final woe! Methinks I hear them crying out for help—for speediest help! Their misery speaks the louder, because they have not hearts to ask for help themselves. Many a time have I known that I had some hearers of higher fancies, that looked for rarities, and were addicted to despise the ministry, if I told them not something more than ordinary; and yet I could not find in my heart to turn from the necessities of the impenitent, for the humoring of them; nor even to leave speaking to miserable sinners for their salvation, in order to speak so much as should otherwise be done to weak saints, for their confirmation and increase in grace. Methinks as Paul's 'spirit was stirred within him,' when he saw 'the Athenians wholly given to idolatry,' so it should cast us into one of his paroxysms, to see so many men in the greatest danger of being everlastingly undone. Methinks, if by faith we did indeed look upon them as within a step of hell, it would more effectually untie our tongues, than Crœsus' danger did his son's. He that will let a sinner go down to hell for want of speaking to him, doth set less by souls than did the Redeemer of souls; and less by his neighbor than common charity will allow him to by his greatest enemy. O therefore, brethren, whomsoever you neglect, neglect not the most miserable! Whatever you pass over, forget not poor souls that are under the condemnation and curse of the law, and who may look every hour for the infernal execution, if a speedy change do not prevent it. O call after the impenitent, and ply this great work of converting souls, whatever else you leave undone."

"These powerful and impressive observations," says the editor of Baxter, "we cannot too earnestly recommend to the attention of ministers. We have no hesitation in saying that the most of preachers whom we have known, were essentially defective in the grand and primary object of the Christian ministry,—*laboring for the conversion of souls.* From the general strain of some men's preaching, one would almost be ready to conclude that there were no sinners in their congregations to be converted. In determining the proportion of attention which a minister should pay to particular classes of his congregation, the number of each class, and the necessities of their case, are unquestionably the principal considerations which should weigh with him. Now in all our congregations we have reason to fear the unconverted constitute by far the majority;—their situation is peculiarly pitiable; their opportunities of salvation will soon be forever over; their danger is not only very great, but very imminent; they are not secure from everlasting misery, even for a single moment. Surely then the unconverted demand by far the largest share of the Christian minister's attention, and yet from many they receive but a very small share of attention—their case, when noticed at all, is noticed only, as it were, by the bye. This no doubt is a principal cause that among us there are so few conversions by the preaching of the word, and especially in the congregations of particular ministers. We feel this subject to be of such transcendent importance that we trust we shall be excused for here introducing a quotation connected with it, from another work of our author, which has been introduced into the series of 'Select Christian Authors.'"

"It is not," says he, in his "Mischiefs of Self-Ignorance," "a general dull discourse, or critical observations upon words, or the subtile decision of some nice and curious questions of the schools; nor is it a neat and well-composed speech, about some other distant matters, that is likely to acquaint a sinner with himself. How many sermons may we hear that are levelled at some mark or other which is very far from the hearers' hearts, and therefore are never likely to convince them, or open and convert them? And if our congregations were in such a case as that they needed no closer quickening work, such preaching might be borne with and commended. But when so many usually sit before us that must shortly die, and yet are unprepared for death; and that are condemned by the law of God, and must be pardoned, or finally condemned; that must be saved from their sins that they may be saved from everlasting misery—I think it is time for us to talk to them of such things as most concern them, and that in such a manner as may most effectually convince, awaken, and change them.

"A man that is ready to be drowned is not at leisure for a song or a dance; and a man that is ready to be hanged, methinks should not find himself at leisure to hear a man show his wit and reading only, if not his folly and malice, against a life of holiness. Nor should you think that suitable to such men's case that doth not evidently tend to save them. But, alas! how often have we heard such sermons as tend more to *diversion* than *direction;* to fill their minds with other matters, and find them something else to think of, lest they should study themselves, and know their misery! A preacher that seems to speak *religiously,* by a dry, sapless discourse, that is called a sermon, may more plausibly and easily ruin him. And his conscience will more quietly suffer him to be taken off the necessary care of his salvation, by something that is like it, and pretends to do the work as well, than by the grosser avocations or the scorn of fools. And he will be more tamely turned from religion by something that is called religion, and which he hopes may serve the turn, than by open wickedness, or impious defiance of God and reason. But how often do we hear sermons applauded, which force us, in compassion to men's souls, to think, 'Oh what is all this to the opening of a sinner's heart unto himself, and showing him his unregenerate state? What is this to the conviction of a self-deluding soul, that is passing into hell, with the confident expectation of heaven? What is this to show men their undone condition, and the absolute necessity of Christ, and of renewing grace? What is in this to lead men up from earth to heaven, and to acquaint them with the unseen world, and to help them to the life of faith and love, and to the mortifying and pardon of their sins!' How little skill have many miserable preachers in the searching of the heart, and helping men to know themselves, whether Christ be in them, or whether they be reprobates! And how little care and diligence is used by them, to call men to the trial, and help them in the examining and judging of themselves, as if it were a work of no necessity. 'They have healed the hurt of the daughter of my people slightly, saying, Peace, peace, when there is no peace,' saith the Lord."

Oh what preachers we should be, could we drink in the spirit of these powerful passages! May God impress them on our hearts, and lead us to mould our discourses after this fashion. I would, however, by no means wish to be thought unmindful of the importance of building up the believer on his holy faith. Not only must the children of the redeemed family be born, but they must also be fed, watched, guided, and nourished up to manhood. The growth in grace and in knowledge of the heirs of immortality must be an object of deep solicitude with the faithful pastor. His children in the faith are not glorified, as soon as converted, but are carried through a probation, and often a long one, of conflict, trial, and temptation; and it is his business, by the instrumentality of the truth, deeply searched, carefully expounded, and appropriately applied, to conduct them through the perplexities and the dangers of the divine life. Hence, therefore, it is the duty of the minister, not to be always dwelling on first principles, nor teaching the mere alphabet of Bible knowledge, but to lead his people "on unto perfection;" yet still, amidst all this, he is never to forget that by far the greater number of those who are before him do not experimentally know these first principles, and have not learnt even this alphabet of practical piety. I once had a member of my church, who had been brought out of the literary world to a deep, experimental knowledge of divine truth. She was a woman of uncommonly fine and tasteful mind. After her conversion she dwelt for a season in London; and on her return from the metropolis, in giving an account of the various preachers she had heard, expressed her surprise and regret that their sermons, however excellent, seemed to be addressed, almost exclusively, to true believers, as if they took it for granted that their congregations were composed wholly of such, and contained none who were dead in trespasses and sins. And I know a devoted and consistent Christian, who, upon leaving a minister whom he had heard for several years, declared he had scarcely ever heard one thoroughly practical sermon from him during the whole time: there had been much doctrinal statement, much theological science, much religious comfort; but no vivid and pungent appeals either to saints or sinners. No wonder he knew of no conversions there: and yet this preacher is not an Antinomian.

SECONDLY. Earnestness implies *that the subject has not only been selected, but that it has taken full possession of the mind, and has kindled towards it an intense desire of the heart.*

It is something more than the correctness of theory, and the deductions of logic; more than the cool calculation of the judgment, and the play of the imagination—earnestness means that the understanding, having selected and appreciated its object, has pressed all the faculties of both mind and body into its pursuit. It urges the soul onward in its career of action at such a speed, that it is set on fire by the velocity of its own motion. The object of an earnest man is never, for any long period of time, absent from his thoughts. He meditates on it by day, and dreams of it by night: it meets him in his solitary walks as some bright vision which he loves to contemplate, and it comes over him in company with such power, that he cannot avoid making it the topic of his conversation, till he appears in the eyes of those who have no sympathy with him in the light of an enthusiast.

FOSTER, in his "Essay on Decision of Character," has alluded to HOWARD as supplying a fine illustration of this mental quality. I furnish one extract bearing more directly than perhaps any other on our present theme. It relates to the singular fact that this great philanthropist turned not a moment from his course, when traversing those scenes most calculated to awaken curiosity, and to enkindle enthusiasm by the associations of ancient glory with which they are connected—even Rome itself. "The importance of his object held his faculties in a state of excitement which was too rigid to be affected by lighter interests, and on which, therefore, the beauties of nature and art had no power: like the invisible spirits who fulfil their commission of philanthropy among mortals, and care not about pictures, statues, and sumptuous buildings. It implied an inconceivable severity of conviction that he had *one thing to do;* and that he who would do some great thing in this short life must apply himself to the work with such a concentration of his forces as, to idle spectators, who live only to amuse themselves, looks like insanity. It was thus he made the trial, so seldom made, what is the utmost effect which may be granted to the last possible effort of a human agent; and therefore what he did not accomplish, he might conclude to be placed beyond the sphere of mortal activity, and calmly leave to the disposal of Omnipotence."

There, again, is the representation of the really and intensely earnest minister of Jesus Christ, and of the manner in which he regards the object of his ministry, the salvation of immortal souls. He has drunk in the inspiration of those inexpressibly sublime and solemn words, so often already quoted, "They watch for your souls as they that must give account, that they may do it with joy and not with grief." This declaration has come over him like a spell, from the fascination of which he neither tries nor wishes to escape. Whether seated in his chair in his study; or carrying on the exercises of devotion in the closet; or preaching the gospel in the pulpit; or enjoying the pleasures of Christian friendship in the social circle; or recreating his energies amidst the beauties of creation; the words of Solomon stand out conspicuously before his mind's eye,

"He that winneth souls is wise;" while, ever and anon, the thunder of Christ's awful inquiry comes pealing over his ear, "What shall it profit a man if he gain the whole world, and lose his own soul, or what shall a man give in exchange for his soul?" To be useful in converting souls is his constant and practical aim: with a view to which, his texts are chosen, his sermons are composed and delivered, and his language, figures, and illustrations are selected. That word USEFULNESS has the same meaning in his ear, the same power over his soul, as the word "victory" has over the mind of the hero: and the preparation and delivery of the most eloquent sermons, with all the plaudits that follow them, will no more satisfy his ambition, than the skilful evolutions, the military splendor, and the martial music of a field day, however they may be admired by the multitudinous spectators, will content the desires of the patriot warrior who burns to defeat his country's foe upon the field of battle, and to rescue the liberties of his enslaved nation from the grasp of a tyrant. By the earnest minister, the salvation of souls is sought with the obligation of a principle, and the ardor of a passion. It is impressed upon his whole character, and is inseparable from his conduct. It distinguishes him among, and from, many of his brethren. When the congregations, either at home or abroad, go to hear him, they know what to expect, and consequently do not look for the flowers of rhetoric, but for the fruit of the tree of life; not for a dry crust of philosophy, not for a meatless, marrowless bone of criticism, but for the bread which cometh down from heaven; not for a display of religious fire-works, splendid but useless, but for the holding up of the torch of eternal truth in all its clear shining light to guide the wandering and benighted souls to the refuge of the lost. He has, by the usual style of his pulpit discourses, [illegible] is character as a *useful* preacher, and those who go to hear him, would as soon expect to listen to a mere poetical or classical effusion, instead of directions for health, from a physician whom they consulted in a time of sickness, as such matters from this servant of Christ, instead of a sermon calculated and designed to do good to their souls. He could possibly be eloquent, profound, or learned, and when these things can aid him in securing his one great end, he does not scruple to employ them. His aim is at the heart and conscience, and if the poetic, the literary, the logical, the scientific, will at any time so polish and plume the shaft, or sharpen the point of the arrow, he will not reject them, but will avail himself of their legitimate uses, that he may the more certainly hit the mark. This is his motto, "If by any means I might save some."

But this touches a THIRD thing implied in genuine earnestness, and that is *the studious invention and diligent use of all appropriate means to accomplish the selected object.* An earnest man is the last to be satisfied with mere formality, routine, and prescription. He will often survey his object, his means, and his instruments; will look back upon the past to review his course, to examine his failure, and success, with the causes of each; to learn what to do, and what to avoid for the future. His inquiry will often be, What next? What more? What better? And as the result of all this, new experiments will be tried, new plans will be laid, and new courses will be pursued. With an inextinguishable ardor, and with a resolute fixedness of purpose, he exclaims "I *must* succeed—*How?*"

And shall we ministers possess nothing of this, if we are in earnest for the salvation of souls? Shall dull uniformity, stiff formality, everlasting repetitions, and rigid routine satisfy *us?* Shall we never institute the inquiry, "Why have I not succeeded better in my ministry? How is it that my congregation is not larger, and my church more rapidly increasing? In what way can I account for it, that the truth as it is in Jesus, which I believe I preach, is not more influential, and the doctrine of the cross is not as it was intended to be, the power of God unto the salvation of souls? Why do I not more frequently hear addressed to me, by those who are constantly under my ministry, the anxious inquiry, 'What shall I do to be saved?' I am not wanting, as far as I know, in the regular discharge of my ordinary duties, and yet I gather little fruit of my labors, and have to utter continually the prophet's complaint, 'Who hath believed our report, and to whom is the arm of the Lord revealed?'" *Do* we indeed indulge in such complaints? Have we earnestness enough to pour forth such lamentations? Or is it of little consequence to us, provided we get our stipend, keep up the congregation to its usual size, and maintain the tranquillity of the church, whether the ends of the ministry are accomplished or not? Are we ever seen by God's omniscient eye pacing our study in deep thoughtfulness, solemn meditation, and rigorous inquisition; and after an impartial survey of our doings, and a sorrowful lamentation that we are doing no more, questioning ourselves thus—"Is there no new method to be tried, no new scheme to be devised, to increase the efficiency of my ministerial and pastoral labors? Is there nothing I can supply, correct, or add? Is there anything particularly wanting in the matter, manner, or method of my preaching, or in my course of pastoral attentions?" Surely it might be supposed that such inquiries would be often instituted into the results of such a ministry as ours, that seasons would be not unfrequently set apart, especially at the close of the year, for such a purpose.

Here it may be proper for us to look out of our own profession, and ask if the earnest tradesman, soldier, lawyer, philosopher, and mechanician, are satisfied to go on as they have done, though with ever so little success? Do we not see in all other departments of human action, where the mind is really intent on some great object, and where success has not been obtained in proportion to the labor bestowed, a dissatisfaction with past modes of action, and a determination to try new ones? And should we who watch for souls, and labor for immortality, be behindhand with them? In calling for new methods, I want no new doctrines; no new principles; no startling eccentricities; no wild irregularities; no vagaries of enthusiasm, nor frenzies of the passions; no, nothing but what the most sober judgment and the soundest reason would approve;—but I do want a more inventive, as well as a more fervid zeal in seeking the great end of our ministry. Dull uniformity, and not enthusiasm, is the side on which our danger lies. I know very well the contortions of an epileptic zeal are to be avoided, but so also is the numbness of a paralytic one; and after all, the former is less dangerous to life, and is more easily and frequently cured, than the latter. We may, as regards our preaching, for instance, examine whether we have not dwelt too little on the alarming, or on the attractive themes of revelation; whether we have not clothed our discourses too much with the terrors of the Lord, and determine to try the more winning forms of love and mercy, or whether we have not rendered the gospel powerless by an everlasting repetition of it in common-place phraseology; whether we have not been too argumentative, and resolve to be more imaginative, practical, and hortatory; whether we have not addressed ourselves too exclusively to believers, and determine to commence a style of more frequent and pungent address to the unconverted; whether we have not been too vague and general in our descriptions of sin, and become more specific and discriminating; whether we have not been too neglectful of the young, and begin a regular course of sermons to them; whether we have not had too much sameness of topic, and adopt courses of sermons on given subjects; whether we have not been too elaborate and abstract in the composition of our discourses, and come down to greater simplicity; whether we have not been too careless, and bestow more pains; whether we have not been too doctrinal, and in future make all truth, as it was intended to do, to bear upon the heart, conscience, and life.

Nor must the inquiry stop here. There must be the same process of rigid scrutiny instituted as to the labors of the pastorate. We must review the proceedings of this momentous department, for here also is most ample scope for invention as to new plans of action. Perhaps upon inquiry we shall find out that we have neglected various channels through which our influence might have been poured over the flock committed to our care, and shall discover many ways in which we can improve upon our former plans in the way of meeting the inquirers after salvation, giving our aid to Sunday schools, setting up Bible classes, or visiting the flock. What is needed, is an anxious wish to be wanting in nothing that can conduce to our usefulness, a diligent endeavor to make up every deficiency, and a mind ever inquisitive after new means and methods of doing good. Could we all but adopt the plan of setting apart a day at the close of every year for solemn examination into our ministerial and pastoral doings, for the purpose of ascertaining our defects and neglects, to see in what we could improve, to humble ourselves before God for the past, and to lay down new rules for the future, we should all be more abundantly useful than we are. And does not earnestness require all this? Can we pretend to it if we do not? The idea of a minister's going on from year to year with either little success, or none at all, and yet never pausing to inquire how this comes to pass, or what can be done to increase his efficiency, is so utterly repugnant to all proper notions of devotedness, that we are obliged to conclude that the views of such a man of the design of his office are radically and essentially defective.

FOURTHLY. Earnestness implies *a purpose and power of subordinating everything it meets with, selects, or engages in, to the accomplishment of its one great object.*

An earnest man has much sagacity in discerning objects, even at a distance, that are favorable to his purpose; much power in seizing them as they approach; and much tact in pressing them into his service, and weaving them into his schemes. He avoids at the same time the folly of letting go his main object in the pursuit of lesser ones, and of thus converting means into ends. The operations of his mind resemble those of a vast machine, in which the ruling power subjects to itself the thousand little wheels and spindles that are set in motion, and makes them all accomplish the purpose for which the engine has been set up. Or the current of his thought and feeling may be compared to the majestic flow of some noble river, which receives into its stream, and bears forward in its course, the numerous rivulets by which its waters are swollen, and its power increased. So acts the earnest minister. There are various matters which he may attend to, and ought not to neglect, which may with great propriety be considered as means, but which cannot be viewed as the end of his high and holy calling.

The FIRST of these which I mention is *learning*, and indeed, *general knowledge* of all kinds. Literature, science, and philosophy, however excellent in themselves, and however subservient they may be rendered as means to accomplish the great ends of the ministerial office, must never, I repeat, be exalted into the place of the ends themselves. Viewed as subordinate and subsidiary, they cannot be too highly valued, nor too diligently sought. There is not any kind of knowledge, nor any degree of it, which may not be made tributary to the ends of gospel ministrations. All other things being equal, he is likely to be the most useful preacher, who is the most learned one. There is nothing, there can be nothing, in literature and science, which of themselves can be injurious to a minister of Christ: the pride and vanity which produce such a result are but as those weeds which flourish in a shallow and sandy soil, but which wither and die in rich, deep loam. The man who decries learning as mischievous *per se* to the ministry, is fit only to be torch-bearer to another Caliph Omar, and to act the part of an incendiary to all the libraries of the world. A minister may have too little piety, too little solicitude for the salvation of souls, too little devotedness, too little care to render his acquisitions subservient to the ends of his vocation, but he can never have too much knowledge.

"Perhaps the best answer that can be given to those inconsiderate Christians who say that religion needs not such foreign and meretricious aids as human learning, is that of SOUTH,—'If God hath no need of our learning, he can have still less of your ignorance.' In the spiritual temple, as wel. as in the ark of the covenant, there is room not only for those humbler gifts, the skins and hair cloth, but also for the gold and silver of human learning: and even the sciences themselves, daughters as they are of the uncreated wisdom, may receive consecration from seraphic piety, and be made priestesses of the Most High, by the very service in which we employ them." How beautiful is the following language of Dr. WISEMAN, and how correct the sentiment which it clothes and adorns: "You all, I doubt not, have often admired those exquisite paintings in the ceilings of the Borgia apartments of the Vatican, wherein the sciences are represented as holding their separate courts; each enthroned upon a stately chair, with features and mien of the most noble and dignified beauty, surrounded by the emblems and most distinguished representatives of its power on earth, and seeming to claim homage from all that gaze upon it. And judge what would have been the painter's conception, and to what a sublimity of expression he would have risen, had it been his task to represent the noblest of all sciences, our divine religion, enthroned, as ever becomes her, to receive the fealty and worship of these her handmaids. For if, as hath been proved, they are but ministers to her superior rule, and are intended to furnish the evidences of her authority, how much above theirs must be the comeliness and grace, and majesty and holiness, with which she must be arrayed! And what honor and dignity must be conferred on him who feels himself deputed to bear the tribute of these fair vassals; and how must his admiration of their graces be enhanced, by finding himself brought so near her presence."*

* Dr. WISEMAN'S "Lectures on the Connection between Science and Revealed Religion." Vol. II., p. 317.

This splendid passage expresses what I would urgently enforce, that literature and science may be subservient, but must be *only* subservient, to the ends of the ministerial office.

Having thus quoted a passage from a Roman Catholic author, let me subjoin to it another from a Protestant, of a different kind indeed, but by no means inharmonious with it. "O my brethren," says the amiable and pious DODDRIDGE, in his incomparable sermon on "The Evil and Danger of Neglecting Souls," "let us consider how fast we are posting through this dying life, which God has assigned to us, in which we are to manage concerns of infinite moment; how fast we are passing on to the immediate presence of our Lord, to give up our account to him. You must judge for yourselves, but permit me to say for my own part, I would not for ten thousand worlds be that man, who when God shall ask him at last how he has employed most of his time, while he continued a minister of his church, and had the care of souls, shall be obliged to reply, 'Lord, I have restored many corrupted passages in the classics, and illustrated many which were before obscure; I have cleared up many intricacies in chronology or geography; I have solved many perplexed cases in algebra; I have refined on astronomical calculations, and left behind me many sheets on these curious and difficult subjects; and these are the employments in which my life has been worn out, while preparations for the pulpit, and ministrations in it, did not demand my more immediate attendance.' Oh sirs, as for the waters that are drawn from *these springs,* how sweetly soever they may taste to a *curious* mind that thirsts after them, or to an *ambitious* mind that thirsts for the applause they sometimes procure, I fear there is too often reason *to pour them out before the*

Lord, with rivers of penitential tears, as the blood of souls which have been forgotten, whilst these trifles have been remembered and pursued."

This is the language of a scholar, a critic, and a man of varied knowledge; but whose piety as a Christian, and whose devotedness as a minister, were equal to his other attainments. In a foot-note to this admirable discourse, which we ministers should do well to read once a month, is a quotation from a sermon of a Scottish minister, preached before the Synod of Glasgow, which also I may with propriety introduce here:—"A just sense of the relation we stand in to our flocks, and a genuine feeling of that affection which is due to them, will not allow us to hesitate one moment, whether that part of our time is most worthily employed, which is taken up in doing real offices of friendship among them, or that part of it which is spent in perusing the finest writings of the greatest genius that ever appeared in our world, or in polishing any little compositions of our own. Is the arranging of words, the beautifying of language, or even storing our own minds with the divinest sentiments, an employment of equal dignity and importance in itself, or equally pleasing in reflection, with that of composing differences or extinguishing animosities, searching out modest and indigent merit, and relieving it, comforting a melancholy heart, giving counsel to a perplexed mind, suspending pain by our presence and sympathy, suggesting to an unfurnished mind proper materials for meditation in the time of distress, or laying hold of a favorable opportunity of conveying valuable instruction and religious impressions to a mind little susceptible of them on other occasions? There is no need of saying anything in confirmation of this: it was the glorious character of Jesus, that he wen about doing good.'

It might be admitted, and shall be conceded, that we live in an age when, to carry out the main purpose of the Christian ministry, and to render it efficient for the salvation of souls, there requires a higher standard of ministerial qualifications, and larger acquirements of general knowledge, than at some former periods.

It will, I hope, be clearly seen from all this, that I am not decrying education, or learning, or the greatest diligence in ministers for the acquisition of knowledge; quite the contrary; but I am enforcing with all the earnestness I can command, the indispensable necessity of rendering all acquirements subordinate to the great work of saving souls. Learning, as an ultimate object and for its own sake, is infinitely below the ambition of a holy and devoted servant of Christ; but learning employed to invigorate the intellect, to enrich the imagination, to cultivate the taste, to give power to thought, and variety to illustration; to add to the skill and energy with which we wield the weapons of our warfare, is in some cases indispensable, and in all invaluable. Unhappily it is not uncommon for those who have made large acquisitions in varied learning, and acquired a scientific, philosophic or literary taste, to yield to the seductions of the objects of their pursuits, and to allow themselves to be led astray from the simplicity that is in Christ Jesus. If there is one man to be admired, envied, and imitated above all others, it is he who has baptized large classic and scientific acquirements at the font of Christianity,—has surrendered them at the foot of the cross, and gathered them up into the nerve of his strength, as a preacher of the gospel. To hear such a man chastening and guiding, but not checking or freezing the gushing utterances of a full heart, by the rules of genuine eloquence; and warming and sanctifying the finest specimens of rhetoric by the glow of a soul on fire with the passion of love to God and souls; to see the genius of Tully and Demosthenes clothing themselves with the mantle of Paul, Peter, and John, and under the constraining love of Christ, employing all its resources of diction and of metaphor, to persuade men to be reconciled to God,—is an object of surpassing interest: to such preachers we can almost fancy that not only men, but angels, must listen with delight.

There is, however, too much truth in the following remarks of Dr. VAUGHAN: "The effect of learning and of elegant scholarship, in the modern pulpit, has commonly been to render men incapable of producing impressions of this nature in any degree. In the case of such preachers, neither the diction they use, nor the mould into which they cast their expressions and sentences, nor the comparisons they introduce, nor anything belonging to their rhetoric, has been an object of study with a view to its fitness to secure attention, and to move the thoughts and passions of such assemblies as are generally convened by the preacher—assemblies made up from the popular, much more than from the thoroughly educated classes of society. The great object of this class of preachers has been to acquit themselves learnedly, or to acquit themselves elegantly. It is grievous to witness the mischiefs which have resulted from this conventionalism in pulpit taste. If our pulpit lessons must be veiled in the language of a particular kind of scholarship, then the people generally, and even men of good natural parts, who have not been initiated into that sholarship, will fail to perceive our meaning, and will begin, as the consequence, to cast about for some better employment than listening to the utterance of our unknown tongue."*

I go on now to mention another qualification for the sacred office, and which the earnest minister will anxiously cultivate with a view to the great object of his life and labors, and to which I advance with a praying mind, an anxious heart, and a trembling hand, ardently desirous to set it forth in such manner as shall secure for it the attention which its importance demands; I mean PERSONAL RELIGION. We are weak in the pulpit, because we are weak in the closet. An earnest man will not only train his mind to understand his object, and draw around him the resources of ways and means for its accomplishment, but will discipline his heart; for there, within, is the spring of his energies, the seat of impulse, and the source of power. If the heart beat feebly, the whole circulation must be sluggish, and the frame inert. So is it with us ministers: our own personal religion is the mainspring of all our power in the pulpit. We are feeble as preachers, because we are feeble as Christians. Whatever other deficiencies we have, the chief of all lies in the heart. The apostle said, "We believe and therefore speak." We not only speak *what* we believe, but *as* we believe; if the faith be weak, so will be the utterance. In another place the same inspired writer said, "Knowing the terrors of the Lord, we persuade men." It was when standing as amidst the solemnities of the last judgment, that apostles besought men to be reconciled to God. The flame of zeal which in their ministrations rose to such a height and intensity as to subject them to the charge of insanity, is thus accounted

* Modern Pulpit, pp. 23, 24.

for, "The love of Christ constraineth us." We have too much forgotten that the fount of eloquence is in the heart; and that it is feeling which gives to words and thoughts their power. An unrenewed man, or one with a lukewarm piety, may preach elaborate sermons upon orthodox doctrines; but what are they for power and efficiency, when compared with those of the preacher, who feels as well as glories in the cross, but as the splendid coruscations of the aurora borealis to the warm and vivifying rays of the sun?

The Christian minister sustains a double relation, and has a double duty to perform; he is a preacher to the world, and a pastor to the church, and it is impossible he can fulfil, or be in earnest to fulfil, the obligations he is under to either, without a large measure of personal godliness. As regards the church which is committed to his care, and of which he is made by the Holy Ghost the spiritual overseer, he has not only to increase their knowledge, but their holiness, their love, and their spirituality; to aid them in performing all the branches of their duty, and in cultivating all the graces of their sanctification. And what is the present spiritual condition of the great bulk of the professors of religion? Amidst much that is cheering, there is, on the other hand, much that is discouraging and distressing to the more pious observer. We behold a strange combination of zeal and worldly-mindedness; great activity for the extension of religion in the earth, united with lamentable indifference to the state of religion in the soul; in short, apparent vigor in the extremities, with a growing torpor at the heart. Multitudes are substituting zeal for piety, liberality for mortification, and a social for a personal religion. No careful reader of the New Testament, and observer of the present state of the church, can fail to be convinced, one should think, that what is now wanting is a high spirituality. The Christian profession is sinking in its tone of piety; the line of separation between the church and the world becomes less and less perceptible; and the character of genuine Christianity, as expounded from pulpits and delineated in books, has too rare a counterpart in the lives and spirit of its professors.

How is this to be remedied, and by what means is the spirit of piety to be revived? May we not ask a previous question—How came this spirit of slumber over the church? Was it not from the pulpit? And if a revival take place in the former, must it not begin in the latter? Is the ministry of the present day in that state of earnest piety which is likely to originate and sustain an earnest style of preaching, and to revive the lukewarmness of their flocks? I do not mean for a moment to insinuate that the ministers of the present day among the Dissenters, or Methodists, or the evangelical clergy of the Church of England, are characterized by immorality, or even a want of substantial holiness; or that they would suffer, as regards their piety, in comparison with those of some other periods of the history of their denominations: but what I am compelled to believe, and what I now express, is that our deficiencies are great as compared not only with what is always required of us, but is especially required by the circumstances of the times in which we live. Amidst the eager pursuits of commerce; the elegancies and soft indulgences of an age of growing refinement; the high cultivation of the intellect, and the contests of politics, the church needs a strong and high barrier to keep *out* the encroachment of tides so adverse to its prosperity, and needs equally a dam to keep *in* its spiritual feeling. And where shall we find this, if not in the pulpit? It is not in the nature of things to be expected that the spiritua character of the church should ever be superior to that of the ministry; and it is perfectly consistent with what we know of human nature to expect that it will always hold itself excused for being inferior. It will not tread a path which its spiritual guides are slow to pursue; and will deem it an affectation of sanctity and presumptuous ambition to attempt to advance beyond them. How else than by believing in a deficiency of our piety can we account for the fact of a diminished efficiency in our ministry?

I cannot resist the temptation of giving here a long extract from that beautiful tract entitled "A Revived Ministry our only hope for a Revived Church;" a tract so eminently excellent, and so adapted to promote the end of the pious and accomplished writer, that it is a proof that we have little wish to be raised to higher attainments in piety, that such a heart-searching, soul-reviving production has yet reached only a second edition.*

"And for such a revived ministry there would be the most hopeful preparation of mind. The object to be aimed at would be distinctly conceived; it would be loved and cherished as the noblest to which a redeemed being can consecrate himself; and there would be a readiness to yield everything to the urgency and grandeur of its claims, together with the simplicity and guilelessness of intention, which would mightily aid the judgment in seeing its best way to the best methods of achieving it. In such circumstances, all the distracting influences arising from indistinct

* A pious clergyman of this town was so impressed with the beauty, fidelity, and earnestness of this tract, that he purchased a hundred copies for distribution among his brethren.

views, a divided heart, and infirmity of purpose, would be withdrawn, and leave the minister of Christ free to take a decided and energetic course. The subjection of the church and the world to the dominion of the truth, in a pure heart and holy life, would be ever present to his mind as the sole and sublime end of his ministry; and, drawing after it the full tide of his sympathies, and permitting no diversion of his strength to any inferior object, it would command all his powers, and dispossess him of every wish but that of living and dying for it. And that moment would be the dawn of an era of prosperity.

"Everything which he did would be enlivened by the presence of a warmer and holier zeal: but it would be the public administration of divine truth, in the ordinance of preaching, in which the stronger and healthier pulsations of spiritual life would be most signally displayed, and from which the largest results might be expected. In this he would be prepared for acting a new part. Himself saved and eminently sanctified, as well as possessed of the whole treasury of sacred knowledge in the inspired volume, he would be well versed in the respective truths best calculated for awakening the unconverted, and promoting the highest sanctification of the church, and administer them with improved wisdom and force. The wretchedness of the soul as guilty, depraved, and hastening to the judgment-seat; the blessedness of arresting it in its downward course, and of exalting it once more to the glory of the Divine image and favor; the ample means provided for all this in the mediation of Christ; the experience of their efficacy in himself, and the conviction of their undiminished power to do as much for others; the rapid flight of time and the possibility of all the mercy overshadowing that hour being trifled with and lost forever,—these thrill his soul with mingled commiseration, hope, and fear, and urge him to improve to the utmost the fleeting opportunity of snatching sinners from perdition, and adding to the brightness of the Redeemer's crown. How well chosen is his theme! no matter of curious speculation, but some one or more of the solemn verities which concern the instant faith and obedience of every hearer, and bring life or death, as accepted or rejected. Away with those artificial rules which some have prescribed, as if to prepare a sermon were something like composing an epic! He has a truth to enforce, a moral effect to produce, and the sense of its unutterable importance brings to bear upon it all the resources of a judicious, intelligent, and impassioned mind. Bent on winning souls to God, or quickening them to higher obedience, this one desire possesses and inflames him, and gives a unity and completeness to his subject, a force and compactness of argument, a felicity of speech and manner, an ardor and impressiveness of appeal, which the art of the rhetorician could never have supplied. He feels, moreover, that his strength is in God, and that the pleadings of human wisdom and pity never availed apart from a higher inspiration. Would there not be more than HOPE from a ministry like this? In itself so convincing and persuasive, rendered still more so by the practical exhibition of all the faith, uprightness, benevolence, and spirituality which it inculcates, looking to God, and owning its weakness without his blessing, it would have all the characteristics from which the susceptibilities of the human mind, and the solemn promises of the Almighty, authorize the expectation of enlarged success. When was such a ministry known to be long in contact with the minds of men, without producing the happiest effects? 'The word of the Lord would have free course and be glorified,' converts press into the church, and the church be raised to a higher renovation.

"And the minister thus revived would have unwonted power in individual intercourse with the members of his flock. Living only for their advancement in faith and holiness, the warmth and tenderness of his concern for it would make him prompt to seize every opportunity of promoting it, and give an appropriateness and weight to his sayings which a colder and less earnest piety would never have dictated; while the objects of his solicitude, feeling the point and force of his words, and impressed with his singleness of purpose, and still more with that uniform display of the Christian virtues, which was the best voucher of his deep sincerity, would find themselves drawn along by a combination of influences so pure and commanding, that they must tread in the steps of his piety, and bend to his hallowed purpose of extending the limits of the church, and giving it a holier aspect. Every faithful minister can look back upon seasons when, under the kindlings of a warmer love and zeal, and a more affecting sense of external things, he was animated to increased exertion; and he has found that, not only did his preaching fix the attention and touch the souls of his hearers more than at other times, but that, when he went among them in private, the elevation of his spirit, the seriousness of his converse, and the solemnity and unction pervading his petitions, produced an evident impression, and that he left them with improved feelings and resolves. All emotion is contagious, and easily propagates itself to other bosoms; but, beside this, the wakefulness of his zeal, and his steadiness of purpose, made him eager to extract the highest amount of good from every opportunity, stimulated ingenuity, and gave an aptness and charm to all that he said, which fell with happy effect on the understanding and the heart. And had the ardor and determination of those seasons been permanent, the equable and healthy excitement of every day's labor, instead of soon relapsing into the feebler sensibility of other times, his ministry would, doubtless, have told a different history, and been far more richly laden with precious fruit."

Happy shall I feel if this feeble tribute, not only of the recommendation of my pen, but of my heart's gratitude for the benefit I have derived from this production, shall induce any of my brethren to peruse this precious gift which has been offered to them by a writer who veils himself under the modest title of "One of the least among the brethren."

Do we want examples and patterns of eminent and earnest piety, how richly are they supplied both in number and in quality in the pages of our own denominational history. Where is the deep, ardent, experimental religion of our ancestors, the fathers and founders of Protestant nonconformity? What a theologian was OWEN when he wrote his Exposition of the Hebrews! What a polemic when he penned his controversy with BIDDULPH! What an ecclesiastic when he drew up his treatise on Church Government! But what a *Christian* when he indulged in his "Meditations on the Glory of Christ," and gave us his treatise "On Spirituality of Mind and the Mortification of Sin!" What a logician and divine was HOWE, when he produced his "Living Temple;" but what a Christian when, in the shadow of this noble structure of his holy genius, he poured out his heart in his work on "Delighting in God," and "The Blessedness of the Righteous." And then think of holy BAXTER, who gained repose from the labors of polemic strife, and relief from the tortures of the stone, in the believing anticipations of "The Saint's Rest." Was their piety the result of their suffering? Then for one I could be almost content to take the latter, so that I might be possessed of the former. Lead me to the spots, I do not say where they trimmed their midnight lamp, and continued at their studies till the morning star, glittering through their casement, chided them to their pillow; but to those more hallowed scenes where they held their nightly vigils, and wrestled with the angel till the break of day. Mighty shades of OWEN and BAXTER; HOWE and MANTON; HENRY and BATES; GOODWIN and NYE—illustrious and holy men, we thank you for the rich legacy you have bequeathed to us in your immortal works; but oh, where has the mantle of your piety fallen!

God of our fathers! be the God
Of their succeeding race.

Here then let us begin, where indeed we ought to begin, with our own spirits; for what should be the piety of that man on the state of whose heart depends in no small degree the spiritual condition of a whole Christian community? If we turn to any department of human action, we shall learn that no one can inspire a taste, much less a passion, for the object of his own pursuit, who is not himself most powerfully moved by it. It is, as I have said, the scintillation of his own zeal flying off from his own glowing heart, and falling upon their souls, which kindles in them the fire which burns in himself. Lukewarmness can excite no ardor, originate no activity, produce no effect: it benumbs whatever it touches. If we inquire for the sources of energy, the springs of activity, in the most successful ministers of Christ, we shall find that they lay in the ardor of their devotion. They were men of prayer and of faith. They dwelt upon the mount of communion with God, from whence they came down like Moses to the people, radiant with the glory on which they had themselves been intently gazing. They stationed themselves where they could look at things unseen and eternal, and came with the stupendous visions fresh in their view, and spoke of them under the impression of what they had just seen and heard. They drew their thoughts and made their sermons from their minds and from their books, but they breathed life and power into them from their hearts, and in their closets. Trace either WHITFIELD or WESLEY in their career, and you will see how beaten was the road between the pulpit and the closet: the grass was not allowed to grow in that path. This was in great part the secret of their power. They were mighty in public, because in their retirement they had clothed themselves, so to speak, with Omnipotence. The same might be said of all others who have attained to eminence as successful preachers of the gospel. If then we would see a revival of the power of the pulpit, we must see first of all a revival in the piety of those who occupy it: and when this is the case, then "He that is feeble among us shall be as David, and the house of David shall be as God, as the angel of the Lord before them."

CHAPTER III.

NATURE OF EARNESTNESS, CONTINUED,

AS EXEMPLIFIED IN THE MATTER AND MANNER OF PREACHING.

FIFTHLY. Earnestness will manifest itself by *energetic and untiring action in the use of those means by which its object is accomplished.* It does not satisfy itself with contemplation, however enraptured; schemes, however well concerted; wishes, however fervent, or anticipations, however lively: but proceeds to vigorous and well-adapted exertion. An earnest man must of necessity be an active one: he is the opposite and the contrast of an idle dreamer. "I see my object," he exclaims; "it stands out in bold relief, clearly defined before my eyes, and I will leave no effort untried to accomplish it. I have made up my mind to labor, self-denial, and fatigue; and if I do not succeed it shall not be for want of determined and continuous effort." Such is his resolution, and his practice is like it. He is always at work. You know where to find him, and how he is employed. He is the very type of diligence. Labor is pleasure. No difficulties deter him, no disappointments dishearten him. The ignorant do not understand him, the indolent pity him, but the intelligent admire him. There is something in his earnestness commanding, grand; especially when the object of it is worthy.

Apply this to the ministry: there are two means by which this accomplishes its end, *preaching* and the *pastorate.*

In reference to the former, I advert first to the MATTER of our ministrations. And this must consist, of course, of those topics which bear most obviously and directly upon the great ends we are seeking to accomplish. Earnestness will take the nearest and most direct road to its object; nor will it be seduced from its path by beautiful prospects and pleasant walks, that lie in another direction. "I want to reach that point, and I cannot allow myself to be attracted by scenes, which, however agreeable and appropriate to others, would, if I stayed or turned to contemplate them, only hinder me in my business." Such is the language of one intent upon success in any given scheme. Now what is the end of our office? The reconciliation of sinners to God, and their ultimate and complete salvation, when so reconciled. It is easy then to see that the matter of our instruction and persuation must be, *the ministry of reconciliation.* Of course it must be our purpose to declare the whole counsel of God, and to remember "that all scripture is given by inspiration of God, and is profitable for doctrine, for reproof, for correction, for instruction in righteousness: that the man of God may be thoroughly furnished unto all good works." In the way of exposition a minister should go through the greater part of the whole Bible, fairly and honestly explaining and enforcing it. But since the whole Bible, as explained by the most perfect revelation of the New Testament, directly or indirectly points to Christ, or may be illustrated and enjoined by considerations suggested by his mission and work, our preaching should have a decidedly evangelical character. The divinity, incarnation, and death of Christ—his atonement for sin—his resurrection, ascension, intercession, and mediatorial reign—his spiritual kingdom, and his second coming; the offices and work of the Holy Spirit in illuminating, regenerating, and sanctifying the human soul; the doctrine of justification by faith, and the new birth; the sovereignty of God in the dispensation of his saving gifts—these and their kindred and collateral topics should form, so to speak, the staple of our public ministrations and teaching. It surely must be this which the apostle meant when he said, "I determined not to know anything among you save Jesus Christ and him crucified." "The Jews require a sign, and the Greeks seek after wisdom, but we preach Christ crucified, to the Jews a stumbling-block, and unto the Greeks foolishness: but unto them which are called, both Jews and Greeks, Christ the power of God and the wisdom of God." If there be any meaning in language, this must imply that the apostle in his ministry dwelt chiefly upon the work of Christ, as the theme of his discourses. His epistles all sustain this view of his meaning, They are all full of this great subject. We may perhaps smile at the simple piety of the individual who was at the trouble of counting the number of times that the apostle mentioned the name of Jesus in all his epistles, but at the same time something is to be learnt from the fact that he found it to reach between four and five hundred. This teaches us how thoroughly Christian, how entirely imbued with evangelism, his mind and his writings were. His morality was as evangelical as his doctrine, for he enforced all the branches of social obligation by motives drawn from the cross. His ethics were all baptized with the spirit of the gospel, so that the believer, in reading the writings of Paul, has his eye as constantly kept upon the crucified one, in the progress of his sanctification, as the sinner's eye is turned towards the same object, for his justification. Here then was the earnestness of the apostle, one constant, uniform, and undeviating endeavor to save men's souls by the truth as it is in Jesus.

A question now arises whether it is the duty of modern preachers to adopt the same method, and whether, inasmuch as their ends are the same with those of the apostle, they are to seek them by the same means. One should suppose there can be no rational doubt of this. If the apostles were the inspired teachers of Christianity, and have given us in their writings a full exhibition of what Christianity really is; and if it is our business to explain and enforce their writings; it seems to follow as a thing of course that our teaching as to the matter of our discourses must resemble theirs: and will any one pretend that this resemblance can be established unless our preaching is richly and prevailingly evangelical? I am aware it is sometimes said that the times are altered since the apostles' days, and that the state of the world is different from what it then was. But is not human nature in all its essential elements the same? Is it not the same in its moral aspect, impotency, and necessities? Does it not as much need, and as much depend upon the gospel scheme, as it did then? Is not the evangelical scheme as accurately adapted to its miserable condition as it was then? Can sin be pardoned in any other way than through the atonement of Christ; or the sinner be justified by any other means than faith in the Lord our righteousness; or the depraved heart be renewed and sanctified by any other agency than that of the Holy Spirit? Are not all the motives of evangelical doctrine as adapted, as powerful, and as efficacious now, as they were then? No alteration of subject then can be called for now, to meet the advancing state of society, since the gospel is intended and adapted to be God's instrument for the salvation of man, in all ages of the world, in all countries, and in all states of society. We reject alike the ancient practice of conforming the evangelical scheme to the systems of philosophy, and the modern Puseyite notion of the progressive development of Christian doctrine. To the men who would revive the former, we say, "Beware lest any man spoil you through philosophy and vain deceit, after the traditions of men, after the rudiments of the world, and not after Christ:" to the latter we say, "Jesus Christ, the same yesterday, and to-day, and forever. Be not carried about with divers and strange doctrines: for it is a good thing for the heart to be established with grace." It appears to me that something like the same attempts are being made in this day to corrupt the gospel by superstitious additions on the one hand, and by philosophic accommodations on the other, as were carried on in the early days of Christianity. Our danger lies in the latter.

It should never be forgotten that the time when the apostles discharged their ministry was only just after the Augustan era of the ancient world. Poetry had recently bestowed some of its golden favors on the empire of letters in the works of Virgil and Horace. The light of philosophy, though waning, still shed its lustre on Greece. The arts, and their most splendid creations in architecture, sculpture, and painting, still lived, though they had ceased to grow. It was at such a time, and amidst such scenes, the gospel began its course. Apostolic voices were listened to by sages and their pupils who basked in the sunshine of

Athenian wisdom, and were reverberated in echo from temples and statues that had been shaken by the thunders of Cicero and Demosthenes; yet these holy men conceded nothing to the demands of philosophy, but held forth the cross as the only object they felt they had a right to exhibit. They never once conceived such an idea as that they must accommodate themselves to the philosophy or the taste of the age in which they lived, and the places in which they ministered. It is true the philosophy of that day was a false one, but it was not known or acknowledged to be such at the time. Whether the apostle addressed himself to the philosophers on Mars Hill, or to the barbarians in the island of Melita; whether he reasoned with the Jews in their synagogues, or with the Greeks in the school of Tyrannus; he had but one theme, and that was Christ, and him crucified. And what right, or what reason, have we for deviating from this high and imperative example? Be it so, that we are in a literary, philosophic, and scientific age, what then? Is it an age that has outlived the need of the gospel for its salvation; or to the salvation of which anything else can supply a means, but the gospel? The supposition that something else than the gospel, as the theme of our pulpit ministrations, is requisite for such a period as this, or that the gospel must be presented in a more philosophic form, appears to me a most dangerous sentiment, as being a disparagement to the gospel itself, and containing the very germ of infidelity. Let the taste be cultivated as it may by literature, or the mind be enlightened by science, or the reason disciplined by philosophy, the heart is still deceitful and wicked, the conscience still burdened with guilt, and the whole soul in a state of alienation from God. The moral constitution is mortally diseased, and nothing but the gospel is God's saving health, which is as much required for the spiritual restoration of the polished son of science, as for that of the savage of New Zealand, or the Hottentot of South Africa. All else is but pretence and empiricism; and the man who would be in earnest, and successful in the salvation of souls, must have a clear conviction and a deep impression of these facts.

But perhaps the danger to which the evangelical ministry of the present age is exposed, is not so much a philosophizing spirit, or an attempt to conform the gospel to any metaphysical theory, as an effort to attain to a high intellectuality in setting forth received truths. We hear a great deal about this in modern times. It is become a kind of cant term, (for there is a high cant as well as a low one,) to speak of some men as very *intellectual* preachers. If by an intellectual preacher be meant a man who applies the acquirements of a vigorous and well-trained understanding to explain and enforce the great topics of evangelical truth; or the application, in the most attractive form, of whatever knowledge such a mind, in the pursuit after information of all kinds, can obtain, to the great end of the Christian ministry; or the employment of sound logic and natural eloquence to make the doctrines which are unto salvation bear down upon the heart and conscience; in that case a man cannot be too intellectual: the great and glorious doctrines of revealed truth and life eternal, deserve and demand the mightiest energies of the noblest intellects. But if, as is too generally the case, this intellectuality means the cold, dry, argumentative discussion of *religious* truth, rather than *evangelical* subjects, or even of the latter in an abstract and essay-like form; a mere heartless exercise of the understanding of the preacher, and intended or adapted only to engage the understanding of the hearers, without either interesting their affections or awakening their conscience; such intellectuality will do nothing but empty the places of worship in which it is exhibited, or at best draw together a congregation of persons who cannot do without some religion, but who prefer the cold abstractions of the head to the warm affections of the heart.

Here I would not be misconstrued to mean that every sermon must be on strictly evangelical themes; but that these must be the prevailing topics of the man who is in earnest for the salvation of souls. Nor would I go so far as to say that each sermon must contain as much of the gospel as would make every hearer of it acquainted with the way of salvation, though he never should listen to another discourse. There is such a thing as treating these subjects so carelessly, so familiarly, and so frequently, as to deprive them of all their power to interest and impress. A man whose soul is possessed with the passion for doing good, will make almost any and every topic adapted for usefulness. Subjects, which in other hands will be dry and uninteresting, will in his be invested with the glow and the warmth which live in his own soul, and which he imparts to everything he touches. His heart beats with an action so strong, so steady, and so healthful, that his fervid and holy intelligence circulates an evangelical vitality through what in others would be a cold and torpid frame, and thus causes the principle of gospel life to reach to the very extremities of the system of general truth. Still even he, though he dwell occasionally on every topic which can with propriety be brought into the pulpit, will, like the apostle, "glory only in the cross of Christ." Resisting the temptations to neglect a plain gospel, and to go in quest of airy speculations and unprofitable novelties, his aim will not be to gratify the imaginative by what is tasteful and poetic, the philosophical by what is profound, the metaphysical by what is subtle, or the curious by what is strange, but by manifestation of the truth to commend himself to every man's conscience in the sight of God. Alas that any preacher of the gospel should take any other aim, and seek any other object, than this! Do we want subjects for eloquence, where can we find them in such abundance, grandeur, and sublimity, as in the gospel scheme? The cross is a fount of the purest, most impassioned, and most pathetic eloquence in the world, from which genius may go on to draw its streams without ever exhausting it. Compare the most finished orations and sermons of MASSILLON, BOSSUET, or BOURDALOUE, with McLAURIN's discourse on "Glorying in the Cross;" and though the former are more perfect as models of composition, more decorated by all the artifices and graces of rhetoric, yet how far below that incomparable sermon in the sublimity of its theme, and the grandeur of its evangelical eloquence, are these boasted models of the French pulpit. Even the soul of BLAIR kindled into something like a glow of pious warmth when he came, which he seldom did, within the attraction of this object; and though it was but as moonlight, compared with the ardor of his colleague WALKER, yet in his sermon on "The Death of Christ," his frigid elegance becomes enlivened by his theme, and furnishes a standing proof that the heathen morals of Epictetus are a barren source of eloquence, compared with the Christian doctrines of the apostle Paul. I make no apology for requoting a passage from an American author which I have already given to the public in my Address to Students: "My dear brethren, why are we not more impressive? Theology affords the best field for tender, solemn, and sublime eloquence. The most august objects are presented · the most important interests are discussed; the most tender motives are urged. God and angels; the treason of Satan; the creation, ruin, and recovery of a world; the incarnation, death, resurrection, and reign of the Son of God; the day of judgment; a burning universe; an eternity; a heaven and a hell—all pass before the eye. What are the petty dissensions of the states of Greece, or the ambition of Philip; what are the plots and victories of Rome, or the treason of Cataline, compared with this? If ministers were sufficiently qualified by education, study, and the Holy Ghost; if they felt their subject as much as Demosthenes and Cicero did, they would be the most eloquent men on earth, and would be so esteemed wherever congenial minds were found."*

To know what themes contain the greatest potency over the public mind, and which should form the subject of an earnest ministry, we have only to consult the pages of ecclesiastical history. It is unnecessary, after what I have already written, to dwell upon the matter of apostolic preaching. It was by the purest evangelism that Christianity was planted in the earth, and it was when this gave place to a religion of forms and ceremonies, that the power and vitality of true godliness declined, and a mass of splendid corruption grew up, in the dark shadow of which the man of sin erected his throne, and the Papacy commenced its bloody reign. During the long night of the middle ages the sound of the faithful preacher was not heard, and the voice of Zion's watchman was silent, except in a few obscure nooks and corners of the earth; but wherever it was *then* heard, the same effects followed. It was this

* Dr. GRIFFIN's Sermon on the Art of Preaching.

subject with which CLAUDE, of Turin, when nearly all the world were wondering after the Beast, awakened in the ninth century the inhabitants of Piedmont, and commenced that glorious work which was carried on, more or less, for centuries, amid the seclusion of Alpine rocks and valleys, and which the concentrated power and fury of the Papacy could never entirely subvert. It was this evangelism which our WICLIFF preached in England in the fifteenth century, and by it kindled a fire, amidst the smouldering ashes of which lay concealed the embers that were again to ignite when fanned by the breath of the reformers a century afterwards. By what means did LUTHER achieve his immortal triumph over the powers of the Vatican, and smite off the fetters which had enslaved the judgment, heart, and conscience of man? By the potency of what subject did he lift up into freedom and dignity the prostrate intellect of the human race? What was the instrument with which he struck the empire of darkness, and inflicted a blow which resounded through the civilized world? It was the great evangelical doctrine of justification by faith. By what means did WHITFIELD and WESLEY rouse the slumbering piety of our nation, and call up a spirit which is going on from strength to strength to this day? By the evangelical system of divine truth. What called forth the missionary enterprise, and constructed all that moral machinery which is at work upon the world's conversion? Before what system of truths have the inhabitants of Polynesia and New Zealand surrendered their licentious habits and bloody rites; and the Hottentots and Esquimaux dropped their barbarism, and risen up into the form and manners of civilized men? What is the doctrine by which our missionaries are taking possession of India and China? I answer in one word, the doctrine of the cross.

Here then is a fact attested by authentic history, and uncontradicted by any one who is acquainted either with the present or the past, that all the great moral revolutions of our world, during the time of the Christian era, have been effected by one simple process, by one set of means, —and that process is the preaching of the gospel. Providential events may have prepared the way by levelling mountains and filling up valleys, and making smooth the course of the herald of the cross: but it was that herald's mighty voice proclaiming, "Behold the Lamb of God which taketh away the sins of the world," which by the power of God's Spirit has changed the moral aspect of our dark and dreary world. All this has not been done by learning, science, and philosophy; it is not the result of profound speculations on any theory of morals or of fine processes of reasoning; or of splendid creations of poetic genius; or of the subtleties of metaphysical discussion; no, but of the simple testimony of the gosple. While the philosopher has been theorizing in his closet, and the moral arithmetician has been carrying on his calculations in his study, the preacher has gone forth into the midst of the people, ignorant, wicked, and wretched as they were, has lifted up the great truth of a loving God, a dying Saviour, and a regenerating Spirit, and has by those means, as an instrument of God, changed the aspect cf society, and revolutionized the moral habits of the nations.

Strange that with the knowledge of these facts, any of our preachers should think of substituting these glorious truths, which have wrought such wonders in the world, by any other themes; or should act as if weapons that had proved their adaptation and their power, should be wielded now with a doubtful mind, and with a hesitating hand. If we would know how we are to convert souls to God, we have only to ask, how *has* God converted them? Nor is it necessary to go back to past ages, or abroad to other countries. Let us only look round upon our own country; let us go to our largest congregations and our most numerous churches, and ask what kind of preaching has done all this; what doctrine, and how handled, has drawn this multitude together; what magnet has put forth its attractions here? And the secret is soon discovered, and it will be found that here is an exemplification of our Lord Jesus Christ's words, "And I, if I be lifted up, will draw all men unto me." Go into other places where an evangelical intellectuality is substituted for the vital truths of the gospel; where philosophical abstractions take the place of popular addresses on great fundamental doctrines, and cold, logical essays are read, instead of heart-stirring sermons being preached; and the attenuated and still declining congregations proclaim the want of adaptation in the pulpit ministrations, and prove that for the popular mind there can be no substitute for the cross of Christ. Nor does this apply exclusively to the uneducated, or partially educated classes. Human nature in all its prevailing features, tastes, necessities, and enjoyments, is the same in the king and in the peasant; in the savage and the sage. All men are made susceptible of emotion, as well as capable of feeling; and all men love to feel, as well as to think. A tradesman, or professional man, who has been at work all the week, having had his mind strained with hard thinking, as well as his body by hard labor, when he takes his seat in his pew on a Sabbath morning, wants something for his heart, as well as for his head. With a sermon, however intellectual it may be, which has nothing that comes home to his affections, and causes him to *feel*, he is sure to be disappointed and dissatisfied. A dry essay on some gospel subject, which only proves a point he never doubted, or starts a difficulty he never dreamt of, is like giving him a stone when he asks for bread. He wants to be made to *feel* there is something higher and better than this world. He desires to enjoy the luxury of hallowed emotion, he covets the joy and peace of believing, and the anticipations of that world, where the weary are at rest, and the din of business will be forever hushed. That man, tired and jaded by the cares, anxieties, and toils of six days, wants to lie down and take repose on the soft green of evangelical truth, and not on the hard rocks of abstract speculation. It is true, that being a man of education and reading, his heart must be reached through his intellect, and though it must be the substantial bread of evangelical truth with which he is fed, yet it must not be coarse or chaffy; it must not only be prepared and made of the finest of the wheat, but it must also be well mixed, and made palatable to a refined taste by a skilful hand.

Before I pass from this part of the subject, it may be proper to remark that perhaps there are few expressions more misunderstood, and on which more mistakes have been made, than "*preaching the gospel.*" Many by the use of this phrase aim to exclude from the pulpit almost every topic but a perpetual and almost unvarying exhibition of the death of our Lord, and consider this specifically, and this only, as preaching Christ. But it is strangely forgotten by the preachers of this school, that as the scheme of mediation by the Saviour is founded on the eternal obligation and immutable nature of the law of God, and was intended, not to subvert, but to uphold its authority, the moral law must be explained and enforced, in all its purity, spirituality, and extent. Repentance towards God is no less included in the apostolic ministry, than faith in our Lord Jesus Christ; and how can a sinner repent of his transgressions against the law, if he know not the law he has violated? for "sin is the transgression of the law;" and "by the law is the knowledge of sin." So that no man can know sin without knowing the law; and herein appears to me one of the prevailing defects of modern preaching, I mean the neglect of holding up this perfect mirror, in which the sinner shall see reflected his own moral image. It is true that some are melted down at once into a sense of wickedness, and brought to the exercise of both repentance and faith, by an exhibition of divine love in the death of Christ; but I do not think this is so usual a method of conversion as the first awakening of the sinner by an exposition and application of the perfect law. Dr. DWIGHT says, "Few, very few, are ever awakened or convinced by the encouragements and promises of the gospel: but almost all by the denunciations of the law. The blessings of immortality, the glories of heaven, are usually, to say the least, preached with little efficacy to an assembly of sinners. I have been surprized to see how dull, inattentive, and sleepy such an assembly has been, amidst the strongest representations of these divine subjects, combining the most vivid images with a vigorous style and an impressive elocution."* This is a strong testimony, but it is perhaps a little overstated. Still I am persuaded there is much truth in it, for it seems to stand by reason, that men will care little about pardon till they are convinced of sin, and as the apostle says, it is by the law that they come to the knowledge of sin. In this particular there appears to me a superior adaptation in the American preaching to the work of conviction, than in the British pulpit; there is

* Vol. II., p. 417.

more of this exposition of the law, and of the application of it to the sinner's conscience more that is calculated to make him feel at once his obligations and his guilt; more of that which silences his excuses, unravels the deceitfulness of his heart, strips him of self-righteousness, makes him thoroughly acquainted with himself and his entire need of a Saviour; in short, more of what the apostle calls commending himself to every man's conscience in the sight of God. With this, however, is I think associated a want of evangelical fulness and tenderness. I remember a discussion, by a large company of ministers in my vestry, o one occasion, as to what style of preaching had been foun in their own experience to be most useful; and it was pretty generally admitted, and some of them had been among our most successful preachers, that sermons on alarming and impressive texts had been most blessed in producing conviction of sin, and first concern about salvation. At the same time it must be recollected, that though descriptions of sin may affect—exhibiting the consequences of it may affright—vehement censures of it may alarm—reasoning concerning it may open the gloomy road to despair—this alone will not convert. Law without gospel will harden, as gospel without law will only lead to carelessness and presumption: it is the union of both that will possess the sinner with a loathing of himself, and love to God. Still our danger in this age lies not so much in neglecting the gospel, as in omitting to associate with this the preaching of the law. It is worthy of remark that Jesus Christ, who was incarnate love itself, the living gospel, yea, the way, the truth, the life, was the most alarming preacher that was ever in our world. It is, however, especially incumbent upon us not to mistake grossness for fidelity, nor harshness for earnestness. The remarks of Mr. Hall on this, are as correct as they are beautiful. "A harsh and unfeeling manner of denouncing the threatenings of the word of God, is not only barbarous and inhuman, but calculated, by inspiring disgust, to rob them of all their efficiency. If the awful part of our message, which may be styled the burden of the Lord, ever fall with due weight upon our hearers, it will be when it is delivered with a trembling hand, and faltering lips." The look, the tone, the action, when such subjects are discussed, should be a mixture of solemnity and affection—the awfulness of love. To hear such topics dwelt upon in strong language, vehement action, and boisterous tones, strikes us as being an utter violation of all propriety, and in every hearer of the least discernment, is likely to excite horror and revulsion. Real earnestness is the result of deep emotion, and the emotion excited by the sight of a fellow-creature perishing in his sins is that of the tenderest commiseration, which will express itself, not in stormy declamation and thundering denunciations, but of solemnly chastened expostulation and appeal.

CHAPTER IV.

NATURE OF EARNESTNESS CONTINUED.

EARNESTNESS IN REFERENCE TO MANNER.

I NOW pass from matter to *manner;* and when I say manner, I wish to be understood as including in that term, not simply the method of communicating truth by voice and gesture, but the cast of thought and the style of composition in reference to the truth so enunciated; and what is wanted for the pulpit is a vivacious, in opposition to a stiff, formal, and dull method. Style must of course to a considerable extent vary with the subject matter, and be regulated by it. In exegetical preaching, or in that part of a sermon which is merely expository, all that is required, and what *is* required, is a calm perspicuity, a flow of clear, limpid, quiet thought, which shall instruct the understanding, and gently draw after it the heart, without being expected to move, in any great degree, the passions. We have some beautiful specimens of this in the elegant discourses of Dr. WARDLAW. Well would it be if, after his manner, we could be critical without being pedantic; exegetical without being scholastic; and invest exposition with charms which should make it attractive to all our congregations. But though a careful analysis of the text should be the basis of almost all our sermons, there needs something more than mere exegesis, however clear or correct.

We have to do not only with a dark intellect that needs to be instructed, but with a hard heart that needs to be impressed, and a torpid conscience that needs to be awakened; and have to make our hearers feel that in the great business of religion, there is much to be done, as well as much to be known. We must give knowledge, for light is as essential to the growth of piety in the spiritual world, as it is to the growth of vegetation in the natural one: and then the analogy holds good in another point, for we must not only let in light but add great and vigorous labor to carry on the culture. We must, therefore, rise from exegesis into exhortation, warning, and expostulation. The apostle's manner is the right one,—"Whom we preach, *warning* every man, and teaching every man, that we may present every man perfect in Christ Jesus." There must not only be the directive, but the impulsive manner. All our hearers know far more of the Bible than they practice: the head is far in advance of the heart; and our great business is to persuade, to entreat, to beseech. We have to leal with a dead, heavy *vis inertiæ* of mind; yea more, we have to overcome a stout resistance, and to move a reluctant heart. If all that was necessary to secure the ends of our ministry was to lay the truth open to the mind; if the heart were already predisposed to the subject of our preaching, then, like the lecturer on science, we might dispense with the hortatory manner, and confine ourselves exclusively to explanation: logic, unaccompanied by rhetoric, would suffice. But when we find in every sinner we address, an individual acting in opposition to the dictates of his judgment, and the warnings of his conscience, as well as to the testimony of Scripture; an individual who is sacrificing the interests of his immortal soul to the vanities of the world, and the corruptions of his heart; an individual who is madly bent upon his ruin, and rushing to the precipice from which he will take his fatal leap into perdition; can we in that case be satisfied with merely explaining, however clearly, and demonstrating, however conclusively, the truth of revelation? To borrow the allusion which I have already made, should we think it enough, coldly to unfold the sin of suicide, and logically to arrange the proofs of its criminality, before the man who had in his hand the pistol or the poison with which he was just about to destroy himself? Would exegesis, however clear and accurate, be enough in this case? Should we not entreat, expostulate, beseech? Should we not lay hold of the arm uplifted for destruction, and snatch the poison cup from the hand that was about to apply it to the lips? What is the case with the impenitent sinners to whom we preach, but that of individuals bent upon self-destruction, not indeed the present destruction of their bodies, but of their souls? There they are before our eyes, rushing in their sins and their impenitence to the precipice that overhangs the pit of destruction; and shall we content ourselves with sermons, however excellent for elegance, for logic, for perspicuity, and even for evangelism, but which have no hortatory power, no restraining tendency, none of the apostle's beseeching entreaty? Shall we merely lecture on theology, and deal out religious science, to men who, amidst a flood of light already pouring over them, care for none of these things?

It is a question of not a little difficulty, how far the usual rules and qualities of secular eloquence may be carried out in the composition of our sermons. The language of the apostle, in reference to his own preaching, has been thought to forbid all elaboration,—"Christ sent me to preach the gospel, not with wisdom of words, lest the cross of Christ should be made of none effect." A right understanding of his circumstances and ours, will show us that there are differences which forbid too rigid and literal an application of this sentiment to us. Miracles gave a potency to his preaching, which is wanting, of course, in ours. Besides, the wisdom here forbidden was not the selection of the best words, and placing them in the best order for the statement of divine truth, but that combination of false philosophy and artificial rhetoric, which was the usual practice of the Grecian schools; in short, he forbade such a method of setting forth evangelical doctrine as would have brought it into conformity, both as to matter and manner, with the fashionable systems of philosophy. Provided the elaboration is carried on with a view to make the sermon at once perspicuous and impressive, to give it power to command the attention, and, at the same time, to instruct the judgment, engage the affections, and awaken the conscience; to render the subject clearly understood and deeply felt, it cannot be too perfectly done. No elaboration which causes the hearer to forget the preacher, and even the sermon as a production of art, and to think only of himself and the subject; which rivets attention, and makes every one feel that he is in the presence, not only of man, but of God; which lays open the way of salvation so clearly that the most obtuse understanding shall comprehend it, and at the same time, so forcibly that the dullest heart shall feel it, cannot be wrong. If a preacher of the power of Demosthenes were to arise, he would, and must, carry that power into the pulpit, and ought to do so. But, on the other hand, an elaboration that is betrayed in every part of the discourse, and which makes it but too evident to any serious or observant mind, that it was the preacher's aim, not to convert souls, but to catch applause; which, in the view of the fashionable, the giddy, and the frivolous, entitles the sermonizer to the highest rank among pulpit orators; which fills the discourse with flowery diction and gaudy metaphors, with elegant declamation, and fanciful descriptions, with tasteful addresses, and beautiful pictures; which, though it takes the cross for its subject, almost instantly leaves it, and runs out into the fields of poesy, or the labyrinths of metaphysics, for its subtle arguments or its sparkling and splendid illustrations; which, to sum up all, engages the judgment or amuses the imagination, but never moves the heart, or calls the conscience to discharge its severe and awful functions—such preaching may render a minister popular, secure him large congregations, and procure for him the plaudits of the multitude; but where are the sinners converted from the error of their way, and the souls saved from death? Verily I say unto you, if such a preacher has his reward only in the applause of the multitude, whose object and aim were as low as his own—it was what he sought, and all he sought, and let him not complain if he have this, and nothing else. From such preachers may God Almighty preserve our churches, and may he give us men who better know their business in the pulpit, and better do it.

Simplicity of style, then, as opposed to the artificial and rhetorical, is essential to earnestness; for who can believe *that* man to be intent on saving souls, who seems to have labored in the study only to make his sermon as fine as glittering imagery and high-sounding diction could render it? I could as soon believe a physician were intent on saving his fellow creatures from death, who, when the plague was sweeping them into the grave, spent his time in studying to write his prescriptions in beautiful characters, and classical latinity. There are some judicious remarks on the style of the pulpit in two papers which came out some time since, one in the Edinburgh Review, and the other in the Quarterly, on HARE'S "Village Sermons," those admirable models of simplicity.

The object of the reviewer in the Quarterly is to illustrate the nature, to prove the necessity, and to urge the cultivation of simplicity, especially in those sermons which are addressed to congregations which are composed in great measure of the poor. After giving a quotation or two in which Mr. HARE had made mention of "smugglers and poachers," "tea and wheaten bread," the critic remarks:

"We have preachers in our time who would have flinched from expressions so natural and straight-forward, and would infallibly have warned their poor people against holding any intercourse with *the nocturnal marauder on the main or the manor;* and have suggested to them the gratitude they owed for a *fragrant beverage and farinaceous food.* And so might Mr. HARE, if his taste had been less correct, and his desire of doing good less earnest. Affectation is bad enough anywhere; in the pulpit it is intolerable."

In speaking of *illustrations,* the writer goes on to advert to the excessive quaintness which was one of the vices of sermons before and about the time of the Reformation:

"Accordingly, within a century after the Reformation we find THOMAS FULLER, the last man, from natural temperament, one would have thought likely to offer a caution upon such a subject, saying of the faithful minister, 'His smiles and illustrations are always familiar, *never contemptible.* Indeed reasons are the pillars of the fabric of a sermon, but similitudes are the windows which give the best light. He avoids such stories whose mention may suggest bad thoughts to the auditors, and will not use a light comparison to make thereof a grave application, for fear lest his poison go further than his antidote.' Preaching, therefore, now took an opposite tack, and from having been certainly once too succulent, by the time of JOHN WESLEY had become sapless. This was one cause which rendered the new style of preaching adopted by him and his followers so attractive. The standard, according to which the character of the imagery and diction of the pulpit of modern days was regulated, was not fixed before the divines of Queen Ann's time; as the vocabulary of poetry, according to JOHNSON, was not determined before the age of DRYDEN. In both cases the restraint has been injurious to the subject of it. There was a Doric simplicity—'wood-notes wild,'—in the poets before DRYDEN, for which the greater correctness, it may be, of those who have since lived, is but a poor substitute; and there was a homely vigor in the sentiments and phraseology of the pulpit of the first and second Charles, which has been ill replaced by the decorous tameness of later times. Surely it is a morbid taste, and one that requires correction, which would kick at images that satisfied a BARROW; and yet we could point to numbers in his sermons which would now be rejected by the preacher, even the *village* preacher too, as mean and pedestrian. The familiar illustrations, therefore, by which a subject is rendered clear to persons slow to apprehend, and interesting to persons hard to be excited, is a figure not lightly to be renounced in deference to the false refinement of the magnates of a congregation—though doubtless capable of abuse. We say false refinement, for there are parables both in the prophets and in the gospels, against which the same parties might raise the same objections."*

In a similar strain, and with a like object, though with still more expansion of thought, a masterly writer in the Edinburgh Review remarks:

"We have long felt that the eloquence of the pulpit in its general character has never been assimilated so far as it might have

* Quarterly Review, Article II., No. 117.

been, and ought to have been, to that which has produced the greatest effects elsewhere, and which is shown to be of the right kind, alike by the success which has attended it, and by an analysis of the qualities by which it has been distinguished. If we were compelled to give a brief definition of the truest style of eloquence, we should say it was 'practical reasoning, animated by strong emotion;' or, if we might be indulged in what is rather a description than a definition of it, we should say that it consisted in reasoning on topics calculated to inspire a common interest, expressed in the language of ordinary life, and in that brief, rapid, familiar style, which natural emotion ever assumes. The former half of this description would condemn no small portion of the compositions called sermons, and the latter half a still larger portion.

"We would not be misunderstoood. It is far—very far—from our intention to speak in terms of the slighest depreciation of the immense treasures of learning, of acute disquisition, of profound speculation, of powerful controversy, which the literature of the English pulpit exemplifies. In these points it cannot be surpassed. In vigor and originality of thought, in argumentative power, in extensive and varied erudition, it as far transcends all other literature of the same kind, as it is deficient in the qualities which are fitted to produce popular impression. We merely assert that the greater part of 'sermons' are not at all entitled to the name, if by it be meant discourses *specially adapted* to the object of instructing, convincing, or persuading the *common mind.*"

After some admirably judicious remarks on the *topics* of the pulpit, designed to prove that these should be such as are calculated to inspire a common interest in the mass of a common audience, the writer goes on to speak of the *manner* of discussing them, and observes:

"Where the topics are not such as are fairly open to censure, a large class of preachers, especially amongst the young, grievously err by investing them with the technicalities of science and philosophy; either because they foolishly suppose they thereby give their compositions a more philosophical air, or because they disdain the homely and the vulgar. We remember hearing of a worthy man of this class, who, having occasion to tell his audience the simple truth that there was not one gospel for the rich, and another for the poor, informed them, 'that if they would not be saved on general principles,' they could not be saved at all! With such men it is not sufficient to say, that such and such a thing must be, but there is always 'a moral and physical necessity for it.' The 'will' is too old-fashioned a thing to be mentioned, and everything is done by 'volition;' duty is expanded into 'moral obligation;' man not only *ought* to do this, that, or the other, it is always 'by some principle of their moral nature;' they not only like to do so and so, but 'they are impelled by some natural propensity;' men not only *think* and *do*, but they are never represented as thinking and doing without some parade of their 'intellectual processes and active powers.' Such discourses are full of 'moral beauty,' and 'necessary relations,' and 'philosophical demonstrations,' and 'laws of nature,' and *a priori* and *a fortiori* arguments. If some simple fact of physical science is referred to in the way of argument or illustration, it cannot be presented in common language, but must be exhibited in the pomp of the most approved scientific technicalities. If there be a common and scientific name for the same object, ten to one that the latter is adopted. Heat straightway becomes 'caloric;' lightning, 'the electric fluid;' instead of plants and animals, we are surrounded by 'organized substances;' life is nothing half so good as 'the vital principle.' Not only is such language as this obscurely understood, or not understood at all, but even if perfectly understood, must necessarily be far less effective than those simple terms of common life, which for the most part may be substituted for them. The sermons of AUGUSTUS WILLIAM HARE may serve to show how the abstract terms of philosophy may be advantageously translated into simple, racy English."*

* Edinburgh Review, No. 145. On the British Pulpit.

So harmonious are the judgments on the best style of preaching of two writers, belonging to very different schools of literature and religion, whose keen sarcasm it may be hoped will correct the pedantry at which it is aimed, and convince many an ambitious aspirant after popularity, that whatever may be the method which will secure the applause of the frivolous and the ignorant, simplicity is the only way to usefulness and to secure the approbation of the serious, the wise, and the good. An affectation of learning and science in the pulpit is not only a sin against good taste, but betrays an utter want of that watching for immortal souls, which is, or ought to be, the preacher's steady and constant aim. To borrow the homely, but forcible language of DOOLITTLE,—

"The eyeing of eternity should make us ministers painful and diligent in our studies to prepare a message of such weight as we come about, when preaching to men concerning everlasting matters, and should especially move us to be plain in our speech, that even the capacity of the weakest in the congregation, that hath an eternal soul, that must be damned, or saved, might understand in things necessary to salvation, what we mean, and aim, and drive at. It hath made me tremble to hear some soar aloft, that knowing men might know their parts, whilst the meaner sort are kept from the knowledge of it; and put their matter in such a dress of words, in such a style so composed, that the most stand looking at the preacher in the face, and hear a sound, but know not what he saith, and while he doth pretend to feed them, doth indeed starve them. Would a man of any bowels of compassion go from a prince to a condemned man, and tell him in such a language that he should not understand, the condition upon which the prince would pardon him, and then the poor man lose his life because the proud and haughty messenger must show his knack in delivering his message in *fine* English, which the condemned man could not understand?"

I shall not inappropriately introduce here a quotation from that great master of chaste eloquence, ROBERT HALL, whose opinion on any subject, but especially on that of the art of preaching, in which he was himself so extraordinary a proficient, is entitled to peculiar deference:

"A great diversity of talents must be expected to be found among them, (the evangelical clergy;) but it has not been our lot to hear of any, whose labors a good man would think it right to treat with indiscriminate contempt. As they are called, for the most part, to address the middle and lower classes of society, their language is plain and simple; speaking in the presence of God, their address is solemn; and, 'as becomes the ambassadors of Christ,' their appeals to the conscience are close and cogent. Few, if any among them, aspire to the praise of consummate orators—a character which we despair of every seeing associated, in high perfection, with that of a Christian teacher. The minister of the gospel is called to declare the testimony of God, which is always weakened by a profuse employment of the ornaments of secular eloquence. Those exquisite paintings, and nice touches of art, in which the sermons of the French preachers excel so much, excite a kind of attention, and produce a species of pleasure, not in perfect accordance with devotional feeling. The imagination is too much excited and employed, not to interfere with the more awful functions of conscience; the hearer is absorbed in admiration, and the exercise which ought to be an instrument of conviction, becomes a feast of taste. In the hand of a MASSILLON, the subject of death itself is blended with so many associations of the most delicate kind, and calls up so many sentiments of natural tenderness, as to become a source of theatrical amusement, rather than of religious sensibility. Without being insensible to the charms of eloquence, it is our decided opinion that a sermon of Mr. GISBORNE's is more calculated to 'convert a sinner from the error of his way' than one of MASSILLON's. It is a strong objection to a studied attempt at oratory in the pulpit, that it usually induces a neglect of the peculiar doctrines of Christian verity, where the preacher feels himself restrained, and is under the necessity of explaining texts, of obviating objections, and elucidating difficulties, which limits the excursions of imagination, and confines it within narrow bounds. He is therefore eager to escape from these fetters, and, instead of '*reasoning out of the Scriptures*,' expatiates in the flowery fields of declamation."

It appears to me that a want of powerful, eloquent, yet simple and unaffected exhortation, is among the greatest deficiencies of the modern pulpit. Let any one read the sermons of our great nonconformist ancestors, of CLARKSON, DOOLITTLE, MANTON, HOWE, OWEN, BATES, FLAVEL, and especially of BAXTER, and mark the all but overwhelming force of persuasion which is put forth in the application of their powerful discourses; let him see how these great men exerted the mightiness of their strength to make all they had said to the judgment reach the heart and awaken the conscience. And to come to more modern times, let him read the sermons of WHITFIELD, JONATHAN EDWARDS, and DAVIES of New Jersey; and to advance to still *more* modern productions, let them peruse the sermons of Mr. PARSONS of York, and many of the best preachers on the other side of the Atlantic, SPRING, BARNES, SKINNER, BEECHER, GRIFFIN, CLARKE, and SPRAGUE. Also ROBERT HALL's sermon on "Marks of love to God," and BRADLEY's sermon on "Our lamps are gone out," for fine specimens of this hortatory method; this bearing down with the truth on the sinner's heart and conscience; this beseeching men to be reconciled to God. Some specimens of this method will be given in the following chapter. Now *this* is earnestness in preaching; when a man is seen to feel the truths he discusses; when it is evident to all that he believes what he says, in affirming that his hearers are sinking into perdition, and that he is laboring to persuade them to forsake their evil courses; when his sermons are full of close, pointed, personal addresses; when, in short, through the whole discourse, the preacher is seen moving onward from the understanding to a closer and closer approximation to the heart in the conclusion, and the hearer feels at length the hand of the preacher seizing it with a mysterious and resistless power.

CHAPTER V.

NATURE OF EARNESTNESS.

ILLUSTRATED BY SPECIMENS FROM VARIOUS AUTHORS.

FAMILIAR as most of the readers of this work are with examples of the kind of manner intended by me, I have thought it would help to illustrate and enforce my meaning if I introduced a few extracts from different authors by way of specimens. Those which are here presented are not selected as possessing anything very extraordinary, or as being the best of the kind that could be selected from the same authors; but they are sufficient to answer my purpose. Nor are they exhibited as models to be in every particular imitated in modern composition, but as pervaded by that one quality of intense earnestness, which it is the object of this work to recommend.

The first extract which I shall quote is from a sermon of Mr. DOOLITTLE. This eminent minister of Christ was ejected by the Act of Uniformity, in 1662, from the church of St. Alphage, London Wall. He was a man of extraordinary courage, power, and success in preaching; and, after his expulsion from his living, educated young men for the ministry. The extract which follows is taken from a discourse contained in that valuable series called "The Morn ing Exercises,"* and is entitled, "How we should eye eternity so that it may have its influence on all we do." It is perhaps the most solemn and awful sermon in the English or any other language; and is overcharged sadly with terminology, which, though it should be sparingly introduced, ought not to be altogether excluded from the modern pulpit, even in this fastidious age. The sickly sentimentalism which would "never mention hell to ears polite," should be abjured with as much disgust as a gross and almost profane familiarity with these awful realities. It was not only DOOLITTLE's fault, but it was the vice of the age, to approach somewhat too near to the latter extreme. But then after this admission is made, let us look at the burning and overwhelming earnestness of the sermon.

"Is there an eternal state; such unseen eternal joys and torments? Who then can *sufficiently lament* the blindness, madness, and folly of this distracted world, and the unreasonableness of those that have rational and eternal souls, to see them busily employed in the matters of time, which are only for time, in present honors, pleasures, and profits, while they do neglect everlasting things: everlasting life and death is before them, everlasting joy or torment is hard at hand; and yet poor sinners take no care how to avoid the one, or obtain the other. Is it not matter of lamentation to see so many thousands bereaved of the sober, serious use of their understandings? That while they use their reason to get the riches of this world, they will not act as rational men to get the joys of heaven; and to avoid temporal calamities, yet not to escape eternal misery. Or if they be fallen into present afflictions, they contrive how they may get out of them: if they be sick, reason tells them they must use the means, if they would be well, if they be in pain, nature puts them on to

* A new edition of this work has been lately published by TEGG, and let every young minister be sure to purchase a copy.

seek after a remedy; and yet these same men neglect all duty, and cast away all care concerning everlasting matters; they are for seen pleasures and profits, which are passing from them in the enjoyment of them; but the unseen eternal glory in heaven they pray not for, they think not of. Are they unjustly charged? Let conscience speak, what thoughts they lie down withal upon their pillow; if they wake or sleep, fly from them in the silent night, what a noise doth the cares of the world make in their souls? With what thoughts do they rise in the morning? Of God, or of the world? Of the things of time, or of eternity? Their thoughts are in their shops before they have been in heaven; and many desires after visible temporal gain, before they have had one desire after the invisible, eternal God, and treasures that are above. What do they do all the day long? What is it that hath their endeavors, all their labor and travel? their most painful industry and unwearied diligence? Alas! their consciences will tell themselves, and their practices tell others, when there is trading, but no praying; buying and selling, but no religious duties performed: the shop-book is often opened, but the sacred book of God is not looked into all the week long.

"O Lord! forgive the hardness of my heart, that I can see such insufferable folly among reasonable creatures, and can lament this folly no more: good Lord, forgive the want of compassion in me, that can stand and see this distraction in the world, as if the most of men had lost their wits, and were quite beside themselves, and yet my bowels yearn no more towards immortal souls that are going to unseen miseries in the eternal world. To see distracted men busy in doing things that tend to no account is not such an amazing sight, as to see men that have reason for the world, to use it not for God, and Christ, and their own eternal good: to see them love and embrace a present dunghill world, and cast away all serious, affecting, and effectual thoughts of the life to come: to see them rage against the God of heaven, and cry out against holiness as foolish preciseness, and serious godliness as madness, and melancholy.

"Let us call the whole creation of God to lament and bewail the folly of man, that was made the best of all God's visible works; but now by such wickedness is bad beyond them all, being made by God for an everlasting state, and yet minds nothing less than that for which he was principally made.

"O sun! why is it not thy burden to give light to men to do those works, and walk in those ways that bring them to eternal darkness? O earth! why dost thou not groan to bear such burdensome fools that dig into thy bowels for gold and silver, while they do neglect everlasting treasures in the eternal world? O ye sheep and oxen! fish and fowl! why do ye not cry out against them that take your present life to maintain them in being, that only mind present things, but forget the eternal God that gave them dominion over you, to live upon you while they had time to mind eternal things, but do not? O ye angels of God, and blessed saints in heaven, were ye capable of grief and sorrow, would not ye bitterly lament the sin and folly of poor mortals upon earth? Could ye look down from that blessed place where ye do dwell, and behold the joy and glory which is to us unseen, and see how it is basely slighted by the sons of men, if ye were not above sorrow and mourning, would not ye take this up for a bitter lamentation? O ye saints on earth! whose eyes are open to see what the blind deluded world doth not see, do ye bitterly take on, let your heads be fountains of water, and your eyes send forth rivers of tears, for the great neglect of eternal joys and happiness of heaven? Can you see men going out of time into eternity in their sin, and in their blood, in their guilt, and unconverted state, and your hearts not moved? your bowels not yearn? Have ye spent all your tears in bewailing your own sin, that your eyes are dry when you behold such monstrous madness, and unparalleled folly of so many, with whom daily ye converse? Ye sanctified parents, have ye no pity for your ungodly children? Nor sanctified children, for ungodly parents?"

The next extract I give, is from holy BAXTER, under whose ministry DOOLITTLE was converted, and from whom he appears to have borrowed his own manner of preaching.

"O sirs, they are no trifles or jesting matters that the gospel speaks of. I must needs profess to you that when I have the most serious thoughts of these things, I am ready to wonder that such amazing matters do not overwhelm the souls of men; that the greatness of the subject doth not so overmatch our understandings and affections, as even to drive men beside themselves, but that God hath always somewhat allayed it by distance; much more do I wonder that men should be so blockish as to make light of such things. O Lord, that men did but know what everlasting glory and everlasting torments are! Would they then hear us as they do? Would they read and think of these things as they do? I profess I have been ready to wonder when I have heard such weighty things delivered, how people can forbear crying out in the congregation; and much more do I wonder how they can rest, till they have gone to their ministers, and learned what they shall do to be saved, that this great business should be put out of doubt. O that heaven and hell should work no more upon men! O that eternity should work no more! O how can you forbear when you are alone, to think with yourselves what it is to be everlastingly in joy or torment! I wonder that such thoughts do not break your sleep, and that they do not crowd into your minds, when you are about your labor! I wonder how you can almost do anything else! How can you have any quietness in your minds? How can you eat, or drink, or rest, till you have got some ground of everlasting consolations. Is that a man or a corpse, that is not affected with matters of this moment —that can be readier to sleep than to tremble, when he hears how he must stand at the bar of God? Is that a man or a clod of clay that can rise up and lie down without being deeply affected with his everlasting state—that can follow his worldly business, and make nothing of the great business of salvation or damnation, and that when he knows it is so hard at hand? Truly, sirs, when I think of the weight of the matter, I wonder at the best saints upon earth, that they are no better and do no more, in so weighty a case. I wonder at those whom the world accounts more holy than needs, and scorns for making so much ado, that they can put off Christ and their souls with so little; that they do not pour out their souls in every prayer; that they are not more taken up with God; that their thoughts are not more serious in preparation for their last account. I wonder that they are not a thousand times more strict in their lives, and more laborious and unwearied for the crown, than they are. And for myself, as I am ashamed of my dull and careless heart, and of my slow and unprofitable course of life, so the Lord knows I am ashamed of every sermon that I preach: when I think what I am, and who sent me, and how much the salvation and damnation of men is concerned in it, I am ready to tremble, lest God should judge me a slighter of his truth, and the souls of men, and lest in my best sermon I should be guilty of their blood. Methinks we should not speak a word to men in matters of such consequence without tears, or the greatest earnestness that possibly we can. Were we not too much guilty of the sin which we reprove, it would be so. Whether we are alone, or in company, methinks our end, and such an end, should still be in our mind, and as before our eyes, and we should sooner forget anything, or set light by anything, or by all things, than by this."

The third extract I give, is from the works of that great and serene spirit, JOHN HOWE, whose surpassing grandeur of thought and expression places him, in this respect, above all his compeers. His sermon on the "Inquiry whether we love God," is one of the finest pieces of solemn, heart-searching expostulation, which can be found in the whole range of English theology, from which I give the following pages, the spirit of which should enter into the soul of every minister and student who reads them.

"For further direction take heed of passing a false judgment in this case, a judgment contrary to the truth: for—

"*First*, That is to no purpose, it will avail thee nothing, you cannot be advantaged by it, for yours is not the supreme judgment. There will be another and superior judgment to yours, that will control and reverse your false judgment, and make it signify nothing it is, therefore, to no purpose. And,

"*Secondly*, It is a great piece of insolency, for it will be to oppose your judgment to his certain and most authorized one; who, if this be your case, hath already judged it, and tells you 'I know you, that you have not the love of God in you.' It belongs to him, by office to judge: 'The Father hath committed all judgment to the Son,' as a little above in this chapter; from which, will you depose him? dethrone him? disannul his judgment? condemn him? that you may be righteous? (to borrow that, Job xl. 8.)

"*Thirdly*, It is most absurd, supposing such characters as you have heard do conclude a man in this case, yet to judge himself a lover of God. If against the evidence of such characters a man should pronounce the wrong judgment, it would be the most unreasonable and absurd thing imaginable; for then let us but suppose, how that wronged judgment must lie related to those fore-mentioned characters that have been given you. Let me remind you of some of them: he that never put forth the act of love to God, cannot say he hath the principle—he that is not inclined to do good to others for the sake of God, 1 John iii. 17—he that indulges himself in the inconsistent love of this world, 1 John ii. 15—he that lives not in obedience to his known laws, John xiv. 14, 1 John v. 3, with many more. Now if you will pass a judgment in your case against the evidence of such characters, come forth then, let the matter be brought into clear sight, put your sense into plain words, and this it will be:—'I am a lover of God, or I have the love of God in me, though I cannot tell that ever I put forth one act of love towards him in all my life; I have the love of God in me, though I never knew what it meant to do good to any for his sake, against the express words of scripture: How dwelleth the love of God in such a man? I have the love of God in me, though I have constantly indulged myself in that which he maketh an inconsistent love: Love not the world, nor the things which are in the world: if any man love the world, the love of the Father is not in him. I have the love of God in me, though I would never allow him to rule me, though I never kept his commandments with a design to please him, and comply with his will. I have the love of God in me, though I never valued his love. I have the love of God in me, though I never cared for his image, for his presence, for his con verse, for his interest and honor.' I beseech you consider how all this will sound! Can anything be more absurdly spoken? and shall it be upon such improbabilities or impossibilities as these, that any man will think it fit to venture his soul! 'I will pawn my soul upon it, I will run the hazard of my soul upon it, I am a lover of God for all this!' Would you venture anything else so besides your soul? Would you venture a finger so, an eye so? It is to place the name where there is nothing of the thing; it is to place the name of the thing upon its contrary. The soul of man cannot be in an indifferency towards God; but if there be not love and propension, there is aversion, and that is hatred. And what! is hatred to be called love? If you bear that habitual disposition of soul towards God, to go all the day long with no inclination towards him; no thought of him; no design to please him, to serve him, to glorify him; if this be your habitual temper and usual course, will you call this love? Shall this contrariety to the love of God be called love to him? You may as well call water fire, or fire water, as so grossly misname things here; and therefore, again,

"That we may advance somewhat; plainly and positively pass the true judgment. If the characters that you have heard do carry the matter so, come at last plainly and positively to pass the true judgment of your own case, though it be a sad one; and tell your own souls, 'Oh my soul! though I must *sadly* say it, I must say it, all things conclude and make against thee: the love of God is not in thee.' Why, is it not as good this should be the present issue at your own bar, and at the tribunal of your own conscience, as before God's judgment-seat? Why should you not concur and fall in with Christ the authorized Judge, whose judgment is according to truth? Why, this is a thing that must be done, the case requires it, and God's express word requires it, 1 Cor. xi. 31. Other previous and preparatory duty plainly enjoined, doth by consequence enjoin it, and requires that it follow, 2 Cor. xiii. 5. What is examination for, but in order to judgment? It must, therefore, be done, and I shall show how it must be done, and proceed to some further directions.

"*First*, You must do it solemnly. Take yourselves aside at some fit season or another, inspect your own souls, review your life, consider what your wonted frame and your ordinary course has been. And if you find by such characters as heretofore were given, this is the truth of your case, then let judgment pass upon deliberation: Oh my soul! thou hast not the love of God in thee, whatsoever thine appearances hitherto have been; and whatsoever thy peace and quiet hath been, thou hast not the love of God in thee. Let it be done with solemnity.

"*Secondly*, Do it in the sight of God as before him, as under his eye, as under the eye of Christ. That eye that is as a flame of fire, that searches hearts, and tries reins; arraign thyself before him: 'Lord, I have here brought before thee a guilty soul, a delinquent soul, wretchedly and horribly delinquent, a soul that was breathed into me by thee, an intelligent, understanding soul, a soul that hath love in its nature, but a soul that never loved thee.'

"*Thirdly*, Judge thyself before him as to the *fact*, and as to the *fault*. As to the *fact*: 'I have never yet loved thee, O God. I own it to thee; Lord, I accuse, I charge my soul with this before thee, this is the truth of the fact, I have not the love of God in me.' And charge thyself with the *fault*: 'Oh horrid creature that I am! I was made by thee, and don't love thee; thou didst breathe into me this reasonable, immortal spirit, and it doth not love thee; it is thine own offspring, and does not love thee. It can never be blessed in anything but thee, and it does not love thee.' And then hereupon,

"*Fourthly*, Join to this *self-judging* and *self-loathing*. That we are to *judge ourselves* is a law laid upon us by the supreme Lawgiver, the one Lawgiver, that hath power to save and to destroy. And his word that enjoins it as plainly tells us what must go with it, that this self-judging must be accompanied with *self-loathing*, Ezek. vi. 9; xx 43, and xxxvi. 31. Do God that right upon thyself that thou mayst tell him, 'Blessed God! I do even hate myself, because I find I have not loved thee; and I cannot but hate myself, and I never will be reconciled to myself, till I find I am reconciled to thee.' This is doing justice: doth not the Scripture usually and familiarly so represent to us the great turn of the soul to God; when poor sinners become penitents and return, that they are brought to hate themselves, and loathe themselves in their own eyes? And is there anything that can make a soul so loathsome *in itself*, or ought to make it so loathsome *to itself*, as not to love God, to be destitute of the love of God? And then,

"*Fifthly*, Hereupon, too, *pity* thyself, *pity* thy own soul. There is cause to *hate* it, to *loathe* it, and is there no cause to *pity* it? to lament it? Doth not this look like a lamentable case, 'Oh! what a soul have I, that can love anything else, that can love trifles, that can love impurities, that can love sin; and cannot love God, Christ, the most desirable good of souls. What a soul have I! What a monster in the creation of God is this soul of mine!' Methinks you should set yourselves, if any of you can find this to be the case, to weep over your own souls. Some may see cause to say, 'Oh my soul, thou hast in thee other valuable things, thou hast understanding in thee, judgment in thee wit in thee; perhaps learning, considerable acquired endowments in thee; but thou hast not the love of God in thee. I can do many other commendable or useful things, I can discourse plausibly, argue subtilly, I can manage affairs dexterously, but I cannot love God. Oh my soul, how great an essential dost thou want to all religion, to all duty, to all felicity! The one thing necessary thou wantest, thou hast everything but what thou needest more than anything, more than all things; and oh, my soul, what is like at this rate to become of thee? Where art thou to have thy eternal abode? To what regions of horror, and darkness, and woe art thou going? What society can be fit for thee—no lover of God! no lover of God! what, but of infernal, accursed spirits, that are at utmost distance from him, and to whom no beam of holy vital light shall ever shine to all eternity! Thou, oh my soul, art self-abandoned to the blackness of darkness forever. Thy doom is in thy breast, thy own bosom; thy no love to God is thy own doom, thy eternal doom; creates thee a present hell, and shows whither thou belongest.'

"*Sixthly*, * * * All disobedience and rebellion is summed

up in this one word—*Having been no lover of God;* and won't it make any man's heart to meditate terror, to think of having such a charge as this likely to lie against him in the judgment of that day; that day, when the secrets of all hearts are to be laid open? Every work must then be brought into judgment, and every secret thing, whether it be good or evil, Eccles. xii. 14. And it will be to the confusion of many a one. It may be your no love of God was heretofore a great secret; you had a heart in which was no love of God, but it was a secret, you took not care to have it writ in your forehead; you conversed with men so plausibly, nobody took you to be no lover of God, to have a heart disaffected to God. But now out comes the secret, that which you kept for a great secret all your days; out comes the secret; and to have such a secret as this disclosed to that vast assembly, before angels and men! Here was a creature, a reasonable creature, an intelligent soul, that lived upon the divine bounty and goodness so many years in the world below, and hid a false, disloyal heart by a plausible show and external profession of great devotedness to God, all the time of his abode in that world: oh what a fearful thing would it be to have this secret so disclosed! And do you think that all the loyal creatures that shall be spectators and auditors in the hearing of that great day, will not all conceive a just and a loyal indignation against such a one when convicted of not loving God; convicted of not loving him that gave him breath, him whose he was, and to whom he belonged, whose name he bore? What a fearful thing will it be to stand convicted so upon such a point as this! And sure in the meantime there is great reason for continual fear, why a man's heart should *meditate terror!* One would even think that all the creation should be continually every moment in arms against him! One would be afraid that every wind that blows should be a deadly blast to destroy me; that when the sun shines upon me all its beams should be turned into vindictive flames to execute vengeance upon me! I would fear that even the very stones in the streets should fly against me, and everything that meets me be my death! For what? I have not the love of God in me! What, to go about the streets from day to day with a heart void of the love of God! What a heart have I! *Fear* ought to be exercised in this case; we are bid to fear if we do evil against a human ruler: 'If thou do that which is evil, be afraid, for he beareth not the sword in vain.' Rom. xiii. 4. But if I be *such an evil-doer* against the supreme Ruler, the Lord of heaven and earth, have I not reason to be afraid, and to think sadly with myself, what will the end of this be?"

The next extract is from JONATHAN EDWARDS' sermon on "Pressing into the Kingdom of God." This extraordinary man presents a remarkable proof and illustration that the most acute logician and the most subtle metaphysician, may be at the same time the most earnest preacher. His sermons are some of the most impressive and alarming in print, but certainly not a little wanting in the tenderness and melting pathos of the gospel of salvation. They may be read with admirable effect to teach us how to expound the nature and enforce the obligations of the moral law, so as to awaken the slumbering conscience of the unconverted sinner. His astonishing usefulness shows the adaptation of his preaching to the age and state of society in which he lived, but his method could not be rigidly followed, except in its earnestness, in the present day.

"1. I would address myself to such as yet remain unawakened. It is an awful thing that there should be any one person remaining secure amongst us at such a time as this; but yet it is to be feared that there are some of this sort. I would here a little expostulate with such persons.

"When do you expect that it will be more likely that you should be awakened and wrought upon than now? You are in a Christless condition, and yet, without doubt, intend to go to heaven; and therefore intend to be converted some time before you die: but this is not to be expected till you are first awakened, and deeply concerned about the welfare of your soul, and brought earnestly to seek God's converting grace. And when do you intend that this shal. be? How do you lay things out in your own mind, or what projection have you about this matter? Is it ever so likely that a person will be awakened, as at such a time as this? How do we see many, who before were secure, now roused out of their sleep, and crying, What shall I do to be saved? But you are yet secure! Do you flatter yourself that it will be more likely you should be awakened when it is a dull and dead time? Do you lay matters out thus in your own mind, that though you are senseless when others are generally awakened, that yet you shall be awakened when others are generally senseless? Or do you hope to see another such time of the pouring out of God's Spirit hereafter? And do you think it will be more likely that you should be wrought upon then, than now? And why do you think so? Is it because then you shall be so much older than you are now, and so that your heart will be grown softer and more tender with age? or because you will then have stood out so much longer against the calls of the gospel, and all means of grace? Do you think it more likely that God will give you the needed influences of his Spirit then than now, because then you will have provoked him so much more, and your sin and guilt will be so much greater? And do you think it will be any benefit to you to stand it out through the present season of grace, as proof against the extraordinary means of awakening there are? Do you think that this will be a good preparation for a saving work of the Spirit hereafter?

"2. What means do you expect to be awakened by? As to the awakening, awful things of the word of God, you have had those set before you times without number, in the most moving manner that the dispensers of the word have been capable of. As to particular solemn warnings, directed to those that are in your circumstances, you have had them frequently, and have them now from time to time. Do you expect to be awakened by awful providences? Those also you have lately had, of the most awakening nature, one after another. Do you expect to be moved by the deaths of others? We have lately had repeated instances of these. There have been deaths of old and young: the year has been remarkable for the deaths of young persons in the bloom of life, and some of them very sudden deaths. Will the conversion of others move you? There is indeed scarce anything that is found to have so great a tendency to stir persons up as this; and this you have been tried with of late in frequent instances, but are hitherto proof against it. Will a general pouring out of the Spirit, and seeing a concern about salvation amongst all sorts of people, do it? This means you now have, but without effect. Yea, you have all these things together; you have the solemn warnings of God's word, and awful instances of death, and the conversion of others, and see a general concern about salvation; but all together do not move you to any great concern about your own precious, immortal, and miserable soul. Therefore consider by what means it is that you expect ever to be awakened.

"You have heard that it is probable some who are now awakened, will never obtain salvation; how dark then does it look upon you that remain stupidly unawakened! Those, come to adult age, who are not moved at such a time as this, have reason to fear whether they are not given up to judicial hardness. I do not say they have reason to *conclude* it, but they have reason to fear it. How dark doth it look upon you, that God comes and knocks at so many persons' doors, and misses yours! that God is giving the strivings of his Spirit so generally amongst us, while you are left senseless!

"3. Do you expect to obtain salvation without ever seeking it? If you are sensible that there is a necessity of your seeking in order to obtaining, and ever intend to seek, one would think you could not avoid it at such a time as this. Inquire therefore whether you intend to go to heaven, living all your days a secure, negligent, careless life.—Or,

"4. Do you think you can bear the damnation of hell? Do you imagine that you can tolerably endure the devouring fire and everlasting burnings? Do you hope that you shall be able to grapple with the vengeance of God Almighty, when he girds himself with strength, and clothes himself with wrath? Do you think to strengthen yourself against God, and to be able to make your part good with him? 1 Cor. x. 22, 'Do we provoke the Lord to jealousy? are we stronger than he?' Do you flatter yourself that you shal. find out ways for your ease and support, and to make it out tolerably well, to bear up your spirit in those everlasting burnings that are prepared for the devil and his angels? Ezek. xxii. 14. 'Can thine heart endure, or can thine hands be strong, in the days that I shall deal with thee?' It is a difficult thing to conceive what such Christless persons think, that are unconcerned at such a time."

The following extract is from that first of all preachers, WHITFIELD; and who that considers the circumstances under which these flaming periods were enunciated, and the feeling and action which accompanied their delivery, can wonder at the effects they produced?

BESEECHING SINNERS. "O my brethren, my heart is enlarged towards you. I trust I feel something of that hidden but powerful presence of Christ, whilst I am preaching to you. Indeed it is sweet, it is exceedingly comfortable. All the harm I wish you, who without cause are my enemies, is, that you felt the like. Believe me, though it would be hell to my soul to return to a natural state again, yet I would willingly change states with you for a little while, that you might know what it is to have Christ dwelling in your hearts by faith. Do not turn your backs; do not let the devil hurry you away; be not afraid of convictions; do not think worse of the doctrine because preached without the church walls. Our Lord, in the days of his flesh, preached on a mount, in a ship, and in a field; and I am persuaded many have felt his gracious presence here. Indeed, we speak what we know. Do not reject the kingdom of God against yourselves; be so wise as to receive our witness. I *cannot* I *will not* let you go; stay a *little*, let us reason together. However lightly you may esteem your souls, I know our Lord has set an unspeakable value on them. He thought them worthy of his most precious blood. I beseech you therefore, O sinners, be ye reconciled to God. I hope you do not fear being accepted in the Beloved. Behold, he calleth you; behold, he prevents and follows you with his mercy and hath sent forth his servants into the highways and hedges, to compel you to come in. Remember, then, that at such an hour, of such a day, in such a year, in this place, you were all told what you ought to think concerning Jesus Christ. If you now perish, it will not be for lack of knowledge; I am free from the blood of you all. You cannot say I have, like legal preachers, been requiring you to make brick without straw. I have not bidden you to make yourselves saints, and then come to God; but I have offered you salvation on as cheap terms as you can desire. I have offered you Christ's whole wisdom, Christ's whole righteousness, Christ's whole sanctification and eternal redemption, if you will but believe on him. If you say you cannot believe, you say right; for faith, as well as every other blessing, is the gift of God: but then wait upon God, and who knows but he may have mercy on thee? Why do we not entertain more loving thoughts of Christ? Or do you think he will have mercy on others, and not on you? But are you not sinners? And did not Jesus Christ come into the world to save sinners? If you say you are the chief of sinners, I answer, that will be no hindrance to your salvation; indeed it will not, if you lay hold on him by faith. Read the Evangelists, and see how kindly he behaved to his disciples, who fled from and denied him: 'Go tell my brethren,' says he. He did not say, Go tell those traitors; but, 'Go tell my brethren, and *Peter*;' as though he had said, Go tell my brethren in general, and poor *Peter* in particular, 'that I am risen:' O comfort his poor drooping heart, tell him I am reconciled to him; bid him weep no more so bitterly: for though with oaths and curses he thrice denied me, yet I have died for his sins, I am risen again for his justification: I freely forgive him all. Thus slow to anger and of great kindness, was our all-merciful High Priest. And do you think he has changed his nature, and forgets poor sinners, now he is exalted to the right hand of God? No, he is the same yesterday, to-day, and forever, and sitteth there only to make intercession for us. Come then, ye harlots; come, ye publicans; come, ye most abandoned of sinners, come and believe on Jesus Christ. Though the whole world despise you and cast you out, yet he will not disdain to take you up. O amazing, O infinitely condescending love! even you he will not be ashamed to call his brethren. How will you escape, if you neglect such a glorious offer of salvation? What would the damned spirits, now in the prison of hell, give, if Christ was so freely offered to their souls! And why are not we lifting up our eyes in torments? Does any one out of this great multitude dare say, he does not deserve damnation? If not, why are we left, and others taken away by death? What is this but an instance of God's free grace, and a sign of his good will towards us? Let God's goodness lead us to repentance! O let there be joy in heaven over some of you repenting! Though we are in a *field*, I am persuaded the blessed angels are hovering now around us, and do long, 'as the hart panteth after the water-brooks,' to sing an anthem at your conversion. Blessed be God, I hope their joy will be fulfilled. An *awful silence* appears amongst us. I have good hope that the words which the Lord has enabled me to speak in your ears this day, have not altogether fallen to the ground. Your tears and deep attention are an evidence that the Lord God is amongst us of a truth. Come, ye pharisees, come and see, in spite of your fanatical rage and fury, the Lord Jesus is getting himself the victory. And, brethren, I speak the truth in Christ, I lie not: if one soul of you, by the blessing of God, be brought to think savingly of Jesus Christ this day, I care not if my enemies were permitted to carry me to prison, and put my feet fast in the stocks, as soon as I have delivered this sermon. Brethren, my heart's desire and prayer to God is, that you may be saved. For this cause I follow my Master without the camp. I care not how much of his sacred reproach I bear, so that some of you be converted from the errors of your ways. I rejoice, yea, and I will rejoice. Ye men, ye devils, do your *worst:* the Lord who sent will support me. And when Christ, who is our life, and whom I have now been preaching, shall appear, I also, together with his despised little ones, shall appear with him in glory. And then what will you think of Christ? I know what you will think of him. You will think him to be the fairest among ten thousand: you will then think him to be a just and sin-avenging Judge. Be ye then persuaded to kiss him lest he be angry, and so you be banished forever from the presence of the Lord. Behold, I come to you as the angel did to Lot. Flee, flee for your lives; haste, linger no longer in your spiritual Sodom, for otherwise you will be eternally destroyed. Numbers, no doubt, there are amongst you, that may regard me no more than Lot's sons-in-law regarded him. I am persuaded I seem to some of you as one that mocketh: but I speak the truth in Christ, I lie not; as sure as fire and brimstone was rained from the Lord out of heaven, to destroy Sodom and Gomorrah, so surely, at the great day, shall the vials of God's wrath be poured on you, if you do not think seriously of, and act agreeably to, the gospel of the Lord's Christ. Behold, I have told you before; and I pray God, all you that forget him may seriously think of what has been said, before he pluck you away, and there be none to deliver you."

Not to multiply these extracts unnecessarily, I give one more from a preacher who is, perhaps, without any exception, the most impressive living example of earnestness, both in matter and manner; I mean Mr. PARSONS, of York.

"O, do not deceive yourselves! I would strive to tear away the veil, I tell you, O ye whose 'goodness has been as a morning cloud, and as the early dew that goeth away,'—if unchanged you die, and if unchanged you stand before the dread tribunal, where an account must be rendered of all providences, all immunities, and all feelings, you will be found fatally wanting, and will hear a sentence of condemnation that will consign you to realms of everlasting despair. As true as that Jehovah lives, is it that he will thus execute the fierceness of his indignation. Abodes of sorrow await you, where every past benefit will but be an instrument of torture; where memory and conscience will hold up the mirror of by-gone privilege and promise, of abused mercy, of forsworn and perjured vows, only that remorse may strike upon the soul its more than scorpion sting, and where grace and hope can never alleviate the wailings that will reverberate through the dungeons of outer darkness forever and forever! Your doom will be more tremendous, precisely in proportion to the means you possessed, and the signs you gave, of averting it; can *any* doom be worse than *yours?* When these 'terrors of the Lord' are expounded, say if there be not an argument of mighty force why you should now beware, and why you should now hear the voice of God, lest you should be hardened by the deceitfulness of sin, and lest he should swear in his wrath that you shall not enter into his rest!

"But once more to appeal to those for whom this address has been particularly designed. That such there are, *I know*. I could turn round, and fix my eye, and rest my hand, on persons by whom, if so arraigned, the accusation of the text could not be denied or evaded. You have been again visited by the instrumentality which is adapted for the impression of the heart. Do not reject it: do not let it have that insufficient influence which is but to be dissipated for the world, and which makes the end worse than the beginning. No—nothing will avail but the entire surrender of the soul to him who gave it—the determination to live to Christ, and to glory only in his cross. In the name of the great God, who is not willing that any should perish, but that all should come to repentance, I do now abjure you, that you trifle not a moment longer, that you delay not a moment longer, that you resist not a moment longer: 'Come and return unto the Lord:' let *this* be a season of consideration; let *this* be a season of repentance; let *this* be a season of prayer; let *this* be a season of dedication to your God:—*now*, my hearers, now!

"—Minister and people must part once more. The book must be closed again; the voice must be silent again; the congregation must retire again. O Spirit of God, perform thy work! 'Come from the four winds, O breath, and breathe upon these slain, that they may live!' Let there not be one here before thee, of whom, when yonder heavens shall be on fire, and when this earth shall be burned up, it shall be found—that their 'goodness was as a morning cloud, and that as the early dew it went away!'"

These extracts will illustrate what I mean by earnestness, better than any language which I have employed or could select, and they appear to me to answer well to the apostolic method of beseeching entreaty. I do not of course insist that the pulpit should be restricted to the specific variety of preaching which we designate the hortatory method, under which classification these specimens must all be placed. There should be exegesis, as well as application; exposition, as well as expostulation. The judgment must be enlightened in order that the heart may be impressed, and the conscience awakened, and the believer edified, no less than the sinner converted; and for this a less impassioned strain of preaching will not only suffice, but indeed be more appropriate. Yet with regard to that portion of our public ministrations, and it should be no small portion of it, which has reference to the conversion of the impenitent, where shall we find better models on which to construct our sermons than the DOOLITTLES, the HOWES, the BAXTERS, and the WHITFIELDS, of former times, so far at least as their intense earnestness is concerned? It is true the moderns have improved upon these men in matters of taste, in reference to which we cannot of course hold them up for imitation. In their numerous and complicated divisions and subdivisions, through which, as so many little rills and channels, they poured the current of their thought, instead of causing it to roll onward in the channel of their sermon with the majestic flow of a noble river; in their quaintnesses and quirks; in their fantastic imagery and uncouth diction; in their occasional grossness and vulgarity, in which some of them were but too prone to indulge—they are to be studiously avoided. Yet even in reference to some of these things, it may be affirmed, that, though, in their free and reckless resort to every mode of stimulating attention, they were very often betrayed into great violations of taste, the very same audacity of genius often produced felicities of imagery and diction, with which, neither for beauty nor effect, will the blameless common-place and the accurate insipidity of many modern discourses bear any comparison. For pregnancy of thought, for knowledge of the word of God, for raciness of style, for evangelical sentiment, for anatomy of the human heart, for closeness of application, and especially for intensity of feeling, where shall we find their equals? They preached *to* their congregations, and not merely *before* them: they felt that the objects of their addresses were immortal souls in danger of being lost, and knew their business in the pulpit was to save those souls from perdition: they preached as if they expected there and then to achieve the great work of conversion: and felt as if the eternal destinies of their hearers were suspended on the manner in which they discharged their duties, and as if they were to ascend the next moment, after they had finished their sermons, to give an account of them at the bar of God. Do not the extracts given, and which are but a sample of their works, bear out these assertions? This is what we want more of in modern preaching. There may be, and should be, more of classic elegance, more of logical arrangement, philosophic precision, of vigorous and clear argumentation; but still, at the same time, combined with this, there should also be the pointed interrogation, the pungent appeal, the bold apostrophe, the gush of feeling, the forcible expostulation, and the tender invitation: now the gentle flow of deep, and solemn, and placid thought, and then the torrent rush of impassioned sentiment: the beautiful and harmonious combination of reason, imagination, and affection: and all this employed to carry out the purpose for which the gospel is to be preached, and to win souls to Christ. Those who were privileged to hear Mr.

Hall, in his best days, deliver some of his most popular and powerful discourses, will not fail to recollect how strikingly *he* combined the intense earnestness of the passages just quoted, with the chaste and classic elegance of our best writers; and thus, considering the evangelical strain of his preaching, may be said to have poured forth a torrent of the water of life, clear as crystal. He reminded you of one who, in his yearnings for the salvation of sinners, seemed to feel that language was too feeble an instrument for such a purpose, and who, notwithstanding his sovereign command and exquisite selection of terminology, was struggling to burst the barrier by which words limit the communication of thought, that he might, by a still more direct and facile method, reach and grasp the soul of his hearers.

There is, however, hope that our old theological writers will not be quite forgotten or neglected, while such men as Professor Stowell, of Rotherham College, shall employ their talents in writing prefaces to reprints of such works as those of Thomas Adams, and shall lend their authority to recommend the perusal of these monuments of sacred genius. Beautifully and no less correctly has he said, "As Edwards constrains to closeness of thought; as Howe inspires sublimity of sentiment; as Bates lights up the soul with a soft and silvery light; as Owen lades the mind with a harvest of rich knowledge; as Taylor cheers the imagination with a vintage of delicious grapes; as Baxter fires the soul with longings for salvation, first of ourselves and then of others;—even so does Adams lead to those springs of graphic power, of dramatic grandeur, and of subduing pathos, of which it is the fear of many that they are dried up. We believe they are not. We cannot but think there are minds now opening on the awful solemnities of the Christian ministry to whom this example will be inciting: let them look at things with their own eyes, ponder them in silent and lonely thought, pray over the fruits of such meditations, till they kindle into living pictures; and so let them pour out their feelings in the best words they can find; there will then be no just complaint of the want of power and originality in the English pulpit."

CHAPTER VI.

EARNESTNESS OF MANNER, CONTINUED,

AS MANIFESTED IN THE DELIVERY OF SERMONS.

By the delivery of sermons is meant voice and gesture, or what Demosthenes called action; who, on being asked what was the first excellence of an orator, replied, "Action:" what the second, "Action:" what the third, "Action." An impressive admonition, this, from such an authority, to all preachers, on the importance of that part of our subject which we are now considering.

After the death of that flaming seraph, Mr. McCheyne, there was found upon his desk an unopened note from one who had heard his last sermon, to this effect: "Pardon a stranger for addressing to you a few lines. I heard you preach last Sabbath evening, and it pleased God to bless that sermon to my soul. It was not so much what you said, as your manner of speaking it, that struck me. I saw in you a beauty of holiness I never saw before."

This is only one instance out of ten thousand, in which the earnestness of a preacher's manner has secured that attention to his matter which would not otherwise have been paid to it. The power of oratory has its foundations in the principles of our nature. It is not merely that ideas are conveyed by articulate language through the ear to the mind, but that also impression is produced on the affections by agreeable tones and pleasant modulations of the voice. Hence the power of music: and what is human speech *but* music? No instrument has ever yet been constructed which can emit sounds so exquisitely moving as the human voice. Art is in this effect still below nature. True it is, that we must go to the best of voices for this superiority; but even in voices far below the best, there is an expression of the various passions which no instruments can equal. All nations, therefore, savage as well as civilized, have confessed the powers of oratory, not only as a vehicle of instruction, but as a means of impression. It is vain to pretend that matter is, or ought to be, every thing, and manner nothing. Truth, it may be said, ought to make its own way, independently of the accompaniments of good elocution and graceful action. So it should, but then these things are necessary, in many cases, to gain for it attention, and to secure that due consideration without which it can make no impression. Manner is, so to speak, the harbinger and herald of matter, summoning the faculties of the soul to give audience to the truth to be communicated, and holding the mind in a state of abstraction from all other subjects that would divert the thoughts and prevent impression. It is not only the more illiterate and feeble-minded, not only the multitude who are led by feeling more than by reason, that are influenced by good oratory, but men of the sturdiest intellect and the most philosophic cast of mind. The soul of the sage as well as of the savage is formed with a susceptibility to the power and influence of music, and therefore also to the power and influence of elocution. The importance of manner is consequently great, yea, far greater than either tutors or preachers have been disposed to admit. I am aware that a good voice is necessary to good speaking, but not always to *earnest* speaking. Nature must do much to make a graceful and finished orator; but still, in the absence of this, an ardent mind, burning for the salvation of immortal souls, can, by an impressive earnestness of manner, be a more intense and effective speaker, notwithstanding naturally weak and unimpressive organs of speech, than the possessor of the finest voice, who is destitute of a vivacious and ardent enunciation; just as an exquisite performer can bring better music out of a bad instrument, than a bad musician can out of a good one. What may be done, where the mind is resolutely bent on accomplishing it, for supplying deficiencies and correcting faults in elocution, Demosthenes has taught us; and were half or a tenth part of the pains taken by us to obtain a powerful and effective method of pulpit address, which were submitted to by this prince of orators to become an effective speaker; were we as much set upon it as he was, and were we to give ourselves to the same means, by declaiming to the waves of the sea, or to the winds of heaven, determining to overcome every obstacle, we too should be orators, and that in a still better cause than his. And surely if ambition, or patriotism, prompted the Athenian and the Roman orator to such studies and such efforts for self-improvement, ought not the love of souls, zeal for God, and the interests of eternity, to prompt us to similar endeavors? Did they cultivate elocution with such unwearied perseverance to counteract the designs of Philip, or to defeat the conspiracies of Cataline, and shall we not do it, to destroy the works of the devil, and to advance the kingdom of the Redeemer?

It is impossible not to know how much the popularity of some preachers depends upon their manner: they do not say better, or more striking things, than other men;

but they say them in a better and more striking manner. There is a pathos in their tones, a power in their looks, a gracefulness in their gestures, which other men have never studied, and therefore have never acquired. This was eminently the case with WHITFIELD, the greatest of preachers. Much of the wondrous power of that extraordinary man lay in his voice and action. I have already given an extract from his sermons to illustrate his manner as regards style of composition, but who that never heard him, or indeed who that had, could illustrate his manner as regards delivery? Think of such paragraphs as those I have just quoted, delivered in a manner appropriate to their nature; with an eye melting into tears; a voice tremulous with emotion—shrill, yet full, now swelling into thunder, and then dying away again into soft whispers; one moment apostrophizing to God, and the next piercing the sinner's conscience with an appeal that was as sharp arrows of the Almighty; at one time pouring out a stream of impassioned pity for the sinner, and the next moment a torrent of burning indignation against his sin; his very hands all the while, and every gesture, seeming to help his laboring soul and his matchless elocution: and all this, to the conviction of his hearers, not the trickery of an artificial rhetoric, nor the effort of a man striving after popularity, but the spontaneous gushing forth of a heart agonizing for the salvation of their immortal souls! What oratory must that have been which extorted from the skeptical and fastidious HUME the confession that it was worth going twenty miles to hear it—which interested the infidel BOLINGBROKE, and once warmed even the cold and cautious FRANKLIN into enthusiasm? In those discourses which roused a slumbering nation from the torpor of lukewarmness, and breathed new life into its dying piety, you will find no profound speculation, no subtle reasoning, no metaphysical disquisition; for these never formed, and never can form, the staple of pulpit eloquence: but you will find "thoughts that breathe, and words that burn," and which, when enunciated with the magic of his wondrous voice, spoke, by the blessing of God, life into thousands dead in trespasses and sins. As a proof of the all-subduing power of his oratory, take the following scene, extracted from his Life and Times by the Rev. ROBERT PHILIP:—

"In February, 1742, WHITFIELD returned to London, where 'life and power soon flew all around' him again; 'the Redeemer getting himself victory daily in many hearts.' The renewed progress of the Gospel at this time in London, he calls emphatically, 'the Redeemer's *stately steps*.' Well he might; for during the Easter holidays, 'Satan's booths' in Moorfields poured out their thousands to hear him. This determined him to dare all hazards on Whit-Monday, the great gala-day of vanity and vice there. GILLIES' account of this enterprise, although not incorrect nor uninteresting, is very incomplete, considering the fame of the feat at the time. The following account is from the pen of WHITFIELD himself; and written whilst he was reporting, at home and abroad, his marriage.

"For many years, from one end of Moorfields to the other, booths of all kinds have been erected for mountebanks, players, puppet-shows, and such like. With a heart bleeding with compassion for so many thousands led captive by the devil at his will, on Whit-Monday, at six o'clock in the morning, attended by a large congregation of praying people, I ventured to lift up a standard amongst them in the name of Jesus of Nazareth. Perhaps there were about ten thousand in waiting, not for me, but for Satan's instruments to amuse them. Glad was I to find, that I had for once, as it were, got the start of the devil. I mounted my field pulpit; almost all flocked immediately around it. I preached on these words, 'As Moses lifted up the serpent in the wilderness, so shall the Son of man be lifted up,' etc. They gazed, they listened, they wept; and I believe that many felt themselves stung with deep conviction for their past sins. All was hushed and solemn. Being thus encouraged, I ventured out again at noon; but what a scene! The fields, the whole fields seemed, in a bad sense of the word, all white, ready, not for the Redeemer's, but Beelzebub's harvest. All his agents were in full motion, drummers, trumpeters, merrry-andrews, masters of puppet-shows, exhibitors of wild beasts, players, etc., etc., all busy in entertaining their respective auditories. I suppose there could not be less than twenty or thirty thousand people. My pulpit was fixed on the opposite side, and immediately, to their great mortification, they found the number of their attendants sadly lessened. Judging that, like Saint Paul, I should now be called as it were to fight with beasts at Ephesus, I preached from these words: 'Great is Diana of the Ephesians.' You may easily guess that there was some noise among the craftsmen, and that I was honored with having a few stones, dirt, rotten eggs, and pieces of dead cats thrown at me, whilst engaged in calling them from their favorite, but lying vanities. My soul was indeed among lions: but far the greatest part of my congregation, which was very large, seemed for awhile to be turned into lambs. This encouraged me to give notice that I would preach again at six o'clock in the evening. I came, I saw, but what? thousands and thousands more than before, if possible, still more deeply engaged in their unhappy diversions; but some thousands amongst them waiting as earnestly to hear the gospel.

This Satan could not brook. One of his choicest servants was exhibiting, trumpeting on a large stage; but as soon as the people saw me in my black robes and my pulpit, I think all to a man left him and ran to me. For a while I was enabled to lif up my voice like a trumpet, and many heard the joyful sound. God's people kept praying, and the enemy's agents made a kind of roaring at some distance from our camp. At length they approached nearer, and the merry-andrew (attended by others, who complained that they had taken many pounds less that day on account of my preaching) got upon a man's shoulders, and, advancing near the pulpit, attempted to slash me with a long heavy whip several times, but always with the violence of his motion tumbled down Soon afterwards they got a recruiting serjeant with his drum, etc., to pass through the congregation. I gave the word of command, and ordered that way might be made for the king's officer. The ranks opened while all marched quietly through, and then closed again. Finding those efforts to fail, a large body quite on the opposite side assembled together, and having got a large pole for their standard, advanced towards us with steady and formidable steps, till they came very near the skirts of our hearing, praying, and almost undaunted congregation. I saw, gave warning, and prayed to the Captain of our salvation for present support and deliverance. He heard and answered; for just as they approached us with looks full of resentment, I know not by what accident, they quarrelled among themselves, threw down their staff, and went their way, leaving, however, many of their company behind, who, before we had done, I trust, were brought over to join the besieged party. I think I continued in praying, preaching, and singing, (for the noise was too great at times to preach) about three hours.

"We then retired to the Tabernacle, with my pockets full of notes from persons brought under concern, and read them amidst the praises and spiritual acclamations of thousands, who joined with the holy angels in rejoicing that so many sinners were snatched, in such an unexpected, unlikely place and manner, out of the very jaws of the devil. This was the beginning of the Tabernacle society. Three hundred and fifty awakened souls were received in one day, and I believe the number of notes exceeded a thousand; but I must have done, believing you want to retire to join in mutual praise and thanksgiving to God and the Lamb."

I shall perhaps hazard my reputation as a judge of oratorical power, when I venture to pronounce this the greatest achievement of elocution which the history of the world presents, next to the splendid triumphs of the apostle Peter's sermon, over the murderers of Christ on the day of Pentecost. Who that considers the spot on which

WHITFIELD then stood; the scenes by which he was then surrounded; the discordant noises of the motley crew, which then rung in his ears, and in the ears of his audience; who, in short, that recollects what is the wild uproar and the hurly-burly of a London popular fair, must not stand astonished, first at the courage of the man who could erect his pulpit, and preach a sermon in such a scene; and then wonder still more at the marvellous success of his effort, in the conversion of hundreds of souls by that one discourse? What, I ask, was the effect of the orations of Demosthenes on the Athenians, in rousing them against Philip of Macedon, compared with this? The illustrious Grecian had everything which the scenery, and the historic associations that connected themselves with it, everything which the prepared mind of his audience could give, in the way of advantage, to his splendid declamation and its success; but the Christian orator had to combat with, and to triumph over, everything that seemed inharmonious with his theme, and opposed to the accomplishment of his object: and what must have been the magic power of that elocution which could blind the eyes and deafen the ears of an audience to the sights and sounds so near them, and produce such fixedness of attention, and power of abstraction, even there, as to leave them at liberty for those processes of thought, which resulted in the conversion of hundreds to God!

And to what, in the way of instrumentality, shall we attribute this astonishing effect? I answer to the power of his wonderful oratory. This fact has stood for a century upon record, and yet we have been slow to learn from it the lessons it is adapted to teach; and among these lessons the chief is the effect produced by a commanding method of address, in circumstances apparently the most unlikely for such a result. I am not calling upon my brethren to imitate this daring attack upon the very citadel of Satan: even WHITFIELD never, I believe, repeated it, and perhaps ought never to have attempted it; but my object is to show the power of voice and action, and the nature of ministerial earnestness.

I now bring forward another proof of this, which, if it be less grand and commanding in itself, is perhaps as likely to be useful to the readers of this little work, because it is an instance brought nearer to their own times, and to the level of their own circumstances: I mean the truly interesting and much lamented Mr. SPENCER, of Liverpool. In reference to this transcendent young preacher, Mr. HALL remarks, "The writer of this deeply regrets his never having had an opportunity of witnessing his extraordinary powers; but from all he has heard from the best judges, he can entertain no doubt that his talents in the pulpit were unrivalled, and that, had his life been spared, he would, in all probability, have carried the art of preaching to a greater perfection than it ever attained, at least in this kingdom. His eloquence appears to have been of the purest stamp, effective, not ostentatious; consisting less in the preponderance of any one quality requisite to form a public speaker, than in an exquisite combination of them all; whence resulted an extraordinary power of impression, which was greatly aided by a natural and majestic elocution." In this last expression Mr. HALL has disclosed much of the secret of Mr. SPENCER's popularity and usefulness: "a natural and majestic elocution," accompanied with a most engaging countenance and form, setting forth, with simple and unaffected earnestness of manner, the grand doctrines of evangelical truth, constituted the charm, and led to the success, of this most captivating preacher of modern times.

Let the young ministers of this age read his Life and Remains, as published by his gifted successor, Dr. RAFFLES, and also his posthumous sermons which have been since given to the world, and they will find nothing whatever of extraordinary genius; no lofty eloquence, in the usual acceptation of that term; no profound speculation; no splendid imagery or diction;—but at every step they will meet with the doctrine of Christ crucified set forth with manly vigor, in plain, perspicuous language; the utterances of a mind well instructed in the way of salvation, and of a heart overflowing for the good of his fellow-creatures. To what then shall we attribute, under God, his success, not only in filling the large town in which he lived, and the nation at large, with his fame, but what was infinitely more important in itself, and far more eagerly coveted by him, in bringing so many souls to Christ? There is but one answer to be given to this, and that is, it was the fascination of his manner. He was in earnest. The stream of his simple, elegant, but by no means profound thought, flowed forth with a resistless impetuosity that carried away his hearers before it. I know no more important lesson to be learnt, no inference more valuable to be drawn from the short life of this most interesting young man, so mysteriously cut off at the very commencement of his career, than the vast importance of an animated manner of preaching the gospel.

We may here advert to another individual, who was considered to be one of the most impressive preachers, in a particular way, of his times, the late Mr. TOLLER, of Kettering, and who also, no doubt, owed much to his mode of address, for the effect which his sermons produced: and the effect in this instance proves that vehemence, boisterousness, and vociferation, are not essential to earnestness and deep impression, for nothing could be more calm and more subdued, though nothing more solemnly commanding, than his whole demeanor in the pulpit. His printed sermons are characterized by manly strength of thought, uttered in language of great perspicuity, though not irradiated by the coruscations of what might be termed a brilliant genius. "A noble simplicity and careless grandeur," says Mr. HALL, with whom he lived on terms of most intimate friendship, "were the distinguishing features of his eloquence." There was an irresistible charm in his manner, which threw a spell over all his hearers, and which fascinated alike the learned and illiterate; he made the latter to understand, and the former to feel. I never heard him but once, but it was a memorable occasion, on the ordination of Mr. ROBERTSON, of Stretton, when Mr. HALL delivered the admirable charge which was afterwards published under the title of "The Difficulties and Encouragements of the Christian Minister." It is impossible ever to forget, and equally so to describe, the effect produced by two such preachers on such an occasion: it was the first time I had ever heard either of them, and the last that I ever heard Mr. TOLLER, and it almost seemed as if I had never heard preaching before: both were excited, no doubt, and stimulated to do their best, not only by the occasion, but by the presence of each other. The terms employed by Mr. TOLLER's biographer were the most appropriate that could be selected to describe his style and manner,—"simplicity and careless grandeur." It was impossible not to listen; neither eye nor ear played truant for a moment, while he was preaching: his delivery was not the rushing torrent of impassioned eloquence which gushed afterwards from the lips of his wonderful fellow-laborer, but the majestic, silent flow of a noble river. "In the power of awakening pathetic emotions," says Mr. HALL, in his Memoir, "he has excelled any preacher it has been my lot to hear. Often have I seen a whole congregation melted under him like wax before the sun: my own feelings on more than one occasion, have approached to an overpowering agitation. The effect was produced, apparently, with perfect ease. No elaborate preparation, no peculiar vehemence or intensity of tones, no artful accumulation of pathetic images, led the way: the mind was captivated and subdued, it hardly knew how. Though it will not be imagined that this triumph of popular eloquence could be habitual, much less constant, it may be safely affirmed that a large proportion of Mr. TOLLER's discourses afforded some indications of these powers." The following is Mr. HALL's description of the effect of two sermons preached in his hearing by this distinguished man:—

"It was about this period (1796) that my acquaintance with him commenced. I had known him previously, and occasionally heard him; but it was at a season when I was not qualified to form a correct estimate of his talents. At the time referred to, we were engaged to preach a double lecture at Thrapstone, nine miles from Kettering; and never shall I forget the surprise and pleasure with which I listened to an expository discourse, from 1 Peter, ii. 1, 3. The richness, the unction, the simple majesty which pervaded his address, produced a sensation which I never felt before: it gave me a new view of the Christian ministry. But the effect, powerful as it was, was not to be compared with that which I experienced on hearing him preach at the half-yearly meeting of the Association, at Bedford. The text which he selected was peculiarly solemn and impressive; his discourse was founded on 2 Peter, i. 13, 15, 'Yea, I think it meet as long as I am in this tabernacle, to stir you up by putting you in remembrance: knowing that shortly I must put off this my tabernable, etc. The effect of this discours) on the audience was such as I have never witnessed before or since. It was undoubtedly very much aided by the peculiar circumstances of the speaker, who was judged to be far advanced in a decline, and who seemed to speak under the impression of its being the last time he should address his brethren on such an occasion. The aspect of the preacher, pale, emaciated, standing apparently on the verge of eternity, the simplicity and majesty of his sentiments, the sepulchral solemnity of a voice which seemed to issue from the shades, combined with the instrinsic dignity of the subject, perfectly quelled the audience with tenderness and terror, and produced such a scene of audible weeping as was perhaps never surpassed. All other emotions were absorbed in devotional feeling: it seemed to us as though we were permitted for a short space to look into eternity, and every sublunary object vanished before 'the powers of the world to come.' Yet there was no considerable exertion, no vehemence, no splendid imagery, no magnificent description: it was the simple declaration of truth, of truth, indeed, of infinite moment, *borne in upon the heart by a mind intensely alive to its reality and grandeur*. Criticism was disarmed; the hearer felt himself elevated to a region which it could not penetrate; all was powerless submission to the master spirit of the scene. It will be always considered by those who witnessed it, as affording as high a specimen as can be easily conceived, of the power of a preacher over his audience, the habitual or even frequent recurrence of which would create an epoch in the religious history of the world."*

This description, even though some allowance should be made for the eloquence of friendship, which was poured forth by the pen of Mr. TOLLER's admiring friend, is replete with instruction to our rising ministry. They may learn the vast importance of the manner in which a sermon is delivered, as well as the matter of which it is composed;

---

* Memoirs of Mr. TOLLER, by Mr. HALL, prefixed to a volume o Mr TOLLER's sermons.

for, with all his vigorous and manly thought, Mr. TOLLER owed much as a preacher to his method of address. Nor is this the only lesson, nor perhaps the most important one, to be learnt from this short but precious piece of ministerial biography; for we gather what it is that, with minds of the highest order, such as Mr. HALL's, constitutes the nearest approach to perfect pulpit eloquence, and to which even these commanding intellects yield themselves up with the most willing submission—not the artificial elaboration of men intent upon producing a *great* sermon; not the magniloquent diction and splendid imagery, which have been sought with ambitious eagerness by those who aim to shine; nor the cold, abstract, philosophical reasoning of a metaphysical dialectician; but the simplicity and earnestness of a preacher who aims to instruct the judgment, awaken the conscience, and affect the heart. All great minds love simplicity, and detest affectation. This was especially the case with Mr. HALL. His censure of the opposite quality to unaffected earnestness, amounted sometimes to eloquent extravagance and burlesque, and his sarcasms not unfrequently were tinged with uncharitable bitterness; while his admiration of simplicity was occasionally expressed in somewhat exaggerated panegyric. The ambition of a preacher whose aim is usefulness might well be gratified in a remark which he once made after hearing a sermon: "I should not wonder if a hundred souls were converted to-night!"

These are only a few out of innumerable instances which could be adduced, to prove the vast importance which belongs to an effective enunciation. Far greater numbers of our preachers fail for want of this than from any other cause; a fact so notorious as to need no proof beyond common observation, and so impressive as to demand the attention not only of the professors but the committees of all our colleges. It is too generally the case that no sufficient culture is bestowed upon the speaking powers of our students, from the beginning to the end of their course of study. There is great assiduity manifested in giving them a fulness of matter, but far too little in producing an impressiveness of manner. Every assistance is granted to them to make them scholars, philosophers, and divines; but as to good speaking, for the acquisition of this they are left pretty much to themselves. Nay, it is not even inculcated upon them with the emphasis it should be, to try to make good speakers of themselves. A complete system of ministerial education must of necessity include some attention to elocution, and which should commence as soon as a student enters college: so that by the time he is put upon the preaching list he may have some aptitude for the management of his voice, and not have his thoughts diverted then from his matter and his object to his manner. He should by that time have acquired a *habit* of good speaking, so as to be able to practice it with facility, and without study. The great objection to lectures on elocution is that they are apt to produce a pompous, stiff, and affected manner; but this is an abuse of the art, the object of which should be to cure the vices of a bad, and to supply the wants of a defective enunciation, and to form an easy, natural, and impressive delivery.

I entirely concur, therefore, with Dr. VAUGHAN, in his important and impressive remark, "that let our students fail in the matter of a good elocution, and so far as regards their ministry among Protestant dissenters, it will matter little in what else they may succeed." This is sustained by a reference to the great number we observe, who, though soundly orthodox in sentiment, possessed of large acquirements in scholarship and philosophy, partakers of undoubted piety, and even desirous of doing good—yet make no way, can with difficulty procure a situation, and are filled, perhaps, with wonder, that men very much their inferiors in natural talent and literary acquirement, are everywhere followed, while they are everywhere neglected. The problem is easily solved, the mystery soon explained: these inferior men, by their earnest, animated manner, make their slenderer abilities tell more upon the popular mind, and heart, and conscience, than the dull scholars and cold philosophers do their accumulated but useless stores of knowledge.

It should, however, be remarked, that there is nothing more likely to be mistaken than animation in the pulpit. There are some young ministers, who, aware of the importance of a graceful and effective elocution, take no small pains to acquire it, by studying and practicing the most approved rules of the art. It is not, however, this alone for which I contend: for as the lessons of the dancing-master form only a stiff and formal action, where there is no natural ease and elegance, so also the teacher of elocution can do little to form an earnest and energetic speaker, where there is no living source of animation in the soul. It is not a pompous, swelling, *ore rotundo* style of speaking that constitutes the excellence of an orator; not "the start and stare theatric;" not modulations of the voice that sound as if the speaker were regulating tones and cadences by the fugle motions of a teacher standing before him: but the impassioned vivacity of one who feels intensely his subject, and who speaks under the influence of strong emotion. The secret of animation, the nature of earnestness, lie, as we have said, in an intense feeling of the subject of discourse; in a mind deeply impressed, and a heart warmed, with the theme discussed. All men are in earnest when they feel. Hence the anecdote of the pleader, who, on being applied to by a client to undertake her cause, upon perceiving the coldness of her manner in stating her case, told the applicant he did not credit her story. Stung by this reflection upon her veracity, and this disbelief of her grievance, she rose into strong emotion, and affirmed, with expressive vehemence, the truth of the story. "Now," said he, "I believe you."

The hackneyed, but valuable rule of the ancient teacher of eloquence remains, and ever will remain, as true as when it was first uttered—"Weep yourself, if you expect me to weep." Sympathy is the speaker's most powerful auxiliary: there is nothing so contagious as strong emotion. We have most of us, perhaps, seen a large portion of a congregation brought to tears by the pathetic and faltering tones, the tremulous lips and suffused eyes of the preacher. But then it must be on a subject which is worthy of it—must be sincere and not simulated emotion, and must come only when the people's minds are prepared to sympathize; for as there is only a step between the sublime and the ridiculous, the same remark may be made concerning the pathetic. Genuine emotion is the charm of all speaking upon moral and religious subjects, in the absence of which the most measured and stately elocution, whatever pleasure it may impart to the ear, will have little power to affect the heart. We have sometimes listened to lofty and well composed music, to an overture for instance, which we could not but admire; but it was still cold admiration, for the whole piece had not a note of passion from beginning to end: but some simple melody followed it, which, by the pathos of its notes, or the power of its associations, touched every chord in our hearts, and raised in us a tumult of emotion. Thus it is with different preachers: we listen to one, whose excellent composition, and sonorous, perhaps even musical voice, command our admiration; but not a passion stirs, all within is cold, quiet, and without emotion; the speaking is good, but it does not move us: but there is another, with perhaps less talent, yea, less oratory, in one sense, but his tone his looks, his manner throughout, are full of earnest feeling; it is a strain, every word of which comes from the heart, and every word of which awakens by sympathy a correspondent state of feeling in our hearts.

Who is likely to be moved by hearing a man discuss the most awful realities of eternal truth, such as the danger and the doom of immortal souls, the glories of heaven, and the torments of hell, with as much coolness, and with as little emotion as a lecturer on science would exhibit when dwelling on the facts of natural history? Is it probable there can be any earnestness in the hearer, when there is none in the preacher? "How is it," said a minister to an actor, "that your performances, which are but pictures of the imagination, produce so much more effect than our sermons, which are all realities?" "Because," said the actor, "we represent our fictions as though they were realities, and you preach your realities as though they were fictions." It is difficult to believe that a dull, cold, statue-like preacher, whose passionless monotony is a mental opiate for his hearers, can himself credit the message he is delivering. What, that man who never elevates or depresses his voice from one given pitch of soporific dullness; whose tone never falters, whose eye never glistens, whose hand never moves, who speaks as if he were afraid of awakening the slumberers, whom his "drowsy tinklings" had lulled to sleep,—*he* feel the weight of souls; *he* in earnest for their salvation; *he* endeavoring to pluck them as brands from the burning? Who will credit it? It is true he may have no great power of voice, and a naturally phlegmatic mind, with a great deficiency in the natural powers of oratory; but place him by the side of a river where he has seen a fellow-creature fall into the water, and has thrown a plank or a rope to aid the drowning man to escape, will he not have power of voice, and of animated tones, and of persuasive earnestness there, as he directs the object of his solicitude to the means of deliverance? Will he not rise out of his monotone there? Will he not make himself heard and felt there?

By an earnest manner, then, is meant, the enunciation that is dictated by a deep and feeling sense of the importance of our message. We are to persuade, to entreat, to beseech, and these modes of speech have an utterance of their own. What Paul's manner must have been, how impassioned and impressive, when he made Felix tremble and Festus exclaim, "Thou art beside thyself; much learning hath made thee mad." But even the sublime and awful truths of revelation, if they do not press upon the heart, and lay hold of, and possess it, will be but coldly handled and feebly discussed. It is only when the love of Christ constraineth us, and beareth us away as with the force of a torrent, that we shall speak with a manner befitting our great theme. If we are not intensely real, we shall be but indifferent preachers.

This shows us the vast moment of our living under the powerful impression of the truths we preach. We cannot, like the actor, have a stage dress and character to put on for the occasion, and put off when the curtain drops. There may indeed be a factitious earnestness excited by the sounds of our own voice, and by the solemnities of public worship; but this will usually be fitful, feeble, oratorical, and very different from that burning ardor which is the result of eminent piety, and which imparts its own intensity of emotion to the words and tones of the speaker. It was the patriotism of Demosthenes that constituted the fire of his eloquence: he loved his country, and, trembling for the ruin that Philip was bringing upon the liberties of Greece, he poured forth his lightning words, in tones of thunder. His philippics were a torrent of the strongest emotion, bursting from his *heart*, though guided in its course by the established rules of eloquence. He could never have spoken as he did, had not the wrongs of Philip, and the dangers of Greece, entered into his soul. So must it be with us: our animation must be the earnestness, not of rhetoric, but of religion; not of art, but of renewed nature; and not designed to astound, but to move; not the manner studied and intended merely to attract a crowd, and to excite applause, but to save the souls of men from death. For this purpose, whatever means we employ, and whatever rules we lay down, to cure the vices of a bad elocution, and to acquire the advantages of a graceful one—and such an aim is quite lawful—we must ever remember that the basis of a powerful and effective pulpit oratory, will consist of a deep and fervent piety; in the absence of which the most commanding gift of public speaking will be but as sounding brass or a tinkling cymbal.

Dr. COTTON MATHER, in his beautiful and invaluable work, now nearly forgotten, entitled "The Student and Preacher," in speaking on this subject, remarks:—

"It is a pity but a well prepared sermon should be a well pronounced one. Wherefore avoid forever all *inanes sine mente sonos*, and all indecencies; everything that is ridiculous. Be sure to speak deliberately. Strike the accent always upon the word in the sentence it properly belongs unto. A tone that shall have no regard to this is very injudicious, and will make you talk too much in the clouds. Do not begin too high. Ever conclude with vigor. If you *must* have your notes before you in your preaching, and it be needful for you *de scripto dicere*, which even some of the most famous orators, both among the Grecians and the Romans, did, yet let there be with you a distinction between the neat using of notes, and the dull reading of them. Keep up the air and life of speaking, and put not off your hearers with a heavy reading to them. How can you demand of them to remember much of what you bring to them, when you remember nothing of it yourself? Besides, by reading all you say, you will so cramp and stunt all ability for speaking, that you will be unable to make a handsome speech on any occasion. What I therefore advise you to is, let your notes be little more than a guide, on which you may cast your eye now and then, to see what arrow is to be next fetched from thence; and then with your eye as much as may be on them whom you speak to, let it be shot away with a vivacity becoming one in earnest for to have the truths well entertained by the auditory. Finally let your perorations be lively expostulations with the conscience of the hearer; appeals made and questions put unto the conscience, and consignments of the work over into the hands of that flaming preacher in the bosom of the hearer. In such flames you may do wondrously."

Pity that Dr. MATHER had not gone a little farther than this, and affectionately advised his younger brethren in the ministry to begin their career without any notes at all in the pulpit; advice still more necessary in this day, as there seems a rising inclination to adopt the practice. Nothing can be conceived of more likely to repress earnestness, and to hinder our usefulness, than this method becoming general. True it is that some preachers may rise up, who, like a few living examples, may in despite of this practice attain to eminence, to honor, and usefulness, such as rarely fall to the lot of ministers in any denomination; but this will not be the case with the greater number, who, having no commanding intellect to lift them above the disadvantage of this habit, will find few churches willing to accept their dullness, for the sake of the accuracy with which it is expressed. And who can tell how much greater our greatest men would be, if they delivered their sermons without their notes? Think of WHITFIELD, HALL, PARSONS, reading their sermons! What a restraint upon their noble intellects, and their gushing hearts! Where is reading tolerated but in the pulpit? Not on the stage, nor at the bar, nor in the senate. It is conceded that we lose something of precision and accuracy by spoken discourses, as compared with those that are read, but is not this more than made up by what we gain in impression? By him who slavishly reads, the aid borrowed by the preacher from the eye and graceful action is lost; the link of sympathy between his soul and that of the audience is weakened; the lightnings of his eloquence flash less vividly, and its thunders roll less grandly, for this obstruction to their efforts. Perhaps even those who do read are aware of the disadvantages of the habit, and would say to their younger brethren, whose habits are not yet formed, avoid, if you can, the practice of reading your discourses. There are, however, occasions, when from the nature and extent of the subject, this practice is not only allowable, but necessary

Before we pass from the subject of preaching, we may consider with propriety the matter and manner of prayer. Between these two there is a close and obvious connection, for earnest sermons should be ever associated with earnest prayers; and it cannot be doubted that a pious, faithful, and devoted minister, is scarcely less useful, at least in the way of keeping up the spirit of devotion in his congregation, by the latter, than he is by the former. His chastened fervor, like a breeze from heaven, comes over the languid souls of his hearers, and fans the spark of piety in their hearts to a flame: while on the contrary, the dullness and coldness of some public prayers are enough to freeze what little devotion there may be in the assembled people. We have thought too little of this, and have too much neglected to cultivate the gift, and seek the grace of supplication. If entreating and beseeching importunity be proper in dealing with sinners for God, can it be less so in dealing with God for sinners? Our flocks should be the witnesses of both these, and hear not only how we speak to them, but how we plead with God for them; should be the auditors of our agonizing intercession on their behalf; and be convinced how true is our declaration that we have them in our hearts. How such petitions, so full of intense affection and deep solicitude, would tend to soften their minds, and to prepare them for the sermon which was to follow. Who has not beheld the solemnizing and subduing effect of such holy wrestling with God, upon the congregation? they seemed to feel as if God had indeed come down among them in power and glory during the prayer, and was preparing to do some work of grace in their midst. The rudest and most turbulent spirits have sometimes been awed, and the most trifling and frivolous minds made serious, by this holy exercise. We who practice extempore prayer have advantages for this, of which we should not be slow to avail ourselves. Not being confined by the forms of a liturgy, but left to our own choice, we can give a harmony to all the various parts of the service, and make the scripture we read, and the hymns we sing, as well as the prayers we present, all bear upon the subject of the sermon, and thus give a unity of design, and a concentration of effect to the solemn engagements of the sanctuary. This should be an object with every minister, in order that the thoughts of the people may, without being divided or diverted, flow pretty much in one channel, and towards one point. Moral, as well as mechanical effect, depends upon the combination of many seemingly small causes. But more especially should the prayers be in harmony with the sermon, and every preacher knows what the sermon is to be. If he is about to address himself in a strain of beseeching importunity to the impenitent and unbelieving, how much would it tend to prepare them for his appeal if his heart were previously, and in their hearing, to pour forth a strain of fervent pleading with God on their behalf. They would thus be awed and subdued into a state of mind likely to render the forthcoming sermon effectual, by the blessing of God, for their conversion. Such a prayer would be the most appropriate introduction he could give to his discourse. But then especial care should be taken that the hymn, and even the tune, which interposes between the prayer and the sermon, should not be of a kind which would divert the current of thought, much less efface the solemn impressions already produced, and hinder the effect of the discourse about to be delivered. I remember to have heard a preacher, who was going to preach a very solemn sermon, breathe out one of the most impressive strains of intercession for the impenitent I ever listened to, as if even anxious to begin the work of conversion by his prayer, which he hoped to finish by his sermon. The people sat down in solemn awe, when, as if by a prompting of the wicked one, who catches away the seed out of the heart, the clerk gave out a most inappropriate hymn, and the choir, with a band of musical instruments, sung a tune more inappropriate still: as may be easily imagined, the seriousness produced by the prayer was instantly lost, and the preparation for the sermon entirely destroyed. How true is it that the singing seat is often hostile to the usefulness of the pulpit, and the choir in opposition to the effect of the preacher. FINNEY, in his book on Revivals, descends to so minute a specification of the circumstances to be attended to in *preparing* for the revival, as to expose him to the ridicule of many of his readers; and no attempt is here made to defend him, or to recommend his volume; but still there is true philosophy in the *spirit* of his directions, which amounts to this, that the effect of sermons, and indeed of all public speaking, depends often upon very little things. Trifles have great power to divert the current of thought, to break the chain of reflection, and to disturb the process of emotion. Everything connected with public worship should be still, orderly, solemn; as befits a service conducted in the presence of God, and with reference to him.

Returning to the subject of prayer, it becomes every minister to take especial care that this should be conducted with propriety, not only on account of its nature and design, as addressed to God, and as the medium of obtaining blessings at his hand, but because of its moral effect upon the people. We object to pre-composed forms, and we think on sufficient grounds, as wanting in adaptation to the ever-changing circumstances of the congregation, to the events of the times, and to the services of the minister, and as at the same time tending to produce formalism—but then we are bonnd to take care that our *free* prayers are such as are eminently adapted to edification. And is there not room for much improvement in our public devotional exercises? In some cases there is too much elaboration and appearance of study; though in far more, a want of richness and fulness of unction and importunity. The prayers are often too excursive and vague, a mere string of petitions, which have no connection with each other, and which leave the whole without unity of design, or definiteness of object. There are some admirable remarks on the subject of public extempore prayer, in FOSTER's sketch of Mr. HALL's character as a preacher, which go to prove that more concentration of thought on particular topics, would produce a greater effect, than that unrestrained discursiveness which characterizes most of our devotional exercises. We pass too rapidly from one subject to another, and thus as it were surprise our hearers, by their being brought to a new topic before they were aware they had left the preceding one; and it may be safely affirmed that prayers which do not detain the thoughts on any certain things for a few moments, take slight hold on the auditors. "Things noted so transiently, do not admit of deliberate attention, and seem as if they did not claim it." With the liberty of unrestricted variety which we possess, why should it be thought necessary to go always over the same ground, and bring in the same topics, in the same exact order, at much the same length, and in almost the same words? Why may we not sometimes drop everything else, and break out into a continued strain in reference to one selected object? How deep would be the conviction of the audience of the importance which *we*, at any rate, felt to belong to it, and how likely would be such a method to engage them in sympathy with us, in reference to it. We should also be careful to avoid all personalities which would excite curiosity or disturb devotion, and especially all laudatory epithets on the one hand, and criminatory ones on the other. In using our freedom let us take care not to abuse it, and endeavor that the end and object of our preaching shall be helped, and not hindered, by the method of our praying. If pre-composed forms of prayer have their disadvantages, so also has free prayer; and while *we* consider the balance of advantage vastly in favor of the latter, let us recollect that our brethren of the Establishment are of the same opinion respecting their liturgy. Let us therefore charitably bear with, and not reciprocally reproach, each other.

The *manner* of prayer, as well as its matter, demands also our serious attention. While the very nature of the exercise forbids everything showy or elaborately ingenious, everything quaint, familiar, and irreverent, and enjoins the utmost simplicity and spirituality, it no less prohibits all flippancy, carelessness, and pompous oratory. The most serious, reverent, and devotional manner is required, not only on our own account, but on account of the audience. There are some men whose very tones are enough to extinguish all devotional feeling at once. It is almost impossible to conceive that it is a sinful mortal we hear addressing himself to the Holy, Holy, Holy Lord God, before whom the seraphim veil their faces: while on the contrary there are others whose deep, devotional tones, whose subdued manner, whose awe-stricken entire demeanor, seem to remind us that they are indeed speaking to the Almighty. It is not necessary to suppose that earnestness requires *boisterousness;* a mistake too commonly made by many who work themselves up into vociferation and actual contortion. Such vehemence, like a violent blast of wind, puts out the languid flame of devotion, when a gentler breeze would fan it to greater intensity. It were well also to avoid that sing-song tone which we too often hear in those who lead the public devotions. Still there must be earnestness—the earnestness of deep feeling, of lively devotion, of a heart intent upon its own salvation, and the salvation of those who are then and there waiting to hear the word of life.

CHAPTER VII.

EARNESTNESS MANIFESTED IN THE PASTORATE.

This must by no means be omitted. The pulpit is the chief, but not the only sphere of ministerial solicitude and action: just as preaching is God's first, but not his exclusive means of saving souls. Different ministers have fallen into two opposite mistakes; one class have thought to do everything in the pulpit as preachers, but they have neglected the duties of the pastor; while the others have purposed to do everything as pastors, and have neglected the diligent preparation of their sermons. Of the two errors the latter is the more mischievous, inasmuch as no pastoral devotedness, however intense, will long keep together a congregation among Protestant Dissenters, much less collect one, when the preaching is indifferent and unattractive; while, on the other hand, good preaching will of itself do much in the absence of pastoral attentions to keep the flock from being scattered. But why should not both extremes be avoided? Good preaching and good shepherding are quite compatible with each other, and he who is in earnest will combine both. He will be a watchman for souls everywhere, and seek if by any and by all means he can save some. He can never entirely lay aside his anxiety for the objects of his regard, and is ever ready to manifest it on all suitable occasions. His sermons are composed and delivered for this object, and he is afterwards inquisitive for the effect they have produced, and watches and prays for the result. His anxious eye is searching the congregation, even while preaching, to see, not so much who is delighted, but who is seriously impressed. He will not, cannot be content to go on, without ascertaining whether or not his sermons are successful. Like a good physician, who is minutely watchful for the effect of his medicines upon his patients individually, according to their specific varieties of disease, he will endeavor to ascertain the impression which his sermons have produced, and on particular persons. He will aim to attract to him the anxious inquirers after salvation: and for this purpose he will have special meetings for such persons; will invite and encourage their attendance; will cause them to feel that they are most welcome, and by his tender, faithful, and appropriate treatment of their case, will make them sensible that to him they are as truly the objects of deep interest, as the lambs are to the good shepherd. And though he will very naturally wish not to be too frequently broken in upon, in his private studies, by those to whom he has given set times for meeting with him—yet a poor, burdened, trembling penitent will never find him engaged too deeply or delightfully in study, to heal the broken in heart, and to bind up their wounds. It is really distressing to know how little time some ministers are willing to give up from their favorite pursuits, even for relieving the solicitudes of an anxious mind. They read much, and perhaps, as the result, preach well-composed, though possibly not very awakening sermons; but as for any skill, or even taste, for dealing with convinced sinners, wounded consciences, and perplexed minds, they are as destitute of this, as if it were no part of their duty. They resemble lecturers on medicine, rather than practitioners; or are like a physician who would assemble all his patients who were able to attend, in the same room, and then give general directions about health and sickness to all alike, but who does not inquire into their several ailments, nor visit them at their own abodes, nor adapt his treatment to their individual and specific diseases. It is admitted that some men have less tact, and a still greater destitution of taste, than others, for this department of pastoral action; but *some* skill in it, and some attention to it, are the duty of every minister, and may be acquired: and no man can be in earnest without it. He who can only generalize in the pulpit, but has no ability to individualize out of it; who cannot in some measure meet the varieties of religious perplexity, and deal with the various modifications of awakened solicitude; who finds himself disinclined or disabled to guide the troubled conscience through the labyrinths which sometimes meet the sinner in the first stage of his pilgrimage to the skies, may be a popular preacher, but he is little fitted to be the pastor of a Christian church. One half hour's individual conversation with a convinced, but perplexed mind, may do more to correct mistakes, to convey instruction, to relieve solicitude, and to settle the wavering in faith and peace, than ten sermons. True, it requires much love for souls, much devotedness to their salvation, and much anxiety for the success of our ministry, to devote that half-hour to one solitary inquirer after life eternal; but surely no really earnest minister will think his time ill bestowed in guiding that single inquirer into the way of peace.

This individualizing labor is more easily carried on in some situations than in others, and is indeed more important, in some situations, to ministerial success. In small congregations, for instance, especially when they are found in small towns or villages, the objects of such special attention come more under the notice of a pastor, are more accessible, and can have more time given to them, than in large congregations in large towns. To these smaller churches, individuals, though not of more importance or value in themselves, since the soul and its salvation are of equal worth everywhere, are of more consequence to the comfort of the minister, and the prosperity of the cause, than they are where a crowd is gathered. Pastors of large churches are much more occupied, both with the concerns of their own flock, and with public business, than their brethren in more retired situations, and are often so occupied and hurried, as to have too little leisure for the individual attentions now recommended; and are perhaps apt, amidst the aggregate of numbers, to think too little of the units. Still some excuse may be made for *them*, of which the others cannot avail themselves. The accession of a single member to our smaller churches is felt to be of more importance, and produces a more reviving and cheering effect, than the addition of several to the larger ones. We have all something to learn even from the Scribes and Pharisees of ancient times, who compassed sea and land to make *one* proselyte; and also from the Papists of modern times, who pursue a like course: or, to change the examples, we want more of the benevolent disposition of angels, who rejoice over *one* sinner that repenteth. No efforts would be more likely to be successful, none would more amply reward those who make them, than the selection of the most hopeful individuals in the congregation, and following them up with all the assiduities of a special, affectionate and judicious attention. Such a course of pastoral labor, though it would not altogether be a substitute for pulpit attractiveness, and should never be allowed to supersede the most diligent pulpit preparation, would enable many a minister, who may not be gifted with large abilities, to retain a strong hold upon his flock. This is a line along which almost any one may carry on a career of earnestness.

As another object of pastoral attention, may be mentioned *attention to the young:* and these may be divided into two classes—the young persons who belong to the congregation, and those who belong to the Sunday schools. With regard to the former, it is a matter of congratulation that the modern plan of Bible classes is not unfrequent nor unsuccessful: but even at this time, they are rather the exception than the rule. It may be feared that there are some, who, from the beginning to the end of the year, aye, and of their ministry also, take no interest in the youth of their congregations; they have no catechetical classes, no Bible classes, and even rarely preach to the young. Who can wonder that such men have to complain that their young people go off to the Church of England, or, what is far worse, to the world? What have they ever done to attach them to themselves, or to their place of worship? Let no man be surprised that his congregation, diminished by death and removals, continually declines, if he neglects to lay hold of the youth of his flock. Whence does the shepherd look for *his* future flock, but from the lambs? And who are to constitute our future congregations and churches, but our young people?

I am an advocate also for the catechetical instruction of the younger children, and am sorry that this admirable method of imparting religious truth has fallen into such general desuetude. Even the Bible class, however accommodated to the capacity of these junior members of our congregation, is not altogether a substitute for, but should be regarded only as an addition to, the practice of catechising. There is still a great desideratum to be supplied to our denomination, whose thanks would be pre-eminently due to the man who should supply it,—I mean a set of well composed catechisms, which might be introduced to all our families, and thus set up a uniform system of religious instruction for the body. I say, which might be introduced to all our *families;* for it is by no means my wish or my intention to obtrude the pastor between the parent and child, and take the religious instruction of the latter from his natural guardian and teacher, to devolve it upon the pastor. It is to *parents* that the injunction is delivered, "Thou shalt teach these words to thy children diligently, and shalt talk of them when thou sittest in thy house, and bring them up in the nurture and admonition of the Lord." No pastoral attention should be intended, or can be adapted, to supercede or lighten this solemn parental obligation. But then the pastor should labor to the uttermost to keep up the parents who are of his flock, to the right discharge of their duty. There are few of us who are not sorrowfully convinced that little is to be expected from our sermons in the pulpit, or our instructions in the class room, while all our endeavors are so miserably counteracted by the neglect of domestic instruction, and the want of parental solicitude. I do not mean to justify pastoral neglect by advancing the obligations of parental duty, for I believe we have been, and are, all verily guilty of a criminal defect of duty in not giving more of our time and attention to the children of our congregations;—but still even the time and attention we *do* give is all likely to be lost, by the low state of religion in the homes of some of our people.

We might very naturally expect that our churches would be chiefly built up from the families of our members; whereas, the greater number of accessions are from those who were once the people of the world. There is a great mistake on this subject, into which both parents and ministers have fallen; and that is, that the conversion of the children of the professor is to be looked for more from the sermons of the latter than from the instructions of the former; whereas the contrary is the true order of things; and were domestic piety and teaching what they ought to be, this is the order which would be found to exist. There is unquestionable truth in the proverb, "Train up a child in the way he should go, and when he is old he will not depart from it." I believe that were the nature and design of the domestic constitution thoroughly understood, and its religious duties early, judiciously, affectionately, and perseveringly discharged, the greater number of our young people would be converted to God at home.* Were all religious professors, who are parents, real and eminent Christians; were they from the time they became parents to set their hearts upon being the instruments of their children's conversion; were they to do all that prayer, instruction, discipline, and example could do for the formation of the religious character of their offspring; and were they carefully to abstain from everything which would obstruct these ends, I feel confident that it would be within the hallowed precincts of such homes, and not in the sanctuary, that the children of the godly would usually become godly

* I take this opportunity to recommend a most valuable volume, entitled "The Domestic Constitution," by the Rev. CHRISTOPHER ANDERSON; a new and cheaper edition of which is lately published. Every minister should know, by reading it, the worth of this inestimable book, and recommend it to his flock.

themselves. Here, then, should and will be an object with every truly earnest pastor, to bring up the parents in his church to a right sense and discharge of their functions. He will labor to impress upon them the solemn obligations under which they live, to train up their children for God. It will be a matter of prayer and solicitude with him to excite them to their duty and keep them in it; for this purpose, he will not only make his pulpit ministrations bear much upon parental obligation, but he will make it a point of visiting the families which are in his church, to pray with them, and to hold up the hands of the parents in this godly duty. Deeply is it to be regretted that this part of pastoral occupation, as well as catechising, has gone out amidst the bustle and engrossing power of trade, and the public business of modern religious institutions. How little do the families of our people know of us in the character and hallowed familiarity of the pastor? When are *we* seen amidst the domestic circle as the respected and beloved minister of that lovely and interesting group, laboring by our affectionate, serious, and solemn discourse, and by prayer as serious, solemn, and affectionate, to entwine ourselves round the young hearts which there look up to us with reverent regard? Why, why do we neglect such important scenes of labor, and hopeful efforts for usefulness? What power would this give to our sermons, and what efficacy to our ministrations! These young ones would grow up to love us, and it would not be a light or little thing which would break them off from our ministry when we had produced in them such a personal attachment to ourselves. But then we must take especial care that our conduct in the houses of our people should be such as to give weight and influence to *their* religious instruction of the family, and to *ours* in the sanctuary We must be known there as the servants of God, the ministers of Christ, the watchmen for souls; and not merely as the table guest, the parlor jester, the gossiping story-teller, the debating politician, the stormy polemic, the bitter sectarian; much less as the lover of wine. Would God that those of my brethren who have acquired the habit of smoking, if they cannot leave it off, would abstain from this practice in the houses of their friends, and confine it to their own: would that they did not permit the young inquisitive eyes of the junior members of the families which they visit, to see the pipe brought out as their necessary adjunct. Did they know the regrets of their best friends, and consider the power of their example, they would, at any rate, so far abstain as to wait till they had reached their own habitation, before they indulged themselves with their accustomed gratification. Still, it is freely conceded, without justifying the habit, there are some who are addicted to it, so grave, and serious, and dignified in other respects, as to furnish by their general demeanor an antidote against their example in this one particular: but what antidote can be found to neutralize the mischief inflicted by the levity and frivolity of the parlor buffoon, whose highest object in going to the houses of his friends seems to be to tell a merry story and to excite a hearty laugh. In his hands and lips the pages of "Punch" are far more becoming, as they are, perhaps, far more frequent, than those of David, Isaiah, or Paul. Happily we have very few that go to this extreme of lightness and frivolity, but far too many, as is the case with all denominations, and with ours not more than others, of those whose hilarity is destructive at once of their dignity, their seriousness, and their usefulness as ministers of Christ. Not that I contend for sanctified demureness, and solemn grimace, or even a perpetual sermonizing conversation; as if a pastor could not talk, without violating official decorum, upon any topic but religion, and were letting down his dignity, or desecrating his sanctity, if he joined in ordinary conversation, and partook of, or even helped the cheerfulness of the circle. By no means: he is not to appear like a spectre that has escaped from the cloister, to haunt the parlor, striking every face with paleness, and every tongue with silence. He is a man, a citizen, and a friend, as well as a minister; and has a stake and an interest in the great questions which occupy human minds, and engage their conversation; and provided he do not forget what is due to the latter, he need not throw off what belongs to the former. Nay, his very cheerfulness may be made a part of his earnestness, by being taken up and employed as a means to conciliate the affections of all around him. The man who is seriously cheerful, who engages in general conversation, and accommodates himself to the innocent habits of those with whom he associates, and does this in order really to do them spiritual good, and aid him in the great work of saving their souls, will find in the sublimity and sanctity of his end, a sufficient protection against the abuse of the means. This is widely different from the unchecked levity, and unrestrained frivolity in which some indulge, and which make it difficult to imagine how *they* can feel the value of souls, or the obligation of attempting their salvation. Howard at a masquerade, or Clarkson at a fancy ball, would not have been more out of place, nor a physician more out of character who had just come from the ravages of the plague, and was immediately going back to them again, who was seen wasting his time, and amusing himself with the tricks of a merry-andrew, than is a messenger of God's mercy, and a preacher of Christ's gospel, in the circles of folly and vanity, and he himself the Momus of the party.

But we now advert for a few moments to the scope for earnestness which is presented to the pastor, by the children of the Sunday school. By a most fatal error, too many of our ministers deem these institutions as either beyond their circle, or below their notice. They are neither. A pastor is, or ought to be, the head and chief in the department of all the religious instruction which goes on in connection with the congregation under his care. *He* is the teacher, the superintendent, and the responsible organ of religious knowledge for all the flock, and the Sunday school is a part of it. It is a wrong state of things that has grown up among some of us Dissenters, in which two, three. or four hundred rational minds and immortal souls are brought every Sabbath-day to our Sunday schools, and to our places of worship, for the very purpose of receiving religious instruction, and yet all this is to be carried on without its being once thought of by the pastor, that he has something to do in this business; or by the congregation or the teachers, that he has by virtue of his office a right and a reason to interfere. In most cases, the pastor has given the matter out of his hand, and has thus raised up, or has been accessory to there being raised up, a body of young instructors of divine truth, who are acting independently of him, and who, in some few instances, have confederated against him. This is not as it should be. The teachers are, or ought to be, a pastor's special care; to qualify them for their office, and to assist them in its duties, should be thought by him no inconsiderable part of his functions. Nor should even the children themselves be viewed as persons with whom he has nothing to do. There are always, among these, some whose minds have been brought to serious reflection, who are inquiring with solicitude after salvation, and whom he should take under his own teaching and special care, and guide into the way of faith, peace, and holiness: and he should not neglect to give frequent, affectionate, and solemn addresses to the rest. In a Sunday school of two or three hundred children, there are of course two or three hundred *immortal souls*, exposed by their very situation in life to peculiar dangers, yet all capable of eternal blessedness, and all brought weekly under the eye of the pastor: and yet by how many of our pastors is this hopeful object of religious zeal and benevolence thrown off from ministerial solicitude, and handed over to the Sunday school teachers, as if there were no hope of *their* saving the soul of a poor boy, nor any reward for saving a poor girl. This obligation of attending to the souls of the Sunday scholars, while incumbent upon all ministers, is especially so upon those who are laboring amidst much discouragement, in small congregations. Many of these men are continually uttering their complaints over the smallness of their congregations, and the inefficiency of their labors; and yet, perhaps, have never thought of turning their attention to the two or three hundred youthful minds which are every Sabbath day before their eyes, and under the sound of their voice. No minister who ever threw his mind and heart into his Sunday schools had to complain that he labored in vain, and spent his strength for nought. No part of ministerial labor yields a quicker or a larger reward. By some it is made the main pivot on which their whole system of religious instruction turns, and flourishing congregations have risen up under its potency. I have myself been the astonished and delighted witness of this, especially in one well-known instance, and am so deeply impressed with its importance, that I conjure my brethren not to neglect this means of usefulness, not throw away the golden opportunity which the present circumstances of our country still hold out.

Nor is it Sunday school instruction alone which claims our attention, but daily education. In this we must be in earnest also. It is one of the great subjects of the day, and belongs to us as much as to any one. We must not allow the public mind to be wholly taken from us, but must exert ourselves according to our ability and opportunity to train it up for society and God. Others know and feel the importance of this, if we do not. The Roman Catholic priests are aware of it, so are the clergy of the Established Church, and so are the Methodist ministers; and shall Dissenting ministers be behind the most zealous and devoted friends of education? I trust not.

But there are other departments of the pastorate, in which earnestness will manifest itself; such as visiting the sick, especially where the disease is chronic, and leaves the mind at liberty for conversation; and then also there is the difficult, but incumbent duty of rebuke, warning, and ecclesiastical discipline. No devoted servant of Christ can neglect the state of the church, but will be solicitous to maintain such order there, as shall be pleasing to Him to whom the church belongs. Like a good shepherd he will look after his flock, and will endeavor to avoid the denunciations of God delivered by the prophet Ezekiel: "Woe be to the shepherds of Israel that do feed themselves! Should not the shepherds feed the flocks? The diseased have ye not strengthened; neither have ye healed that which was sick; neither have ye bound up that which was broken; neither have ye brought again that which was driven away; neither have ye sought that which was lost."

Impressive description of our duty! May we be found so discharging it as to avoid this fearful woe!

How appropriately may I here introduce the words of the BISHOP of CALCUTTA, in his admirable and heart-searching introduction to the edition of "BAXTER's Reformed Pastor," published by COLLINS, in his series of "Select Authors:"

"What have we been doing as ministers? Lamentably as we have failed in a general estimate of the vast importance of our office, we have failed as lamentably in all those parts of it which relate to personal inspection and vigilance over our flocks. We have confined ourselves to preaching, to ecclesiastical duties, to occasional visits to the sick, to the administration of the sacraments, to the external and secular relation in which we stand to our parishes; but what have we done in personal care and direction, in affectionate catechetical conferences, in going from house to house, in visiting every family and individual in our districts, in becoming acquainted with the characters, the wants, the state of heart, the habits, the attendance upon public worship, the observance of the Sabbath, the instruction of children and servants, the family devotions, of each house? Have we looked after each individual sheep with an eager solicitude? Have we denied ourselves our own ease, and pleasure, and indulgence, in order to 'go after Christ's sheep, scattered in this naughty, wicked world, that they may be saved forever?' What do the streets and lanes of our cities testify concerning us? What do the highways and hedges of our country parishes say as to our fidelity and love to souls? What do the houses and cottages and sick chambers of our congregations and neighborhoods speak? Where have we been? What have we been doing? Has Christ our Master seen us following his footsteps, and going about doing good? Brethren, we are verily faulty concerning this. We have been content with public discourses, and have not urged each soul to the concerns of salvation. Blessed Jesus! thou knowest the guilt of thy ministers in this respect, above all others! We have been divines, we have been scholars, we have been disputants, we have been students—we have been everything but the holy, self-denying, laborious, consistent ministers of thy gospel."

Such, then, is a view, and but an imperfect one, too, of an earnest ministry.

I would have made it more comprehensive and impressive if I could: for the reality can never be overdrawn nor exaggerated. Let any one consider what that object must be which occupied the mind of Deity from eternity; which is the end of all the Divine dispensations of creation, providence, and grace, towards our world; which is the purpose for which the Son of God expired upon the cross; which formed the substance of revealed truth, and employed the lives and pens of apostles; to which martyrs set the seal of their blood: in short, let him recollect that the end of the Christian ministry is the salvation of immortal souls, through the mediation of our Lord Jesus Christ; and then say if anything less than an *earnest* ministry is befitting such an object, or if that earnestness can comprehend in it less than has been set forth in these chapters.

CHAPTER VII.

EXAMPLES OF EARNESTNESS.

The power of example is proverbial. We are constituted to be moved by it, as well as directed. It teaches us *how* to act, and impels us to action. Hence the excellence of Scripture; it is a book of models as well as of maxims. Towering above all the rest, standing out in bold relief beyond all the others, is the character of Christ. He is an example to all persons. To the ministers of the gospel, this beautiful and perfect embodiment of all that is holy and lovely commends itself with peculiar energy. He was himself a minister of the gospel, sent by the Father in the same manner as he has sent others. He is the great model, the divine archetype as a preacher and a teacher, after which they are to copy. In his manner of preaching, as well as in his matter, he is to be imitated; in his liveliness, his tenderness, his fidelity, his solemnity, he is to be closely and constantly followed. We, of all men, are under the most solemn obligations to tread in his steps and do as he did. But I now select from all his qualities, his earnestness. In this as well as in everything else he surpassingly excelled all his most devoted servants. When he came into the world he said, "Lo, I come; in the volume of the book it is written of me, I delight to do thy will, O

God." When he emerged from his obscurity at Nazareth and entered on his public ministry, he commenced a career of increasing and untiring activity. His eye, his heart, his tongue, embraced one object, and one only,—the salvation of souls. We see him always in action, never in repose. Follow him where we will, we find him always working, preaching, praying, or weeping, but never loitering. He gathered up the very fragments of his time, when waiting in the house of Martha for his food, and sitting down at the well of Samaria for his disciples who had gone into the city to purchase provisions, and employed them in doing good. He was the compassionate Saviour, and not the cold and heartless philosopher. His preaching was the breathing of a soul replete with love, his discourse was the overflowing of mercy. He was not a mere personification of reason, but an incarnation of love; and sent forth not the moon-beams of a cold intellectuality, but the sun-rays of a fervid benevolence. To save souls, he scrupled not to go, where, but for this object, we should have never seen him, to feasts and weddings, as well as funerals. From the hour when he thus addressed his mother, "Wist ye not, I must be about my Father's business?" his meat and his drink were to do the will of that Father. He denied himself all that was of a luxurious and self-gratifying nature; his only relaxation was devotion, which, after laboring all day in the city, he sought by prayer upon the mountains and in the midnight air. As a scene of earnestness, never surpassed till he ascended the hill of Calvary, behold him bathed in tears over the guilty city, and choked in his utterance by the sobs with which the foresight of the approaching destruction of Jerusalem convulsed his bosom! O, that was a spectacle which was enough to draw into a sympathy of grief the moral universe! What a heart that must have been, which on such a spot, and at such a time, could find relief for its intense emotions only in tears! Truly has it been said, that melting scene is inferior in pathos, in tender and solemn grandeur, only to Calvary itself. But this was only a prelude to what followed. In prospect of the hour of the solemn and mysterious scenes of Gethsemane and Golgotha, he exclaimed, "I have a baptism to be baptized with, and how am I straitened till it is accomplished." His eagerness for man's salvation was such that the guilty heart of the traitor was too slow in its purpose for his love, and he quickened the movements of Judas by those memorable words, "What thou doest, do quickly." He made haste to the cross. He was almost impatient for the hour of sacrifice. He could brook no delay in love's redeeming work.

Here, ministers of the gospel, here is your pattern. This earnestness is your model. You are to be something like this. The work of Christ in saving souls is to be regarded in a double aspect by you, both as the means of your personal salvation, and the example for your official character. We have too much forgotten the latter. Even though as Christians we may have looked to his conduct as our exemplar, we have too much neglected to do so as ministers. As servants, we have not kept our eyes fixed as we ought to have done upon the Great Master. Shame upon us, how little careful we have been to catch the fire of intense and ardent devotedness from this glowing and divine example.

We have seen the sun, let us now turn to the stars: we have beheld the Master, let us now contemplate the servants. Perhaps the former is so high above you, that you are discouraged by its loftiness and perfection: well, look now at some nearer your own level. First of all observe the apostle Paul; and where shall we find anything so nearly approaching to the earnestness of his divine Lord, as the conduct of this wondrous man? From the moment of his conversion on the way to Damascus, he had but one object of existence, and that was the glory of God in the salvation of souls; and but one way of seeking it, and that was the preaching of the cross. Wherever he went, whatever he did, to whomsoever he addressed himself, he was ever watching for souls. Whether reasoning with the Jews in their synagogues, or discoursing with the philosophers on Mars Hill, or preaching to the voluptuous inhabitants of Corinth, or appealing to the Ephesian elders at Miletus, or pleading in chains the cause of Christianity before the tribunal of Festus in the presence of Agrippa, or writing letters from prison to the churches he had planted, we find him everywhere, and always, the earnest minister of Jesus Christ. There is one expression in his address to the Ephesian elders which reveals, in a short compass, the whole spirit and marrow of his preaching: "Remember that by the space of three years, I ceased not to warn every one of you night and day with tears." The terror of the Roman government could not extract from his firmness a single drop; but the sight of an immortal soul perishing in its iniquity, and pleased with its delusions, altogether unmanned him, and suffused his face with tears, which in other cases would have been the sign of weakness. O those tears, those tears; how they reprove us for our insensibility, and how they prove to us our deficiencies. Every view we can take of this illustrious servant of the cross fills us with astonishment and admiration. His conversion and history seem designed to teach us what energy may be compressed into one human heart, to be developed in one single life; what sufferings may be endured, what power exerted, what results produced, by one mar, who is constrained by the love of Christ, and filled with all the fulness of God ; and what God can accomplish, in fulfilling the purposes of his wisdom and love, by the instrumentality or an individual of our species. There is a short sentence in his epistle to the Philippians, which, in a few words, sums up his whole life and labors,—"FOR ME TO LIVE IS CHRIST." What a compass of meaning, what a manifestation of soul, what a comprehension of purpose and plan, do those few monosyllables contain! "Christ is my life: apart from him and his work I seem to have no separate existence: I have grown into that one object."

This *is* earnestness: and what obligation rested on Paul to cultivate it, which does not rest on us? What was Christ to him, which he ought not to be to us? Why should he thus labor for souls, and not we? Is there a single reason which appertains to him, that does not appertain to us? Ministers of Christ, read this great man's life with a view to know what you ought to be, and how you ought to live and labor. In view of what this blessed apostle was, and how he labored, will you be satisfied with cold intellectuality, flowery orations, subtle metaphysics; with thinking you have answered the end of your calling when you have composed two sermons a week, and kept the people tolerably well satisfied with your labors? Will you think it enough to be a close student, a hard reader, a good writer—though all this while souls are not converted to God, nor the cause of religion advanced in the world? Talk you of hard labor, and severe trials, and scanty incomes, and ungrateful congregations, and fickle friends? listen to his tale, and be silent: "In labors more abundant, in stripes above measure, in prisons more frequent, in deaths oft. Of the Jews five times received I forty stripes save one. Thrice was I beaten with rods, once was I stoned, thrice I suffered shipwreck, a night and a day have I been in the deep; in journeyings often, in perils of waters, in perils of robbers, in perils by mine own countrymen, in perils by the heathen, in perils in the city, in perils in the wilderness, in perils in the sea, in perils among false brethren; in weariness and painfulness, in watchings often, in hunger and thirst, in fastings often, in cold and nakedness. Beside those things that are without, that which cometh upon me daily, the care of all the churches. Who is weak, and I am not weak? who is offended, and I burn not?" Is there to be found in human composition such a passage as this? In reading this who can help asking, What have *I* done or suffered for Christ, that can give me a title to be ranked as a minister of Christ after this?

But perhaps *this* also is too lofty an example to have much weight with you; then take an instance next from the Nonconformist's Memorial. It appears from the diary of that eminent servant of Christ, OLIVER HEYWOOD, that in one year, beside his stated work on the Lord's day, he preached one hundred and fifty times; kept fifty days of fasting and prayer, and nine of thanksgiving; and travelled fourteen hundred miles in the service of Christ and immortal souls. And when we consider that these journeys must have been either on foot or on horseback, this distance was more than ten thousand miles by our modern railways. And then think of BAXTER, that wondrous man, who, though hunted and imprisoned by the demon of persecution, and tortured with the stone, was always preaching and writing, till he had composed and published those hundred and twenty volumes, the very writing of which, as to the mechanical act alone, seemed enough to occupy a whole life, and of the contents of which the celebrated Dr. BARROW said, that "his practical works were never mended, nor his controversial ones ever confuted."

Now turn to those extraordinary men, WESLEY and WHITFIELD; and who of us can read the account preserved to us of their amazing labors, and equally amazing success, without something of a self-reproachful and desponding feeling, as if we were living almost in vain? When we see them dividing their whole lives between the pulpit, the closet, and the class-room; sacrificing all domestic enjoyment and personal ease; encountering savage mobs, and addressing congregated thousands; pacing backward and forward the whole length of the kingdom, and crossing the ocean many times; moving the population of cities, and filling nations with the fame and the fruit of their evangelical labors; breathing little else than the atmosphere of crowded chapels and preaching-rooms, except when they lifted up their voice under the canopy of heaven; regaling themselves, not with the dainties of the table, nor the repose of the soft, luxurious couch, but with the tears of the penitent, and the songs of the rejoicing believer; making it their one and only business to seek the salvation of souls, and their one and only happiness to rejoice in the number of their conversions; indifferent alike to the savage fury of their persecutors, and the fondest flatteries of their followers; sometimes rising from the bed of sickness to address the multitude in circumstances which rendered it probable they would exchange the pulpit for the tomb; to sum up all in one short sentence, wearing out life in labor so great that it looked as if they were in haste to die: when we see this, how can we endure to think of the way in which we are living, or scarcely imagine that we are living at all? How can we read their lives, and not blush for ourselves? How can we witness their earnestness, and not feel as if we knew nothing of the passion for saving souls?

And what shall be said of BRAINERD, the missionary of Christ, and preacher of the gospel to the American Indians? See him harassed by a nervous and gloomy dejection, wearing down by a slow consumption; yet, for the love of souls, dwelling amidst savages, helping to build his own comfortless and ill-furnished hut; living at times on parched corn; travelling and benighted in the woods, sleeping, if sleep he could, wet and cold, in a tree; throwing himself down, on his return to his own solitary dwelling, on his hard bed, with none to comfort him; and, amidst all this, long tried and harassed by the want of success in his apostolical labors—and all this for the love of souls, and the glory of Christ! Where, O where, even among modern missionaries, to say nothing of ministers at home, do we find this rigorous self-denial, this self-sacrificing disposition, this intense desire after the salvation of souls!

We may profitably refer to one more instance of ministerial devotedness—that is, the excellent Dr. PAYSON, of America, whose biography should be read by every Christian pastor. Many *have* read it, and we would hope with no small advantage. During his ministry his solicitude for the salvation of souls was so earnest, that he impaired his health by the frequency of his fastings and the importunity of his prayers. His whole life was spent in one constant series of efforts to produce revivals of religion; and the anguish of his mind when his labors failed, was so acute, as to bring on bodily disease. It was said of him by his biographer, that his language, his conversation, and his whole deportment were such as brought home and fastened on the minds of his hearers the conviction, that *he believed, and therefore spoke.* So important did he regard such a conviction in the attendants on his ministry, that he made it the topic of one of his addresses to his clerical brethren, which he entitled, "*The importance of convincing our hearers that we believe what we preach.*" In the course of this address he remarks, that a minister, "in delivering his message as an ambassador of Christ, would show that he felt deeply penetrated with a conviction of its truth and infinite importance. He would speak like one whose whole soul was filled with his subject. He would speak of Christ and his salvation, as a grateful, admiring people would speak of a great and generous deliverer, who had devoted his life for the welfare of his country. He would speak of eternity, as one whose eye had been wearied by attempting to penetrate its unfathomable recesses, and describe its awful realities, like a man who stood on the verge of time, and had lifted the veil which conceals them from the view of mortals. Thoughts that glow and words that burn would compose his public addresses, and while a sense of the dignity of his official character, and the infinite importance of his subject, would lead him to speak as one having authority, with indescribable solemnity, weight and energy, a full recollection that he was by nature a child of wrath, and that he was addressing fellow men and fellow sinners, mingled with compassion for their wretched state, and an ardent desire after their salvation, would spread an air of tenderness over his discourses, and invest him with that affectionate, melting, persuasive correctness of manner, which is best calculated to affect and penetrate the heart. To say all in one word, he would speak like an ambassador of Him who spake as never man spake, and who would say, 'We speak that we do know, and testify that we have seen!'"

When disabled by increasing disease from preaching, Dr. PAYSON carried with him into his sick chamber all his undiminished earnestness for the salvation of souls. Being present on one occasion at the administration of the Lord's Supper, he rose, and thus addressed his flock: "Ever since I became a minister, it has been my earnest wish that I might die from disease which would allow me to preach a farewell sermon to my people; but as it is not probable I shall ever be able to do this, I will attempt to say a few words now; it may be the last time I shall ever address you. This is not merely a presentiment: it is an opinion founded on facts, and maintained by physicians who know my case, that I shall never behold another spring.

"And now, standing on the borders of the eternal world, I look back upon my past ministry, and on the manner in which I have performed its duties; and oh, my hearers, if you have not performed your duties better than I have done, woe! woe! be to you—unless you have an Advocate and Intercessor in heaven. We have lived together twenty years, and have spent more than a thousand Sabbaths together, and I have given you at least two thousand warnings. I am now going to give an account *how* they were *given*; and you, my hearers, will soon have to give an account how they were *received*. *One* more warning I will give you. Once more your shepherd, who will be yours no longer, entreats you to flee from the wrath to come. Oh, let me have the happiness of seeing my dear people attend to their eternal interests, that I may not have reason to say, 'I have labored in vain, I have spent my strength for nought.'"

After this he entered the chapel but once more. Confined now to his house and to his room, he still carried out his intense desires to be useful in saving souls, by dictating letters and addresses to individuals and to bodies. Persons under anxious concern for their salvation, young converts entering on the Christian life, ministers just commencing the arduous duties of their office, and various *bodies* and *classes* of individuals, among whom were the young men, were sent for to visit him in his sick chamber, and receive his dying counsels and admonitions. What messages also went forth from that scene of agony and of glory, to ministers and friends! His "ruling passion was strong in death." His love for preaching was as invincible as that of the miser for gold, who dies grasping his treasure. Dr. PAYSON directed a label to be attached to his breast, with the words, "*Remember the words which I have spoken unto you, while I was yet present with you;*" that they might be read by all who came to look at his corpse; and by which he being dead, yet spake. The same words, at the request of his people, were engraven on the plate of the coffin, and read by thousands on the day of interment.

Here was a beautiful instance of ministerial earnestness, and if I have dwelt longer on this than on some of the still more illustrious ones which have preceded it, the reason may be found in the fact that it is the example of a minister of our own times, and placed in nearly the same circumstances as ourselves; and also in the wish that many who have not read this most instructive piece of ministerial biography, may be induced by these extracts to peruse the volume. That man's heart must be in a bad state indeed, both as a Christian and a minister, who is not made the holier and more earnest by contemplating this bright and lovely example.

Leaving the ministry, and turning towards the laity for some rares examples of unquenchable ardor, we find two.

deserving, above most, of honorable mention and assiduous imitation—Lady HUNTINGDON, and the late THOMAS WILSON, Esq., of Highbury. In the former we see a peeress, related of course to many noble families, to whom the honors of the court and the elegancies of fashion were accessible, relinquishing, from the hour of her conversion to God, all these pomps and gaities of the world, and consecrating her rank, her influence, and her wealth, to the glory of God and the salvation of souls; quitting the saloons of the gay for the conventicles of the pious; and the society of nobles, statesmen, orators, and wits, to hold converse with itinerant preachers; selling her jewels to enable her to purchase chapels; opening her own drawing-room for religious worship; and unmoved or undiverted by the wonder, the reproach, and the sneers of a proud and scoffing aristocracy; pursuing, with an intensity which they could as little comprehend as they could the object to which it was directed, the spread of evangelical truth and the salvation of immortal souls, both among the rich and the poor. In this one object her whole life was bound up, apart from which she had neither occupation nor enjoyment.

Pretty much the same may be said of the late Treasurer of Highbury College. We waited not for the very valuable and interesting memoir of this inestimable man, with which his son has favored the world, to convince us of this; much as the conviction is deepened, and the impression perpetuated, by the *tout ensemble* of the life and character there presented to our view: those who knew Mr. WILSON—and who in the religious circle of all parties did not know him?—ever considered him as a man of extraordinary zeal and great benevolence, and a most useful specimen of an earnest man. This character will be assigned to him, even by those who differed from him in some views of the object on which he lavished the energies of his active mind, and the resources of his ample fortune. But now that the whole outward career of this indefatigable man is laid before us, and the mechanism of his heart, as the spring of his energy, is disclosed to us in this seasonable and instructive biography, we learn the important lesson how much one man, whose heart is given to the work, may accomplish in the way of evangelizing our dark and wretched world. Perhaps modern times have produced or presented few more striking instances of that quality of character which it is the design of this volume to illustrate and to enforce. He selected his one object of life, and that was the support and spread of evangelical religion, by means of building chapels, and the education and support of ministers, in connection with the denomination to which he belonged For this he retired from business, and consecrated to it his time, his fortune, his influence, and his piety. His journeys *from* home, and his occupation *at* home, were in a great measure devoted to this. He had his office, his clerk, his house of business, his correspondence, in reference to this, as much as the merchant has for his commercial affairs. To this was given his conversation in company, and his musing and letters when alone. The consummation of one scheme of usefulness in his own line of effort, was but the commencement of another. While others talked, he worked. We knew where to find him, and how he was employed. If a voice from heaven had commanded him to build chapels, and educate ministers, he could not have pursued this object with more fixedness of aim, unity of action, and steady perseverance, than he manifested. He knew his object, and therefore needed no counsel: he loved it, and suffered nothing to divert his mind from it; he saw its practicability, and hearkened to no objections. If others would act with him, well; and if not, he would go alone. It was not brilliant talents, nor a princely fortune, nor a commanding eloquence—though he had good abilities, a handsome income, and an easy utterance—but it was earnestness, that made him what he was, and enabled him to do what he did. Yes, THOMAS WILSON was an earnest man: and would to God that all whom he helped to introduce into the ministry partook, in the still more sacred duties of their calling, of the same intensity of action as he did in his.

CHAPTER IX.

MOTIVES TO EARNESTNESS,

AND THE INDISPENSABLE NECESSITY OF IT.

I. *It is demanded alike by the theme and the object of it.*

When Pilate proposed to the illustrious prisoner at his bar the question, What is truth? he placed before him the most momentous subject which can engage the attention of a rational creature; and if Christ refused to give an answer, his silence is to be accounted for by the captious or trifling spirit of the querist, and not by any supposed insignificance of the question, since truth is the most valuable thing in the universe, next to holiness; and it is truth that is the theme of our ministry, even that which by way of eminence and distinction is called *the* truth. Take any branch of general science, be it what it may, and however valuable and important it may be considered, its most enthusiastic student and admirer cannot claim for it, *par excellence,* that supremacy which is implied in the definite article, *the* truth. Who shall adjust the claims for this distinction, between the various sciences of natural and moral truth, and declare which is the rightful possessor of the throne, against the false pretensions of usurpers? Who? The God of truth himself: and he has done it.

and placing the Bible on the seat of majesty in the temple of truth, has called upon all systems of philosophy whatever, to fall down and do it homage. This is our subject: eternal, immutable truth—truth given pure from its divine source, and given with the evidence and impress of its own omniscient Author. Oh, what are the loftiest and noblest of the sciences;—chemistry, with its beautiful combinations and affinities; or astronomy, with its astounding numbers, magnitudes, distances, and revolutions of worlds; or geology, with its marvellous and incalculable dates of by-gone millions of ages;—to the truths of revelation? What is dead, inert matter, with its laws of materiality,—however diversified, classified, or combined,—compared with the world of mind, of souls, of immateriality and immortality, and with the laws of moral truth by which they are regulated? What is nature, to the God of nature? what the heavens and the earth, to the glorious mind that looks out upon them through the organ of vision, as from a window that commands the grand and boundless prospect? what the fleeting term of man's existence upon earth, with its little cycles of care, and sorrow, and labor, compared with the eternal ages through which the soul holds on her course of deathless existence? The works of creation are a dim and twilight manifestation of God's nature, compared with the grandeur and more perfect medium of redemption. The person of the Lord Jesus Christ is itself a wonder, and a mystery, which shall shine all other displays of Deity into darkness; this is the shekinah in the holy of holies of the temple of God's creation, towards which, as they bend over the mercy-seat of his work of redemption, all orders of created spirits, from the most distant parts of the universe, reverently turn and do homage to the great God our Saviour. This, this is our theme—

the truth *of* God, and *concerning* him; the truth of an incarnate Deity; the truth of man's redemption by the cross; the truth of the moral law, the eternal standard of rectitude, the tree of knowledge of good and evil; the truth of the gospel, as the tree of life in the midst of the paradise of God; the truth of immortality, and of heaven, and of hell; the truth couched under the symbols of the Levitical law, and the predictions of inspired prophets, and fully exhibited in the gospels of evangelists, and the inspired letters of apostles. Again I ask exultingly and rapturously, what are the discoveries of NEWTON, or of DAVY, or the inventions of WATT, or of ARKWRIGHT, compared with these? Viewing man in his relation to immortality, as a sinful and moral agent, what is art or science, compared with revealed truth? And shall we, can we, be otherwise than earnest in the promulgation of *this* truth? Shall we touch such themes with a careless hand, and a dronish mind? Shall we slumber over truths which keep awake the attention, and keep in activity the energies of all orders of created intelligences, and which are the object and the resting-place of the uncreated mind? Let us look at the earnestness with which the sons of science pursue their studies: with what enthusiasm they delve into the earth, or soar on the telescope to the heavens, or hang over the fire; with what prolonged and patient research they carry on their experiments, and pursue their analyses; how unwearied in toil, and how enduring in disappointment, they are; and then how rapturously they hold up to the world's gazing and wondering eye some new particle of truth, which they have found out after all this peering and prying into nature's undiscovered secrets! Ministers of the gospel, is it thus with the men who have to find out the truths of nature, and shall we, who have the volume of inspired, revealed truth opened before us, drone, and loiter, and trifle over such momentous realities? Shall the example of earnestness be taken from him who analyzes man's lifeless flesh, to tell us by the laws of organic chemistry its component parts, rather than from him who has to do with the truths that relate to the immortal soul? Shall he whose discoveries and lessons have no higher object than our material globe, and no longer date than its existence, be more intensely in earnest, than we who have to do with the truth that relates to God and the whole moral universe, and the truth that is to last through eternity? What deep shame should cover us for our want of ardor and enthusiasm in such a service as this!

And then what is the purpose for which this truth, so grand, so awful, so sublime, is revealed by God, and to be preached by us? Not simply to gratify curiosity; not merely to conduct the mind seeking for knowledge, to the fountains where it may slake its thirst; no, but to save the immortal soul from sin, and death, and hell, and conduct it to the abodes of a glorious immortality. The man who can handle such topics, and for such a purpose, in an unimpassioned, careless manner, and an icy heart, is the most astounding instance of guilty lukewarmness in the universe: to his self-contradiction no parallel can be found: and he remains a fearful instance how far it is possible for the human mind to go in the most obvious, palpable, and guilty inconsistency. A want of earnestness in the execution of that commission which is designed to save immortal souls from eternal ruin, and raise them to everlasting life, is a spectacle which, if it were not so common, would fill us with amazement, indignation, and contempt. We have read the speeches of the great masters of eloquence, both of ancient and modern times; and have read also of the intense anxiety, and untiring effort, with which they have sustained by corresponding efforts, the mighty periods that flashed from their burning souls: and do we condemn as enthusiasts the Athenian orator who thus agonized to save his country from the yoke of Philip; the majestic Roman who roused the indignation of the republic against the treason of Cataline; or our own Wilberforce, who for twenty years lifted his voice, and appealed to the justice and mercy of a British Parliament, against the atrocities of the slave trade? On the contrary, we deem no eulogy sufficient to express our admiration of their noble enthusiasm. But our panegyric upon them is a condemnation upon ourselves; for how far short of them do we fall in earnestness, though the salvation of a single soul, out of all the multitudes that come under the influence of our ministrations, is an event, which in its consequences is inconceivably more momentous, because enduring through eternity, than all the objects, collectively, for which these men exhausted the energies of their intellect and life. Do we really believe that we are either a savor of life unto life, or of death unto death, to them that hear us? Or is this mere official phraseology, which is never intended to be understood in its ordinary import? Is it a matter of fact, or only the solemn garnish of a sermon, the trickery and puffing of pulpit vanity, that souls are perpetually rising from beneath our ministry into the felicities and honors of the skies, or dropping from around our desk into the bottomless pit? Are companies of immortal spirits continually emigrating from our congregations to colonize eternity, to people heaven or hell, to swell the numbers of the redeemed, or to add to the multitude of the lost? If this be true, and we are gross deceivers, mere pulpit actors, reverend hypocrites, if we do not believe in their truth,—then where is the earnestness that must give consistency to our professions, and which is appropriate to our situation, and adequate to our convictions? Have we really become so carelessly, so criminally familiar with such topics as salvation and damnation, that we can descant upon them with the same calmness, coolness, not to say indifference, with which the public lecturer will discuss one of the minutest branches of natural philosophy? O where is our reason, our religion, our consistency?

II. *Earnestness is imperatively demanded by the state of the human mind, viewed in relation to the truths and the object just set forth.*

This was glanced at in an earlier part of the work, but must be now resumed and amplified. The entreating and beseeching importunity employed by the apostle, and which are found to be no less necessary to us, presuppose, on the part of its objects, reluctance to come into a state of reconciliation with God, which must be assailed by the force of vehement persuasion. Although we have to treat with a revolted world, a world engaged in mad conflict with Omnipotence, yet, if the guilty rebels were weary of their hostilities, and in utter hopelessness of success, were prepared, on the first offer of mercy, to throw down their arms, and in the spirit of contrition to sue for pardon, ours would be an easy mission, and we might spare ourselves the trouble of earnestness and expostulation. But the very reverse is the case. "The carnal mind is enmity against God, and is not subject to the law of God, neither indeed can be." The hearts of men are fully set in them to do evil. We find them taken up, occupied, influenced, governed, by the palpable and visible things of the present life; and our business is to engage them in a constant resistance of the undue influence of the things which are seen and temporal, and to do this by a vigorous faith in things that are unseen and eternal. Our aim and labor are, by the power of the unseen world to come, to deliver them from the spell of the present state, with whose pageantry they are enamored, and under whose fascination they are well pleased to continue. And then, apart from, or at any rate in connection with this, they are so occupied by the pursuits of business, so engrossed by the cares, the comforts, and the trials of life, engaged in such breathless haste to pursue, such distracting bustle to possess, and such ardent hope to enjoy, the various objects of their earthly desires, that when we call their attention to serious religion, as the one thing needful, we are as one who would stop another in a race to offer him an object foreign to that for which he is contending, and who, by the competitor for the prize, is deemed intrusive, impertinent, and obstructive.

But the difficulty stops not here: if this were all, we should have only a very small share of the opposition which now calls forth our energy and requires our most strenuous efforts; for when we have succeeded in gaining a hearing and arresting attention, we have to contend, not only with an indisposition to receive the truth, but a determined hostility against it. We have, as our first business, to fasten a charge of guilt upon men naturally disposed to think well of themselves: to produce a sense of utter worthlessness and depravity in those, who, in the utmost length to which their concession will go, admit only some few imperfections and infirmities; to displace a feeling of complacency by one of self-condemnation and abhorrence; and to substitute for a general and unhumbled dependence upon divine mercy, such a conviction of exposure to the curse of a violated law, as makes it difficult for the trembling penitent to see how his pardon can be harmonized with the claims of justice; to offer salvation upon terms which leave not the smallest room for self-gratulation, or the operation of pride; indeed, to carry such a message as frequently excites disgust, and calls forth the bitterest enmity of the human heart, and arms all its passions in determined hostility. And then the salvation exhibited in the gospel is not only opposed to the pride, but to the passions of the soul of fallen man. It requires the excision of sins dear as a right hand, the surrender of objects which have enamored the whole soul, the breaking up of habits which have grown with our growth, and strengthened with our strength. Sometimes we have, in addition to all this, to summon our hearers to a war without, as well as a conflict within, and to verify the words of Christ, that he came to send a sword instead of peace, and to set parents against children, and children against parents. What minister has not sometimes felt his very courage ready to quail, and his steadfastness in danger of faltering, when called to lead on some persecuted convert to brave the cruel mockings and reproaches, the frowns, the threats, and the violence, of his nearest and dearest earthly connections? I agonize as I write, to think what I, among others, have witnessed of this kind. Verily it is through much tribulation, that some, even in these peaceful times, are called to enter into the kingdom of heaven. And then, to follow on the difficulties of the Christian ministry, to prevent the irst impressions of divine truth from vanishing like the cloud, or exhaling like the dew; to guide the inquirer from finding repose anywhere but at the cross of Christ; to guard the feeble, and to inspire the timid with courage; to detect the deceit of the heart, and to aid the novice in breaking off from besetting sins; to inspire the resolution to crucify the flesh, and to stimulate the soul to an ever onward progress in sanctification; to meet the epidemic malady of our nature, which assumes so many shapes, and appears under such a variety of symptoms, with a proportionate and well-adapted variety of treatment; to help the believer to beat down his foes under his feet, and amidst all his various trials, temptations, and difficulties, to continue steadfast, immovable, and always abounding in the work of the Lord, notwithstanding the conteracting influence of much unremoved corruption in his heart;—this, all this, must require in him who has to do it, earnestness of the most collected and concentrated kind. To carry on the ministry of reconciliation in this revolted world, with the intention and desire of recovering its inhabitants from sin and Satan unto God, when the opposition to be overcome is considered, must appear to every reflecting mind the most hopeless of all human undertakings, apart from the promised aid of the Holy Spirit. It is this alone that could induce us to continue in the ministry another hour. Without this agency, we must retire in utter despair. But then, even this is not to be viewed, much less expected, apart from human instrumentality; and man's earnestness is that very species of instrumentality which the Divine Agent employs. It is not the feeble ministrations of the lukewarm and the negligent that God blesses for the conversion of souls, but the heart-breathed, fervent wrestlings of the ardent and the diligent. He maketh the winds his messengers, and flames of fire his ministers. Here, then, is a double argument for earnestness, in the difficulties which are to be subdued in the accomplishment of our object, and the co-operating agency of the Spirit of God. The former shows its indispensable necessity, and the latter encourages us o put it forth. Without it, we cannot look for the aid of the Spirit; and without the aid of the Spirit, it would be exerted in vain. May we be able to take a right view of our obstacles and our resources.

III. *Consider the aspect of the times, as affecting the human mind, and the objects of our ministry.*

The view which has been just given of the difficulties that lie in the way of the faithful minister, applies to all countries and to all times, inasmuch as the depravity of human nature is co-extensive with the race of man. But still there may, and do, exist circumstances in one age and country, to give greater force to these difficulties, which are not found, at any rate to the same amount, in others. The features of our own age are strikingly impressive, and in no small degree hostile to the success of the gospel, and the prevalence of evangelical piety.

The sphere of human pursuits, whether we consider the active or speculative departments, is filled with unusual energy and excitement. Earnestness is the characteristic of the age. If we turn our attention to TRADE, we see men throwing their whole soul into its busy occupations, and laboring as if their salvation in another world depended upon their success on earth. What ardor of competition; what rage for speculation; what looking about for novel schemes, and what eagerness to embrace them when offered; what hazardous and reckless gambling, do we see going on all around us,—leaving out the impetus to all this which the railway system has introduced, and saying nothing of the multitudes who, instead of plodding onward in the beaten path of regular trade, endeavor, by watching the share market, to make a bound to wealth,—how engrossing are the pursuits of secular business, in these days of large returns and small profits. Think of the consumption of time, and the absorption of soul, which are necessary to maintain credit and respectability; and also the strength of religious principle which is indispensable to follow the things that are just, and true, and honorable, and of good report. How many professors are in danger of being carried away, how many *are* carried away, by the tricks, artifices, and all but actual dishonesties of modern trade: and what but a powerful and energetic ministry can be expected to rouse and help God's professing people to bear up against, and to keep in check, much more to subdue, this sordid and selfish spirit? What can be sufficient but an intense devotedness on the part of ministers to make things unseen and eternal bear down the usurping power of things seen and temporal? Who but the man that knows how to deal with invisible realities, and wield the powers of the world to come, can pluck the worldling from the whirlpool of perdition which sucks down so many in the torrents of earthly-mindedness, or prevent the professing Christian from being drawn into it? If our own minds are not much impressed with the awful glories and terrors of eternity, we shall not and cannot speak of these things in such a manner as is likely to rescue our hearers from the ruinous fascinations of mammon. How in such an age we seem to want a BAXTER and a DOOLITTLE; an EDWARDS and a HOWE; a WHITFIELD and a WESLEY; to break in with their thunder upon the money-loving, money-getting spirit of this grossly utilitarian age.

Then think of the engrossing power of POLITICS. What a spell has come over the popular mind, from this source, since that tremendous outburst, the French Revolution! For more than half a century the potency of this subject has been perpetually augmenting, till the rustic of the village, as well as the merchant of the city, the recluse student of the cloister, no less than the man of the exchange, have alike yielded themselves up to the fascinations of the newspaper, now accommodated, not only to every party in politics, but to every creed in religion, and at the same time cheapened down to almost the poorest member of society. This is matter neither of surprise, nor, provided it do not thrust out other and still more important matters, of regret. It is but the constitution of our country developing the energies of its popular element. The people are claiming their share of power and influence: may they prepare themselves by knowledge and piety to exercise it rightly. The stream and tendency of opinion in Europe at large, as well as in our own country, is evidently democratic; but without education and religion, the nations will daily become desirous of more liberty, and at the same time less capable of enjoying and preserving it. The less they feel of outward force and of the compulsion of secular power, the more they need the control of moral principles. At such a time, when the elements of good government are, so to speak, in a high state of excitement, and amidst much repulsion and attraction amongst themselves, are settling into their proper order, there will be such an unusual degree of interest felt in this great matter, as to throw into the shade matters of still deeper moment.

In sight of this, will any one deny that we want an earnest ministry to break in some degree the spell, and leave the soul at liberty for the affairs of a kingdom which is not of this world? When politics have come upon the minds, and hearts, and imaginations of the people for six days out of the seven, invested with the charms of eloquence, and decked with the colors of party; when the orator and the writer have both thrown the witchery of their genius over the soul; how can it be expected that tame, spiritless, vapid common-places from the pulpit,—sermons without either head or heart, having neither weight of matter, nor grace of manner, neither genius to compensate for the want of taste, nor taste to compensate for the want of genius; and what is still worse, having no unction of evangelical truth, no impress of eternity, no radiance from heaven, no terror from hell; in short, no adaptation to awaken reflection, produce conviction, or save the soul,—how can it be expected, I say, that such sermons can be useful to accomplish the purposes for which the gospel is to be preached? What chance have such preachers to be heard or felt, or what claim have they, amidst the high excitement of the times in which they live? Their hearers too often feel, that in listening to their sermons on the Sabbath, as compared with what they have heard or read during the week, they seem as if they were turning from the brilliant and tasteful gas-light to the dim and smoking spark of the tallow and the rush.

Another characteristic of our age is an ever-growing taste for ELEGANCE, refinement, and luxurious gratification. We cannot wonder at this, nor, if it be kept within proper bounds, greatly regret it. It is next to impossible that the progress of art, and the increase of wealth, should not add to the embellishments of life, and multiply the sources of tasteful enjoyment. But then, just in proportion as we multiply the attractions of earth, is our danger of making it our all, of leaving heaven out of sight, and learning to do without it. This is affecting the church, and the hardy and self-denying spirit of Christianity is in danger of being emasculated, and of degenerating into a soft and sickly effeminacy. Elegance and extravagance, luxurious entertainments and expensive feasts, are beginning to corrupt the simplicity that is in Christ; and amidst sumptuous buildings, gorgeous furniture, costly dress, and gay equipages, professors of religion are too much setting their affections on things that are upon the earth, and turning away from the glory of the cross to the glory of the world. Who is to call them off from this pageantry, and make them by God's grace feel how vain are all these things? Who can set up a breakwater against the billows of this ocean of worldly-mindedness, and guard the piety of the church from being entirely swept away by a flood of ungodliness? Who but a pastor that can speak in power and demonstration of the Spirit,—a man who shall rise Sabbath after Sabbath in the pulpit, clothed with a potency to throw into shadow, by his vivid representations of heaven and eternity, all these painted nothings on which his hearers are in danger of squandering their immortal souls?

Akin to this is a continually augmenting desire after AMUSEMENT. A love for pleasure, diversion, and recreation, is an appetite evidently increasing, for which there are those who are ever ingenious and ever busy to furnish a supply. Religion is no enemy to rational enjoyment, even though it be not strictly spiritual; and they who can supplant the low and vulgar sensualities on which the multitude have fed, by a more refined and elevated taste, even if it should not rise into the element of religion, are doing a service to their country and to their species. But still, a taste for amusement, both mental and bodily, may be carried too far, and many foreseeing and deeply reflective minds are of opinion that it is going too far now.

There cannot be a thoughtful mind, one that looks upon our sojourn in this world as a probation for eternity, but must reflect with serious alarm and grief upon the endless devices which are suggested by the wisdom that cometh from beneath, to hide from mankind their duty and their destiny as immortal creatures. It seems as if by common consent, mankind were striving who should be most successful, by inventing new kinds of diversions, in blotting from the mind all considerations of eternity. Pleasure-taking is the rage of the day, a taste which has been excited into a hungry appetite by the railway system. Before this desolating influence, the sanctity of the Sabbath, and with it of course the prevalence of religion, are likely to be destroyed. It may be said that anything is better than the ale-house and the gin-shop. This is freely admitted, but it may be questioned whether some of the modern stimulants to pleasure do not lead to, and not from, these scenes of iniquity. The people, it is affirmed, must have recreation. Be it so: but let it be of a healthful kind, and let the great aim of all who have any influence upon the public mind be to endeavor to implant a taste for the recreations afforded by cheap and wholesome literature, by quiet home enjoyments, and above all, by the sacred delights of true piety.

In connection with this may be mentioned, as one particular species of amusement, the taste for works of HUMOR which has been produced in this country within the last ten years. There is no sin in mirth: man is made to enjoy it, and there is a time to laugh as well as to weep. And he must be a very misanthrope, a vampire which in the dark night of sorrow would suck the last drop of happiness from the human sufferer, who would forbid the smiles of gladness, and everything which ministers to the gratification of the laughter-loving heart. But then it is a different thing from this, to wish to keep down this propensity within due bounds, and to remind men that they have other things to do in this world than to laugh and be merry. Dr. VAUGHAN says:—

"We are not certain that some of our wise men do wisely, who are going abroad just now, with their cap and bells, in the hope of securing better attention to their lessons from the foolish. A fondness for grotesque jokes and everlasting caricature, bears as little resemblance to manly feeling, as the ecstacies of a young lady over the last new novel. Truth is a grave matter, and can owe little ultimately to the services of a buffoon. It loses half its dignity, if often presented in association with the ridiculous. Those who find their chief pleasure in broad farce, are rarely capable of a due exercise of earnest and reverential feeling. Your great wits do not spare their best friends, and your votaries of fun are generally persons prepared to sacrifice anything to their god. The mind which is wont to pay much homage to the laughers, too often forgets to pay a real homage to anything higher. In such a service the fine edge of moral feeling is almost of necessity worn away. Not that we would send a man to the bow-string, because he has indulged a laugh. On the contrary, the man who cannot so indulge is not a man to our liking. There is something wrong in him, physically, mentally, and morally. All truly healthful men, in the spiritual, as well as in the natural sense, know how to enjoy their laugh. But your great laughers are generally slow workers. To make a merriment of folly is not to displace it by wisdom. Our proper business here is neither to grin nor to whine, but to be men. We say not that good may never be done by means of ridicule, but we are convinced that its general effect is such as we have ventured to indicate. It is an instrument, moreover, which has two edges,—use it, and you have no right to complain of its being used."*

These are wise and true sayings, as seasonable as they are important, and called for by the excessive taste for this

* British Quarterly Review, No. VI. p. 254.

species of composition which now prevails. If anything need be added in corroboration of these *arguments,* it is the *fact* stated by the justly lamented Dr. Arnold, that since the publication of periodical works of humor, he had perceived a visible declension of manly sentiment and serious thoughtfulness among the elder boys of his school. This is strong and decisive testimony as to the influence of a continued indulgence in broad farce. Is there not precisely the same effect produced on the minds of our young men, especially when to this is added the moral tendency of the sentiments which are sometimes clothed in the garb of humor? Nothing can be more opposed to, or destructive of, the serious spirit which true religion requires, than this constant and regular supply of materials for laughter. Nor does the mischief stop with the young and the undecided in religion, for it is infecting the professors of religion. It is hard to conceive how earnestness and spirituality can be maintained by those whose tables are covered, and whose leisure time is consumed, by these bewitching inspirations of the god of laughter. There is little hope of our arresting the evil, except we make it our great business to raise up a ministry who themselves shall not be carried away with the torrent; who shall be grave, without being gloomy; serious, without being melancholy; and who, on the other hand, shall be cheerful without being frivolous, and who by their chastened mirthfulness shall be among the laughers, if not as total abstainers, yet as a moderate man among drunkards, and whose temperance shall check, or at any rate reprove the excesses of their companions. And then what a demand does this state of things prefer for the most intense earnestness in our Sabbath-day exercises, both as to prayers and to sermons. In this modern taste we have a new obstacle to our usefulness, of a most formidable kind, and which can be subdued only by God's blessing upon our fidelity and zeal. Such men are wanted, as shall by their learning, science, and general knowledge, give weight to their opinions and influence to their advice, in their private intercourse with their flocks, and as shall, by their powerful and evangelical preaching, control this taste, and supplant it by a better.

Nor must we omit to notice, and to notice with peculiar emphasis, the impetus that is now given to the human understanding through all its gradations, from the highest order of intellect down to the humblest classes of the laboring population. We have already alluded to this subject, but on account of its importance must here refer to it again, and a little more at length. As regards the laboring classes, education is advancing among them with rapid strides, as far at least as the counteracting tendency of the manufacturing system will allow. The poor must and will be instructed. The change of opinion on this subject that has come over a large portion of the community within the last quarter of a century, is indeed marvellous; and instead of loud descants upon the dangers of an educated people, we now hear little else but as loud descants on the evils of ignorance. This is a happy conversion, and its results will be auspicious; not, however, without some temporary admixture of evil. It is really refreshing to read the programmes of educationary schemes which are drawn up for the culture of the working classes, by those who are promoting their mental improvement. But improvement in education is not confined, and cannot be confined, to the lower classes, but must be carried forward in equal proportion among those that are above them. The universal mind is awakened, and in motion onwards:

it is in a state of intense excitement and irrepressible activity. Discoveries in science and inventions in art come so fast upon us, that we have scarcely recovered from the surprise produced by one, before another calls upon us to indulge in new wonder. Feats of science and art, especially in the department of engineering, are performed or projected which look as if man in the pride of his intellect felt that nothing was impossible to him. As might be expected, all the knowledge thus obtained and accumulated is flowing by the thousand rills of the press and cheap books, through every department of society. The annual expenditure of millions of pounds in cheap literature will show to what extent information on all subjects is reaching the working and other classes. Knowledge is the great idol around which the multitudes are gathering to pay their homage and record their vows. Is there anything in such a state of things at which the friends of religion should take alarm? Quite the contrary. Christianity began her career, as every tyro in history well knows, in the most enlightened age, and amongst the most polished nations of antiquity; and from that moment to the present, has never shrunk from the broadest daylight of learning and science, to skulk in the darkness and gloom of barbaric ignorance; and its ministers should ever be foremost as the patrons of knowledge: but then it is evident that such a state of things requires an indomitable earnestness in the sacred duties of their calling to secure for religion its due pre-eminence amidst all the various claimants upon the public attention. Giving to general knowledge all the importance that is claimed for it, this, apart from religion, is not the sovereign remedy, the grand catholicon, which is to heal the disorders and restore the moral health of diseased humanity. There are some, and, indeed, not a few in our own country, as well as upon the continent of Europe, who dream, and all history proves it to be but a dream, of regenerating the world by the principles of reason and the aid of secular education. They think they can regulate society without religion, and renew the heart of man without God. We might ask them what philosophy did for such purposes in Egypt, its cradle, or in Greece, its temple? They forget that by the permission of Providence a grand experiment was made in the latter country, during the five centuries that preceded the Christian era, by the sages of the schools, to see what knowledge, apart from Divine revelation, could do to reform the moral world, and make it virtuous and happy. We venture to call for the result, and if the advocates of reason refuse to give it, an apostle shall supply the answer,—"*The world by wisdom knew not God.*" It would seem as if, not satisfied with a single demonstration, these men were hazarding a second trial. Again with still greater advantages, and still greater confidence, they are flocking to the ordeal. Education is to be improved and extended; the press is pouring forth its cheap literature; science is broken down to such fragments and measured out in such drops, as even infant minds can receive and digest; and every appliance is to be furnished to give effect to the knowledge thus communicated; lecturers on all subjects are travelling through the country, and are pouring forth streams of information in every direction; while rational and invigorating amusements are to come in to aid the general improvement. By the advocates of the sufficiency of knowledge alone to improve the taste and raise the morals of the nation, the largest expectations are indulged of the regeneration of society, as the result of all these laborious efforts; but which, without a prophet's eye, we may predict, are doomed to certain and bitter disappointment; and may confidently anticipate that the result of the second experiment will be the same as the first, and prove not only that the world by wisdom will never know God, but that nothing less than the foolishness of preaching will achieve its moral reformation.

The state of our popular literature, as moulded to a considerable extent by these men, proves that such an experiment as that of teaching mankind to do without religion is going on. In much of what is read by the masses, there is an unconcealed hostility to Christianity. Infidelity of the boldest and most daring kind is associating itself with a great many of the cheap publications of the day, with an energy and a success that would astound as well as alarm those who are not in the secret. But still there are many of the guides of the popular mind, perhaps most of them, who would not patronize this open assault upon the foundations of our faith—they go a more insidious, though scarcely less injurious way to work; they are acting upon the principle that the best way to attack religion, and the least likely to shock prejudice and excite alarm, is to say nothing about it, to treat the whole subject as a negative, a nonentity, a thing to be forgotten; with which it is no part of their business to concern themselves, and which may be left to float quietly down the stream to the gulf of oblivion. All that is thought necessary to provide for the *million* in the way of reading, is amusement and general knowledge: and, to a very great extent, the object of all this is accomplished. The laboring classes, with increasing knowledge, are more and more alienated from religion. The masses are not yet won to Christianity, but are sullenly standing aloof from it.

In such a state of things, what kind of ministry is it

that is wanted? The answer is easy—men of earnestness; of earnest intellects, earnest hearts, and earnest preaching; men whose understanding shall command respect, whose manner shall conciliate affection, and whose ministrations shall attract by their beauty, and command by their power. The accessibility of the laboring classes gives us an advantage in approaching them. Neither prejudice nor fashion bars us out from them. We have neither to scale the walls of bigotry, nor to silence or evade the dogs of angry intolerance: the door is open, and we may walk in. But we must be men of the age, men who understand it, who are, to say the least, up with it, and know how to avail ourselves of its advantages, and to surmount its difficulties. But I cannot do better here than refer to an admirable article in the Eclectic Review, on the Modern Pulpit, from which the following extract is given:—

"What is good preaching? Alas, how many answers would be given to this question! And yet is not the true answer—the preaching by which souls are saved? Then, the best preaching must be that by which the greatest number of souls are saved. In order to that end, however, men must be brought within the sphere of the pulpit; and to bring the greatest number of men within that sphere is the design of Dr. VAUGHAN in his treatise, (on the Modern Pulpit,) and it is ours. In one word, what we specifically want in the modern pulpit is—ADAPTATION. Now we have read a good deal in our time, not more than enough, of the necessity of adapting the efforts of the pulpit to the constitution of the human mind, to man's moral nature, to his actual condition as fallen, guilty, wretched, and exposed to future punishment. And not seldom have we read most seasonable injunctions, addressed to our young ministers, on the personal adaptation of their discourses to the condition of individual men. All this we regard as of equal importance at all times, and in all conceivable circumstances. But, at present, our aim is to excite as much attention as we can to the truth that along with these general and fixed adaptations, there is required a constantly varying adaptation to the constantly progressive changes of society."

The writer then goes on to explain what he means by this varying adaptation of the pulpit to the advancement in society, in reference to one portion of it—the working classes :—

"Education is raising these great masses of the community into higher degrees of intellectual culture. New powers are at work. Incredible facilities are multiplied for diffusing knowledge, spreading opinions, and increasing the number of thinkers. Now in such an age, to say nothing of other views of society, it is obviously the duty of evangelical preachers to adapt themselves to the circumstances in which they are placed; not, as this talented writer would be among the last to suggest, by withdrawing from the pulpit the great themes of the mediatory system, and substituting for them philosophic truth, or a rationalized gospel, but by such a general line of conduct with reference to the circumstances of a growingly enlightened age, and such a strain of preaching as shall lay hold of the public mind, and bring it under that doctrine which, and which only, is the power of God unto salvation. Let there be a just estimate formed, and which to be just cannot be a low one, of the mental powers of the common people; a judicious and hearty sympathy with their real wants and reasonable wishes; a studious consideration of the means by which the multitude shall be brought back to the sanctuaries of religion, which they have to a considerable extent deserted; an assiduous endeavor to connect the functions of the pastor with the literary cultivation of the people. For these purposes let there be correct information of their state of intellect, their prevailing habits, their peculiar temptations, their literary tendencies and aspirations as to the books they read—let there be all this, but then let it be only as so much power put forth to bring these masses under the influence of the gospel. Oh, it were a noble triumph of the modern pulpit to see men of strong principle, and self-controlling wisdom, gathering round them the most boisterous elements of our social atmosphere, *conducting* the lightnings with which its darkest thunder-clouds are charged, and showing to the nation they have saved, that the preaching of the cross is still the 'power of God.'"

Of course, such an enterprise of home-evangelization will require that our ministers shall be men of *action*.* Adaptation, then, there may be, and should be, in the sermons and the general habits of the ministry, to the age in which they live, in the way of laying hold of public attention, widening the sphere of their action, and adding to their influence as preachers of the cross Stronger intelligence, profounder thinking, more logical argumentation, more varied illustration, more chastened composition, more refined sentiment, more genuine, yet Christian, and unobtrusive philosophy, may be required in one age than another, and in this than in some preceding ages; but then all this must be in harmony with the simplicity that is in Christ, and only so much added to the height or the ornaments of

* Connected with my own congregation is an Institution, partly religious and partly literary, for the benefit of the young men and elder boys of all classes, but chiefly of the working classes, which has existed for more than a quarter of a century, which has a library of nearly 1200 volumes, and to the members of which lectures on miscellaneous subjects are periodically delivered. As a proof of the advantages it has conferred, as well as of the taste of the age, two of *our* members, both of them formerly in *our* Sunday school, took an excursion last summer, through France, up the Mediterranean to Athens, from thence through Southern Greece, back to Sicily, Naples, Pompeii, Rome, and Italy; and on their return delivered in three lectures an account of their travels, that would bear no distant comparison with some other accounts that have been given to the public from the press. They were able to appreciate, and did appreciate with enthusiasm, the remains of antiquity in Greece and Rome, as well as the exhibitions of modern times.

the pedestal which is to exalt the Saviour, and attract a perishing world to the fountain of life.

Having referred to the state of public opinion and feeling with reference to religion among the lower classes, it may not be amiss to glance at the higher and more educated portions of the community. Many of these are moving on two lines, or in a stream that divides into two channels, and flows in two opposite directions—the devout going off to Puseyism, and a large part of the rest to a philosophical infidelity. A loose, unsystematized theism is adopted by many of our men of letters, in some cases a new edition of the opinion of our English deists of the last century, and in others, and a still more numerous class, bearing a strong affinity to the pantheistic or mystic spirit of the German philosophy. Of the disposition of modern science, in the persons of some of its more illustrious votaries, to retire from revealed religion as if ashamed to be seen in its company, we have an affecting instance in the great octogenarian naturalist of Prussia. It is indeed a melancholy spectacle, to witness such a man as HUMBOLDT—whose eye has seen so much of the visible universe, and whose pen has recorded so ably the researches of his vast genius; whose intellect seemed formed by the Creator, not only to study his works, but to proclaim his glories—send forth such a work as "Kosmos," and in that work declare it was no part of his business to trace the wonders he describes to their still more wondrous Author! How deeply painful to see this high priest of nature officiating with such zeal and devotion at the shrine of matter, and yet never throwing one grain of incense on the altar of the Infinite Mind which made the worlds. Yet this is only a specimen of other similar cases. Alas, alas! that such a mind should be so warped by the modes of thinking prevalent among his countrymen, and should have sent forth perhaps his last gift to the lovers of science, in which the Hegelian pantheism is too obviously interwoven.

With such a view of the state and tendency of the educated mind in this age, we see an additional argument for an earnest, and at the same time intelligent and educated ministry. We shall want men, and we are not without them already, who can enter the lists and do battle with the seductive and dangerous forms of error, that have done such mischief on the continent of Europe, and are likely, without great vigilance and stout resistance, to repeat the mischief here also. The spirit of mental philosophy which was called up by LOCKE, and has since been sustained in different schools by REID and KANT, and those who have descended from them, is at the present moment widely diffusing itself through the English and American mind. Education will no longer be confined to literature and natural science. A disposition and determination are formed to explore the world of mind, as well as that of matter, and to give to subjective studies a place, and that a very high one, among the objective ones. Psychology is now, and will be still more so, the favorite pursuit of great multitudes of reflective intellects. The mind of Germany is operating with power and success upon the mind of England, to an extent which is surprising, and, in some views of the case, alarming. It is, one should think, impossible to trace the progress of Transcendentalism from the time of KANT to that of HEGEL, and to see how, as it diverged more and more widely from the metaphysics of our land, it has associated itself with Rationalism in theology, and led on to Pantheism in philosophy, without some apprehension for the result of its introduction to this country. Perhaps the practical character of the English understanding will be one of our safeguards against a system which to the great multitude must ever remain a mere scientific speculation. It may, however, be feared that some of our young ministers, and our students in theology, especially those of speculative habits, captivated by the daring boldness, the intellectual vigor, and the theoretic attractions of the great German philosophers, may too adventurously launch forth on this dangerous ocean, and make shipwreck of their doctrinal simplicity and practical usefulness. Let them be assured that neither the transcendentalism of KANT, nor the eclecticism of COUSIN, are safe guides for men who would be useful in saving souls. The warning voice has already been lifted up in high places on the other side of the Atlantic, where German philosophy was likely at one time to be received with avidity, and there will not be wanting voices to utter words of warning in this country also. It would not only be useless, but unwise to set out this, or any other system of philosophy, as the tree of knowledge of good and evil, which we are forbidden by the command of God, and the flaming sword of the cherubim, to approach: this, as well as every other object of human inquiry, may be studied, and by a cautious and discriminating mind, may of course be studied with advantage. We would by no means contend that there is nothing in the industry of German investigation, in its method of analysis, in its subjective taste, or even in the systems which are the fruits of its researches, which may not be borrowed with advantage by ourselves: but against that willing and entire surrender of their intellects to a school, the masters of which have advanced from one degree of error to another, till they have left us no gospel but a fable, and no God but nature, which some are beginning to manifest in this land, we must raise an emphatic and protesting voice.

A work has lately made its appearance, likely to be extensively circulated among those who have any taste for philosophical studies, or any wish to become acquainted with German literature; a work which cannot fail to command attention, and will certainly secure for its accomplished author the admiration and respect of his numerous readers—I mean the "History of Modern Philosophy," by the Rev. J. D. MORELL. It is impossible to deny to this gentleman the fidelity of the historian, the impartiality and the candor of the true philosopher, and at the same time the excellence of a very able writer. It is on some accounts a happy circumstance that such a subject has fallen into such hands, since Mr. MORELL's attachment to evangelical truth, united with his intimate acquaintance with continental literature, will qualify him, we trust, to be a safe pilot for the English mind through the perilous seas he has undertaken to navigate. It may be hoped that his own attachment to the subjective system of philosophy will not lead his ardent readers and admirers to go further in that direction than his own discriminating and well-balanced mind would wish or approve; and we are quite sure that he would join with many who are perhaps more apprehensive than he is of the influence of German philosophy, in the opinion that no surer way could our young ministers take to hinder their usefulness than to allow such studies to obscure the simplicity of their matter, or to deaden the energy of their manner, as preachers of the gospel, and that he would also most emphatically say, "Beware, lest any man spoil you (as preachers) through philosophy and vain deceit."

From a very able and complimentary critique on Mr. MORELL's work, contained in the twelfth number of the "North British Review," obviously by Dr. CHALMERS, the following appropriate passage may with advantage be introduced here: speaking of CARLYLE, the reviewer says:—

"They are not creeds, but men, who are the objects of his idolatry, which, under the name of hero-worship, he renders alike to those of most opposite opinions—as to LUTHER, and KNOX, and CROMWELL, on the one hand, so with equal veneration to the lofty poets and transcendentalists of Germany, upon the other. He is a lover of earnestness, more than a lover of truth: and it would not be our counteractive at least, to urge that he should be a lover of truth, more than a lover of earnestness. We should rather say that both are best, and would our island only not be frightened from its propriety by the high-sounding philosophy of the continent—neither overborne by its pretensions, nor overawed by its cabalistic nomenclature—would our savans and theologians but keep unmoved on the ground of common sense, and by their paramount demand for evidence at every step, lay resolute arrest on the pruriencies of wanton speculation—then, while they rejected all that was unsubstantial and unsound in the dogmata of the transcendental school, it were well that they imported the earnest and lofty enthusiasm of its disciples into the phlegmatic universities, and no less phlegmatic churches, of our land. We do not need to take down the framework of our existing orthodoxy, whether in theology or in science. All that we require is that it shall become an animated framework, by the breath of a new life being infused into it. Ours has been most truly denounced as an age of formalism; but to mend this, we do not need to exchange our formulas, only to quicken them; nor to quit the ground of our common sense for baseless speculations; nor to substitute the Divine Idea of FICHTE for a personal and living God; nor to adopt for our Saviour a mere embodied and allegorized perfection, and give up the actual and historical Jesus Christ of the New Testament; nor, finally, to go in quest of a chimerical ontology in upper regions far out of mortal ken, and for visions of merest fancy there, to renounce either the certainties of our own palpable and peopled world, or the truths which He who dwelleth in the heavens brought down from heaven, because no man can ascend into heaven, or tell the mysteries and glories of a place which he never entered. What we want is, that the very system of doctrine which we now have, shall come to us not in word only, but in power. As things stand at present, our creeds and confessions have become effete, and the Bible a dead letter; and that orthodoxy which was at one time the glory, by withering into the inert and lifeless, is now the shame and the reproach of all our churches. If there have been the revival of a more spiritual philosophy in France, or elsewhere, it might well humble us; but this is not exactly the quarter from which we should expect our revival to come. Prayer could bring it down from above; and it is only thus, that all which is good in Puritanism—its earnestness without its extravagance; its faith, without its contempt for philosophy; its high and heavenly-mindedness, without the baser admixture of its worldly politics and passions—it is only thus the Augustan age of Christianity in England, an age which Mr. CARLYLE has done so much to vindicate and bring to light, will again come back, to reform our State and bless our families."

From this article it is perfectly evident that if England should have a tendency to go wrong, Scotland will do something to put us right, and that the followers, but improved ones, of REID, will do much to keep the descendants of KANT in check, and hold the balance even between the Scotch and German philosophies. Surely nothing more need be said to show and prove what kind of men we want for such an age, and to indicate that for times of such excitement we must have men of strong intelligence, simple faith, and entire devotedness. It is, in every view we can take of it, an earnest age, and earnest men alone can at such a time do anything anywhere, and least of all in the pulpit. Events, with trumpet-call, summon us to our post, with every faculty awake, and every energy engaged. Amidst the din of business, of politics, of science, and of fashion; amidst the jests of laughers, the eloquence of orators, and the clamor of parties, the voice of the preacher will not be heard, unless he speak loudly, nor listened to unless he speak earnestly: we shall gain no heed for our holy religion, unless we put forth all our strength; it will be pushed aside, overborne, trampled down in the jostling crowd, if we do not put forth our mightiest energies to bear it up, and to make way for it through the strife and the theory of abounding secularities.

Let us not deceive ourselves by substituting anything else for this. It may be all very well and proper in its place to keep pace with the times in which we live, as regards other matters; in classical, mathematical, and philosophical literature, in academic degrees, in tasteful architecture; but these things, in the absence of a living power of intense devotedness, will be but as the flowers which shed their fragrance upon our grave, or as the sculpture which decorates our tomb.

IV. *We may next contemplate the earnestness displayed by some other bodies, with which, it may be truly said, we have to contend.*

And first of all, let us look at the activity of the Church of Rome. What a change has of late years come over that wonderful and dreadful system, so far as its external circumstances are concerned. Many are disposed to think lightly of its present condition, efforts, prospects, and hopes; and it will be acknowledged it is unwise and impolitic for Protestants to lend their aid in magnifying the power, and swelling the pride and expectations of the Man of Sin. But then it is no less unwise and impolitic, on the other hand, to miscalculate his forces, to shut our eyes on his efforts, and to deny his victories. What we need is just so much of alarm as shall rouse us to action, without producing panic; enough of fear to lead us to buckle on our armor, and yet not so much as to paralyze our energy. Look at the present condition and prospects of Popery, as compared with what they were soon after the French Revolution. Weakened by the withering scorn of an infidel philosophy, to which its own corruption had given rise, it was ill-prepared to sustain the shock of that awful outbreak of human passion, and it fell an apparently lifeless corpse before it. The Gallican Church was subverted, its priests were banished, its property confiscated, its places of worship closed. A French army was in possession of Rome, and the Pope was a prisoner in France, while his adherents were trembling and dispersed in all parts of the world. The opponents of Romanism exulted in the confidence that its days were numbered and its end was come. They exulted too soon. That lifeless corpse which lay prostrate in Europe, has since then shown signs of returning animation—its wounds have been healed—it has risen from the earth—and, recovering its full health, is going forth at this time with giant strength to contend with Protestantism for the mastery of the world. Popery has gained political power in England. It is renewing its old fight in France for the education of the people—its chapels, its priests, its bishops, its monks, its missions, are everywhere multiplying—its ancient craft and cruelty are again called into activity, as Tahiti can witness—it is drawing hundreds, I fear, if we include both clergy and laity, of influential persons from the Church of England, and tainting with its spirit hundreds more who remain behind to diffuse the corruption still more widely—it has done much to blot from the memory of statesmen its past history, and to hide from their eyes its hideous form—and with an ardor kindling to an intense flame, and a hope flushed into a stronger confidence by these victories, it is still going on from conquering to conquer. There are, it is true, for Rome fearful and appalling portents to be set off against these bright signs: there is the confiscation of ecclesiastical property and the dissolution of the monasteries in Spain—the rapid defection going on in Germany, under RONGE and CZERSKI —the conversion of whole congregations and parishes in the south of France to Protestantism—the rising spirit of free inquiry even in Italy—with the growth of knowledge and the advance of education everywhere. From all this it is evident that the great battle of the Reformation is to be fought over again, and we are in the field of action, where the forces are mustered and the conflict is going on; and we are unworthy of our position and our occupation if we do not give our energies, the best and the noblest, to the cause. Let us take pattern from our foes, and imitate their intensity of action. They are in earnest if we are not. Were it possible for us to see a perfect disclosure, in one bird's-eye view, of all that is going on in the Vatican, that most astounding instance of centralization out of the bottomless pit; could we see the gigantic intellects that are planning, and the burning hearts that are feeding the fire of their zeal, and the busy hands that are working in that focus of all that is daring in design and mischievous in effect to the world's intellectual and spiritual welfare, we should feel that we are safe from the tyranny of that audacious system, only under the vigilance of an Omniscient eye, and the protection of an Omnipotent arm. But that help and that vigilance are not to be looked for by the supine and lukewarm, and can be expected only in the way of zealous activity and confiding prayer. To whom chiefly should Protestantism look for the instrumentality necessary for its defence, but to its ministers? Let them, in answer to the call which events are making upon their energies, prepare themselves by study, by deep devotion, and by intense action, to grapple with this ancient foe of spiritual Christianity.

But this is not the only instance of earnestness offered to us, which we should contemplate, and from which we should deduce a stimulus to our own activity. We have far more to fear from England than from Italy; from Oxford than from Rome. I do not now allude merely to the Tractarian party; we have little to fear from them, compared with the other section of the Established Church—the evangelical clergy. The Church of England is in earnest. Many of us can recollect the time when it was not so. A pervading secularity characterized her clergy; a drowsy indifference her people: if the former got their tithes, and ate, drank, and were merry, and the latter got christening, confirmation, and the sacrament when they died, it was all they cared for. The only thing that moved either of them to a pang of zeal was the coming of the Methodists into the parish, and when these were mobbed away, they relapsed again into their former apathy. Exceptions there were—bright and blessed ones—but they were only exceptions. Thank God, it is not so now. A vivifying wind has swept over the valley of dry bones, and an army not only of living, but of life-giving men has sprung up. VENN, BERRIDGE, and ROMAINE; NEWTON, CECIL and SIMEON have lived and awakened a new spirit in the church to which they belonged. Look at that church as she is now to be seen, full of energy and earnestness: divided, it is true, into parties as to theological opinion, to a considerable extent Romanized in her spirit, and aggressive in her designs; but instinct with life, and a great deal of it life of the best kind. Even the orthodox and the Puseyite clergy are all now active, preaching, catechising, visiting the sick, instituting and superintending schools. The day is happily gone by when the taunt of fox-hunting, play-going, ball-frequenting parsons could be with justice thrown at the clergy of the State church: they are now no longer to be found in those scenes of folly and vanity, but at the bed-side of the sick man, or in the cottage of the poor one. We must rejoice in their labors and in their success, except when their object and their aim are to crush Dissenters. There are very many among them of the *true* apostolic succession in doctrine, spirit, and devotedness; many whose piety and zeal we should do well to emulate; many with whom it is among the felicities of my life to be united in the bonds of private friendship, and public co-operation. Sincerely and cordially attached to their church, they are laboring, in season and out of season, to promote its interests. Who can blame them? Instead of this, let us imitate them. For zeal and devotedness they are worthy of it. I know their labors, and am astonished at them. Think of a clergyman, and multitudes of such there are, who, beside his other labors, spends four or five hours every day in going from house to house, visiting the sick, instructing the ignorant, comforting the distressed. Can we wonder that such men should lay hold on the public mind? Is it not in the natural course of things that it should be so? It is admitted that the clergyman of a parish has advantages for this species of ministerial occupation which we have not; he considers all the people within certain topographical limits as belonging to him, as being, in fact, his cure; while, on the other hand, most if not all of these persons, except such as by profession really belong to other denominations, look upon him in the light of their minister. This ever-active assiduity, in addition to the Sabbath-day exercises, is admonitory to us. Can we see this new sight, the whole Church establishment, from the Archbishop of Canterbury down to the curate of the smallest village, with all their modern and comprehensive agency of Pastoral Aid Societies, Ladies' District Visiting Societies, Scripture Readers, Church of England Tract Societies, and other means of influence and power, in busy commotion, dotting the land all over with churches and schools, and thus, by all these efforts, laboring to occupy so entirely the nation as to leave no room for, and to prove there is no need of, any other body of Christians—can we see all this constantly before our eyes, and not see the need of an earnest ministry, not only to maintain our ground, but to advance? Not that I mean to assert that the evangelical clergy would altogether wish to push us off the ground. No, I believe there are many who unfeignedly rejoice in the existence, operations, and success, both of the Methodists and Dissenters, and who would consider it a deep calamity for the nation, if they were arrested in their career of evangelical ministration to-morrow. The spirit of the Evangelical Alliance is diffusing itself abroad. Sectarianism is, we hope, beginning to wither at the root, and Christian charity is grappling with the demon of bigotry. But still we are at present not prepared for the fusion and amalgamation of all parties into one, and till then we may learn from each other; and with the most entire good will towards my brethren in the Church of England, without envy or jealousy, I call upon my other brethren within my own denomination to imitate the zeal of which they are the witnesses among the clergy of the Establishment. I am a Dissenter from conviction as well as by education, and know not the lure which would induce me, or the suffering which would terrify me, to abandon my principles. I believe, as I ever have believed, since I reflected upon the subject, that the establishment of religion by the enactments of secular legislation has no sanction from the New Testament, is a corruption of Christianity, and injurious to its spirit; and I believe the time will come when the same views will be entertained by all the genuine followers of Christ: hence I am, and ought to be, anxious, while I cultivate a spirit of brotherly love towards those who differ from me, to uphold, though without wrath, malice, or any uncharitableness, the denomination by which my conscientious opinions are embodied and expressed. Dissenters of England, and especially Dissenting ministers, I say therefore unto you, be in earnest; first of all and chief of all in attachment to the doctrines of Evangelism, to the creed of Protestantism, to the great principles which God has employed in every age and country where true religion has had existence, to vitalize a dead, and purify a corrupt world. Be it your prayer, your endeavor, your hallowed ambition, to possess a ministry of competent learning, and especially of soundly evangelical sentiment; a ministry which, as regards their matter and manner, shall be the power of God to the salvation of souls; a ministry which, in the simplicity of their discourses, and the intensity of their zeal, the fervor of their piety, and the all-comprehending extent of their labors, shall vie with the best specimens of the clergy of the church of England There is earnestness there, and if we would not be swallowed up in the rising tide and increasing torrent of their zeal, let us meet it with a corresponding intensity. Let each minister, in his own separate and individual sphere of action, set himself to work and put forth all his energies without waiting for combination with others. Not that I speak against combination. We have far too little of it, and this is our weakness. In polity we are too independent, and should be vastly improved as regards our internal condition and our external influence, if we were more compact. But as to ministerial earnestness we need not wait for others: each man can do what he wills, and may do much, though no other man do any thing. Ministerial activity, like Christian piety, is a matter of individual obligation, and no one is so dependent upon his neighbors as that he needs to halt till they are ready to march with him.

Nor is it necessary, nor proper, advocate though I be for the Evangelical Alliance, that we should be silent as to our views of the spirituality of Christ's kingdom. As we are not to sacrifice love for truth, so neither are we to sacrifice truth for love nor to throw away a smaller diamond of truth for a larger one. All truth must be held, as well as all love. I differ from some of our brethren in my views of certain confederations for the maintenance and spread of our Nonconformity, because I believe that whatever good they may do in one way, they do more harm in another; but I do not differ from them in my conviction that our principles, as a part of the New Testament, ought to be taught, and to be taught with earnestness too. If true, they must be important, and if important at all, very important: subordinate I know, immeasurably so, to the doctrines whereby men are saved; but still of consequence. Provided the gross misrepresentation, the exaggerated statement, the studied caricature, the uncharitable imputation, the withering sarcasm, the bitter irony, and the malevolent ridicule be expunged from controversy, and there be as much of the delicacy of love, as there is of the firmness of truth, there can be no harm, but must be much good, not only in stating our own opinions, but in answering those who differ from us. All systems of church polity derive their value and importance from their subserviency to the cause of Evangelism. Church of Englandism or Dissent, apart from this, is but as the pole without the healing serpent which it was erected to exhibit; and to be zealous about either except as viewed in reference to the truth as it is in Jesus, is but like contending about the wood of the cross, to the neglect of the Saviour who was crucified upon it.

How, then, are we to meet that abounding zeal which we ourselves perhaps have been in no small degree the occasion of awakening, but by a corresponding vigor of action? We cannot advance, nay, we cannot keep our ground without it. We have to contend against an energy which is astounding and all but overwhelming; and if this cannot move us to earnestness, nothing will.

V. *This state of mind and action is within the reach of every minister of Christ.*

Some men, from a natural physical energy of character, may be more prone to, and better qualified for, this fervid and devoted zeal than some others. They are of a more mercurial temperament than their phlegmatic brethren who creep while the others fly and who require more stimulus to rouse them into activity than is necessary to keep the rest at the full speed of their progress. This is constitutional to a very considerable extent; but it is, after all, more of a moral than a natural inability in many; and the sinners whom they address and call to repentance, and to whom they declare that the only hindrance they have to true religion is an impotence of will, are just as excusable for their want of penitence and faith as any minister under heaven is for a want of earnestness. He may never be able to be a scholar, or a philosopher, or a mathematician, though he may acquire more of all these attainments than he supposes is within his reach, if he will but give himself to early-rising, make a good apportionment of his time, and adopt a well-arranged plan of study. His situation and engagements may be such, however, that he may not hope to rise to eminence in these things; but nothing forbids his activity, zeal, and entire devotedness to the great work of preaching the gospel and caring for men's souls. He may not be a consummate orator, for he has not voice for this; but he may, if he please, use what voice he has with good effect: he may not have the ability for finished composition; but he can, if he give himself time and labor, produce sermons full of spiritual power: he may not be able to attract around him the rich, the literary, or the great; but he can interest the poor, and engage the children of the Sunday School, and perhaps their parents: he may not have ten talents, but he need not wrap up his one in a napkin and bury it in the earth. Every man *has* one talent at least, with which he can busily trade and acquire profit for his employer, and reward for himself. If the pride of some men over-estimate the number of their talents, the modesty, or in some cases the indolence of others, leads them to make too low a calculation of theirs. There is a source of latent energy in most men, which they have been so far from exhausting that they have scarcely touched it; they have in many cases to break up a virgin soil. I knew a minister of Christ, and loved him well, who was in a situation where he had done little, and feared he never should do more. Everything was dull around him, and he was dull with it. It pleased

God to remove him to a new situation, and then he became a new man. He revived from his torpor, and everything revived around him. An activity and energy were now evinced which surprised himself and those who knew him. He formed a new congregation, instituted a variety of religious organizations of a useful kind, and was one of the most earnest men I knew. All this energy was not a new creation, but a resurrection. So it might be with many more. There are the principles of activity within them which are only waiting for the influence of circumstances, or the power of will, to give them life, motion, and vigor. Away then with the excuses of indolence, the fears of timidity, the objections of modesty, and the opiates of conscience; for it is these, and not impossibilities, which prevent any man from being zealously affected in a good thing. Every minister can be an earnest man if he so wills; and he is so when anything in which he has a deep interest is at stake. Let his house be on fire, or his health and life be in danger, or his wife or child be in peril, or some means of greatly augmenting his property be thrown in his way, and what an intensity of emotion and a vehemence of action will be exerted and put in motion! and there needs but the might and pressure of the interests of immortal souls upon his conscience; there needs but a heart constrained by the love of Christ so as to be borne away by the force and impetuosity of this hallowed passion; there needs but a longing desire to be wise in winning men to Jesus; there needs, in fine, but a heart fully set in him to accomplish the ends and objects of his office, to possess that high and noble quality of soul which it is the object of this work to recommend. There are the same constitutional varieties in tradesmen as are visible in ministers, and yet we never hearken to the former when, in justification of their failure for want of energy, they tell us they have no physical capacity for, or tendency to, activity. Our reply to them is that what is deficient in them by nature, must be made up by reason and diligence. We say the same to the preacher of the gospel, and while by this representation we would constrain his conscience by a sense of obligation, we would interest his heart by awakening hope. He may never be able, with his measure of talent, to reach the success of some more gifted and more favored brethren; but he may have a measure of his own, far more than enough to recompense any labor he may bestow to obtain some success; and instead therefore of spending his time in envying others, or sitting down in despair to do nothing, because he cannot do as much as they, let him rise up, and have the blessed consciousness and reward that he has done what he could.

You who may read these pages can possess and exhibit real earnestness; all its delightful excitement, all its blessed results, all its eternal consequences, are within *your* reach. There is no lion in the street, except what your own imagination sees there, and your own sloth has placed there. Make the effort, it is worth the making: try, you can but fail, and it is better to fail than not to make the attempt. Think what a result may issue from a new devotedness. We have never yet any of us rightly estimated the immense importance and momentous consequences of our work. How can we? They are eternal, and who can duly estimate eternity? Do we believe what we preach, that the conversion of a soul is of more consequence than the creation of a world? Is this sober truth, or mere rhetoric? Is this fact, or the mere garniture of a sermon; only a dash of eloquence, an artifice of our oratory? If true, and we know it is so, how momentous! A soul!

weigh it in the balance of the sanctuary, and settle its worth: appraise its value. Salvation! wondrous word, and more wondrous thing. One word only, but containing millions of ideas; uttered in a moment, but requiring everlasting ages, and all the amplitude of heaven, for the unfolding of its meaning. Archbishop WILLIAMS, who was also Lord Keeper in the time of Charles the First, once uttered this memorable speech: "I have passed through many places of honor and trust both in Church and State, more than any one of my order for seventy years before. But were I assured that by my preaching I had converted one soul to God, I should therein take more comfort than in all the honors and offices that have ever been bestowed upon me." What a confession from an archbishop, that he did not know he had been the instrument of converting a single soul to God; what an impressive importance does the confession stamp upon the work of saving souls; and what a stimulus should it supply to us who are engaged in this divine employment!

How vain and worthless a thing is the popular applause, which some receive for eloquence, compared with the proofs of usefulness in the conversion of immortal souls! What are the flatteries of the foolish, or even the eulogiums of the wise; what the honeyed compliments, or the golden opinions of the most distinguished circle of admirers, weighed against the testimony of one redeemed sinner that we have been the instrument of saving him from death, but as the small dust in the balance! How have some men, pre-eminent for their intellectual power and accustomed to fascinate the spell-bound multitude by the power of their eloquence, yearned, amidst all their popularity, for some more substantial, satisfying, and abiding reward of their labor, than that admiration of their talents which they were accustomed to receive. It may be they were not unsusceptible to the emotions of vanity, nor ungratified by the expressions of applause, at the time; but when they found that *this* was all the result of their labors, they sickened of the incense and the honey, and exclaimed in the bitterness of disappointment, and the anguish of self-reproach, "Is this all my reward? Oh, where are the souls I have converted from the error of their ways?" We have a striking proof of this in the late Dr. McAll, whom it was my privilege to call my friend. It was impossible for this extraordinary man to be ignorant either of his great powers, of the estimate in which they were held, or the effect they produced on others by his pulpit exercises. Nor was he by any means unsusceptible of the influence of applause. But how empty did this appear to him as compared with the abiding results of real usefulness; which, if he had not enjoyed in such large measures as some others, it was not for want of any anxiety to obtain it. "Deeply affected was he often," says Dr. Leifchild, "by the fear of not being useful in his ministry." "I have admiration enough," he would say, "but I want to see conversion and edification." He spoke of some other neighboring ministers whose churches, he said, resembled a garden which the Lord had blessed, or whose spots of verdure were more vivid than his own; but added that his emotions in making the comparison, partook of a character that absorbed or overwhelmed sorrow for himself. I remember on one occasion, after a brilliant speech from himself, he listened to a much plainer and less oratorical brother, whose address, however, seemed much more penetrating on the minds of the audience, and produced an appearance of being deeply affected on their countenances. At that moment the speaker, hearing a loud sobbing behind him, turned round; it was McAll. "Ah," said he, afterwards, "that effect, in such a legitimate way, I would give the world to be able to produce." Though the desire thus ardently breathed was elicited on the platform, it extended to every description of ministerial address. "Oh," said he to Mr. Griffin, again and again, "I care nothing what the people may think or say of my abilities, if I may but be useful to souls!" and once, with a kind of swelling indignation, "God knows, I do not want their applause—I want their salvation." This is eminently instructive and impressive, and is one of the most convincing instances which the history of the pulpit can furnish of the worthlessness of almost everything else as an object of ministerial pursuit, and as the reward of ministerial labor, compared with the salvation of immortal souls. This was not the confession and the lamentation of one whose envy led him to depreciate the value of that which he had no hope of obtaining, but of one who was the admiration of every circle into which he entered, and whose surprising talents commanded the plaudits of all who heard him. How much of the power of that vast intellect, and that splendid eloquence, and of the admiration and eulogium which they drew upon him, would Dr. McAll have given up for a portion of that usefulness, which he saw was granted to the humbler but more effective talents of some of his far less gifted brethren. Let the men who are but too apt to envy such displays of genius, and who, when they see the spell-bound multitude listening in breathless silence, or dispersing in audible applause, fret because they cannot do so with their enchantments, study the scene before us: let them follow Dr. McAll home from the crowded, fascinated, admiring congregation, leaving behind him the atmosphere perfumed and vocal with applause, to commune with God and his own heart in his closet, and there hear him exclaiming with a burst of agony, "Lord, who hath believed our report, and to whom has thine arm been revealed?" Let them mark all this, and learn that in the estimation of the most gifted minds, there is no object of pursuit so sublime, nor any reward for ministerial labor so rich, as the salvation of immortal souls.

VI. *We may next direct our attention to the fact that earnestness has usually been successful in the accomplishment of its object, and that little has ever been achieved without it.*

We admit, and in the conclusion of this work shall more emphatically state, the necessity of a Divine influence to convert the soul; but still the Spirit works by means, and by means well adapted to accomplish the end proposed. We do not look for the Spirit to convert souls without the truth; it is by the presentation of this to the judgment, and by the co-working of Divine grace upon the heart, that the great change of regeneration is effected. It is evident, however, that this blessed result can take place only in those cases where the truth is really contemplated. The attention must be fixed upon it, or no result can take place. Attention, and, to a certain extent, abstraction of mind, may be said to be essentially necessary to the work of conversion. Hence those preachers are not only likely to be most useful, but *are* most useful, who have the greatest power of fixing attention upon the truth, and holding the mind in a state of abstraction from all other topics. When the attention is so withdrawn by their manner of preaching from foreign matters and fixed upon the truth then presented, the Spirit in a way of sovereign mercy gives forth his influence, to change the evil bias of the heart towards the truth thus exhibited to the understanding faculty. We perceive in different preachers very various kinds of power to engage the attention: some do it by a commanding eloquence; others by an impressive oratory; others by a burning ardor; others by a melting affection; and some even by eccentricity; but amidst all this specific variety of manner we shall find the one prevailing characteristic to be, an adaptation to arrest and fix the attention. A preacher may be immeasurably inferior to many others in the vigor of his intellect and richness of his imagination, and yet may be very far their superior in seizing and holding the minds of his hearers. We cannot hope to do good if we do not succeed in gaining the attention of the hearers; and our expectations of accomplishing the objects of our ministry may be indulged with much confidence, if we can so preach as to compel our hearers, so to speak, to listen to us. There is a striking incident mentioned in the Life and Remains of Mr. Cecil, of St. John's Chapel, Bedford Row, that master of pulpit eloquence. He was once invited to preach in a village where the joyful sound of evangelical truth was rarely heard in the parish church, and where he thought it probable he should have no other opportunity to proclaim it. To his mortification, when he had got half-way through the sermon he perceived that he had not succeeded in gaining that close attention of the people which he deemed essential to the success of his sermon. The time was going by, the case seemed desperate, and it occurred to him that something must be done, or the opportunity was lost; and pausing for a moment where the subject admitted of his trying his experiment, he said, with some degree of that impressiveness which pertained to him, "Last Monday morning a man was hanged at Tyburn," and then went on to make the recent execution bear upon the subject of discourse. The expedient of course succeeded, the wandering eyes of the congregation were fixed upon the preacher, and their truant minds upon the sermon. He gained their attention, which was riveted to him through the remainder of the discourse. Such self-possession is a noble qualification for a public speaker; and the moral of the anecdote is,—we must have the attention of our congregations, or we can do them no good; and the more we can command this, so as to lead them to think of the truth, the more likely we are to do them good. The history of all successful preachers will prove that, amidst a vast variety of means of gaining this, they each had the power of doing it, and in that power lay the secret of their success.

Let any one who is at all in doubt whether the importance of earnestness is overstated in this work, consider who among departed ministers have been, and who among living ones are, the most distinguished as successful preachers of the word of God. If he apply this to the fathers and founders of Nonconformity, he will find that in the first rank stand BAXTER, BUNYAN, DOOLITTLE, CLARKSON, FLAVEL, HEYWOOD, and HOWE; and when he has read their glowing, and pungent, and powerful appeals to the hearts and consciences of sinners, he will not wonder that such sermons effected the high purpose for which all sermons should be preached, that is, the conversion of sinners. Coming on to later times, it is unnecessary, after what has been said, to mention WHITFIELD and WESLEY, except to reïterate that in addition to other high and nobler qualities, earnestness was the great means of their extensive success. They lived and labored for scarcely anything else than the salvation of immortal souls. As a proof of the intensity of their zeal, reference may be made to the race of men into whom they breathed the fervor of their own souls, and whom they raised up now and then, to carry on their own great work. With here and there an exception, the present race of Methodist and Dissenting ministers are stiff, formal, cold-hearted men, compared with not only the leaders, but the next immediate followers of those illustrious instruments of the modern revival of evangelical religion. How few of us are worthy to be mentioned with COKE and FLETCHER, ROWLAND HILL, BERRIDGE and GRIMSHAW; with CECIL, NEWTON, and ROMAINE. What men were raised up in Wales by the WHITFIELD movement? DANIEL ROWLAND, JONES of Llangan, HOWELL HARRIS, and their successors, JOHN ELIAS, CHRISTMAS EVANS, and WILLIAMS, of Wern; men who caused the mountains of their own romantic country to echo to their mighty voices, and filled its valleys with the fruit of their impassioned oratory. If we look across the Atlantic, what a wonderful man do we discover in JONATHAN EDWARDS, whose printed sermons, and which were only in accordance with his ordinary ministry, are full of such earnestness as is exhibited in the specimen given earlier in this work, whose ministry was so full of its successful results. Call to recollection STODDART, BELLAMY, DWIGHT, DAVIES, who, in the land of the pilgrim fathers, diffused abroad by their unreserved devotedness, the savor of that Name which is above every name. In Scotland there have been the ERSKINES, the McLAURINS, the WALKERS, the DICKSONS, and others of by-gone days, whose remains tell us how they handled the word of God, and whose memoirs inform us with what success. In these venerated men we see the secret of all ministerial power, *a desire amounting to a fervor for the conversion of sinners, and an adaptation to accomplish this in their preaching.*

If the illustrious company of reformers, who present the

most august examples of burning zeal, next to the apostles, be not referred to, if the majestic and mighty LUTHER, the profound CALVIN, the heroic ZUINGLE, the intrepid KNOX, the elegant and classic MELANCTHON, are passed over, it is not only because they are too well known to need a mention, but also because they may be thought too high above the ordinary sphere of ministerial activity to be imitated: and yet if the pattern of the great Master himself is placed before us for contemplation and imitation, surely that of the most renowned of his servants need not be withheld. What singleness of aim, and unity of purpose, and concentration of energy were there in these rare and extraordinary men, and what less could have carried them on through their noble career?

But descending to others, what men have been with us in the recollection of the present generation, and the brilliant horizon of whose setting sun has scarcely ceased even yet to glow with the radiance of their names: the gigantic FULLER, the mighty HALL, the seraphic PEARCE, and the lion-hearted KNIBB; the intellectual WATSON, and the masculine BOGUE; the eccentric yet generous and commanding WILKS, the judicious ROBY, the mild yet persuasive BURDER, the pathetic WAUGH, the wise and tender GRIFFIN, the captivating and lovely SPENCER, and the eloquent McALL. Honored be their names, fragrant their memories, precious be the recollection of their example! May *we* who survive cherish the recollection of their life and labors, and never forget that their greatness and their usefulness arose not more from their talents than from their devoted earnestness in the cause of evangelical truth.

But descending to others and to living examples, more upon the ordinary level, it may be well to look round upon those by whom, in our own day and before our own eyes, the ends of the Christian ministry, and the object of evangelical preaching, are most extensively accomplished, and to inquire by what order of means this has been done. It would be invidious to mention the names of living men, to select from among the multitude those who are pre-eminent above their fellows in usefulness, in popularity, in the constant exhibition of evangelical truth. Two names, however, may here obtain a place, honored by us all, and an honor to us; the names of men of widely differing yet equally conspicuous and acknowledged excellencies, who are too far above us to excite our envy, and whose celebrity will defend this willing, affectionate, and admiring testimony, from the charge of invidious selection or fulsome adulation; and who, each in his own sphere, one in the northern, the other in the southern hemisphere, is shedding the lustre of an evening star, and reflecting upon the church the glory of that great Sun of Righteousness in whose attraction it has been their delight through a long, and holy, and useful life, to revolve; who yet live, and long may they live, that our younger ministry may learn in the holy labors of CHALMERS and JAY, how beautiful and how useful is human genius, when sanctified by grace and devoted to an earnest preaching of the gospel of salvation.

But we are not considering now what may be done, and is done, by the gifted few, who by their rare endowments are fitted, as well as designed, to enrich our theological literature by their valuable works, or to gather around their pulpits the literary or philosophical spirits of the place in which they dwell: these are the exceptions in all denominations to the general rule of preachers, even as those who listen to them are the exceptions to the general rule of hearers. Our remarks apply to the men who move the masses, who operate upon the popular mind as it is most commonly found; and what are *they?* not perhaps men of high scholarship, profound philosophy, or elegant composition; but men of energy and earnestness; men laying themselves out for usefulness; men of tact and of business in the management of their fellow-men; men of heart, of feeling, and perseverance. Where is a large congregation, a flourishing, well-compacted church to be found?—there is an earnest man. Where, in what country, or in what denomination, does one such man labor without considerable success? Where has the faithful, devoted, energetic preacher of evangelical truth, to borrow and use in a figurative sense the words of the Lord's forerunner, had to say, "I am the voice of one crying in the wilderness?" Where do we find small congregations, dissatisfied or declining churches, and empty chapels? Where do the ways of Zion mourn, and her gates languish, because none come to her solemn feasts? Certainly not where the ministers are as flames of fire. No matter where, or under what discouraging circumstances, such a man, who is one of these sacred flames, may commence his labors, he will soon draw around him a deeply interested and attentive congregation: no matter what may be the denomination with which he may be associated, he will not only excite the indifference, or subdue the prejudice, by which he is surrounded, but will awaken interest and conciliate regard. Under the magic power of his devotedness, blessed as it will be by God the Spirit, the verdure and beauty of spring will succeed to the gloom, desolation, and sterility of winter, and the wilderness and the solitary place shall be glad for him, and the desert rejoice and blossom as the rose. In some cases, the change has been as sudden and as complete as in Russia, from hybernal frosts and snows to vernal flowers and fragrance: churches that seemed only the repositories of the dead, and places for monuments and epitaphs, have become crowded with living and listening hearers of the joyful sound; and chapels once far too large for the last remains of a former congregation, have been soon found too small for the new one that has risen up in its place.

It would be no unprofitable exercise for any one to look round upon some of our most successful ministers, and after surveying the extent of their usefulness, to say to himself, "How has that man done this? What have been the means by which, under God, he has accomplished so much?" Unhappily there are a few, perhaps, who are so enamored of what is literary, intellectual, or philosophical, that even in large ministerial success they see little to admire or to covet, if this be not associated with scholarship and science. This is a bad state of mind, indicates a worse state of heart, and proves that the man who is the subject of it, has totally mistaken the end of the ministerial office. There are some of our most useful preachers, who are far more conscious of their literary and philosophical defects, than these supercilious scholars can possibly be; and who would purchase, if they could be obtained by money, at almost any cost, if they had the means, the high attainments which their more limited education never enabled them to acquire: but at the same time they would not give up their usefulness for all the literature of Greece and Rome, with all mathematics and philosophy in addition; and amidst their deficiencies in all that would give them weight and influence in the world of letters, feel adoringly thankful for all that weight and influence which they have acquired in the church. Their labors in the pulpit have gained them an acceptance which is far more surprising to themselves than it can be to others. Peradventure, also, they may have adventured on the sea of authorship, and have had a prosperous course, where many expected they must soon make shipwreck. None can be more sensible than themselves of their defects in composition, and often they have been ready to blame their presumption in taking up their pen, and to resolve to lay it down forever, when perhaps some instance of usefulness has come to their knowledge, as if to reprove their vanity, wounded by a sense of their own deficiencies, and to make them thank God and take courage. They knew their own department of literary action, and aimed at nothing higher than to be useful; willing to bear the sneer of literary pride and endure the lash of critical severity, if this one only object of their ambition could be accomplished, the salvation of immortal souls, and the establishment of believers in their holy faith. Such men there are among us, who owe not their success to a finished education, for it was their misfortune not to enjoy this precious advantage to the same extent to which it is now carried; nor to high scholarship, to which they make no pretensions; but to an intense desire to be useful, and to something of earnestness in carrying out the desires of their hearts: and in addition to the direct usefulness they have accomplished by their own labors, they may be abundantly useful in another way, by showing that where large literary acquisitions cannot be obtained, still simple earnestness without them may be blessed of God, for accomplishing in no inconsiderable extent the great ends of the Christian ministry.

It has been said that a man who has decision of character enough to make up his mind to the determination to be rich; who has a good share of talents to uphold his resolution, and a rigid system of self-denying economy, will ordinarily succeed; and observation seems to a considerable extent to support the remark. With far greater certainty may it be said, that he who enters upon his ministry with an intense zeal for God, an ardent passion for the salvation of souls; and with this, sustained by deep piety, a tolerable share of talents and acquirement, and a fixed purpose in humble dependence upon God's grace, to be a useful minister of Christ, will not fail of his end. The failure of such a man would be a new thing in the earth. We know of no such case, and we may not expect to know it. We say to every sinner, in calling him to repentance. he may be saved if he will: not intending by such an expression, that he can be saved without the Spirit of God; but that he may secure that Divine power if he have faith to receive it: so we may almost venture to say to every minister of Christ, it is his own fault if he is not useful; intending by such an assertion, that as the gospel he preaches is God's own truth; as preaching is his own institute; as the minister is his own servant; and as to all this, he has added the promise of his grace, it would seem as if in the case of entire or extensive failure, he has himself to blame.

But we may look at the power of earnestness, as seen not only in the cause of truth, but of error. It has often served a bad cause as well as a good one. Islamism owes its existence and its wide dominion to this quality, in its extraordinary founder: Mohammed exhibits one of the most wonderful instances of this the world ever witnessed; and with what dreadful results was it followed in his case! We may say the same of Popery: that stupendous fabric of delusion, which throws its dark and chilling shadow over so large a portion of Christendom, owes its erection and its continuance to the intense devotedness with which it has inspired its votaries: it is this that upholds a system constantly at war against the dictates of reason, the doctrines of revelation, and the dearest rights and liberties of humanity. It is this mysterious and indomitable earnestness of the priesthood, which has resisted the attacks of logic, rhetoric, and piety; of divines, philosophers, and statesmen; of wit, humor, and ridicule; and which in this age of learning and science, commerce and liberty, not only enables it to maintain its ground, but to advance and make conquests. The Church of Rome, which would, in the hands of a lukewarm priesthood, fall by the weight of its own absurdity, or be crushed by the hands of its constant assailants, is still strong in the hearts of its members; each of whom, from the Pope down, through all its civil and ecclesiastical gradations, to the most insignificant member, is a type of concentrated and intensely glowing zeal.

The pages of ecclesiastical history furnish us with some extraordinary instances of the power of the pulpit, as exhibited in the cases of some Popish preachers. I do not now refer to the court of Louis the Fourteenth, which, with that grand and licentious monarch at its head, was subdued into a transient frame and season of devoutness by the sermons of MASSILLON, but to the preaching of far inferior, and less known orators, and to effects less courtly, but not less striking. When CONNECTE, an Italian, preached, the ladies committed their gay dresses by hundreds to the flames. When NARNI taught the populace in Lent, from the pulpits of Rome, half the city went from his sermons, crying along the streets, *Lord have mercy upon us, Christ have mercy upon us;* so that in only one passion week, two thousand crowns' worth of ropes were sold to make scourges with; and when he preached before the Pope, to cardinals and bishops, and painted the crime of non-residence in its own colors, he frightened thirty or forty bishops, who heard him, instantly to their own dioceses. In the pulpit at Salamanca, he induced eight hundred students to quit all worldly prospects of honor, riches, and pleasure, and to become penitents in divers monasteries. Some of this class were martyrs too. Here then was the power of earnestness; but being in this case given to the cause of error, being directed rather to the imagination than to the heart, and intended to correct mere ceremonial irregularitics, rather than to lead to repentance towards God, and faith in our Lord Jesus Christ, we are not surprised that the storm of passion soon subsided; that NARNI himself was so disgusted with his office, that he renounced preaching, and shut himself up in his cell, to mourn over his irreclaimable contemporaries; for bishops went back to court, and rope-makers lay idle again. This striking fact is replete with instruction, not only as showing the power of the pulpit, but at the same time the essential feebleness of that religion which does not aim at the renovation of the heart, and the transient nature of that effect which is produced by mere rhetoric, unaccompanied by a sober exhibition of the truth to enlighten the judgment, warm the affections, and awaken the conscience.

But it is not only on this grand scale that we see the power and success of an ardent zeal, even in a bad cause; for there is no system of opinions, nor any course of religious practice, however remote, not only from the truth of revelation, but from the dictates of common sense, and even the decorum of society, but what, if preached and propagated by men of intense ardor, will gain, for awhile, some disciples to believe it, and even some apostles to propagate it. If men are really in earnest in blowing bubbles, some will be found to look at, to admire, and to follow their airy and unsubstantial balloons. It has been already said, that earnestness is contagious : a man in this state of mind and action, is sure to draw some others under the influence of his own example. If this is the case with a bad cause, how much more may we expect it to be so in a good one. Everything, then, combines to prove, that our want of success must be traced up, rather to our neglect of the right means to obtain it, than to any backwardness on the part of God to give his blessing to our own intelligent, judicious, and earnest exertions.

VII. *The state of our denomination demands immediate and devoted attention to the subject.*

In speaking of our own denomination, we find in its general condition, much cause for thankfulness and congratulation. In the number of our churches and the competency of a very large number of their pastors; in our colleges and schools; in our missionary and other organizations; in our periodical and other religious literature; in our public spirit and liberality—we see signs of prosperity, and tokens for good : and if we are true to ourselves and to our cause, we have nothing to fear. Our opponents cannot do us so much harm as we may do to ourselves. With a system of doctrine which we believe is taken from the New Testament, and a system of polity which, in all its general principles, is derived from the same source, we may not only stand our ground, but advance, if we will present the former in all its fullness, and will administer the latter with discretion and charity. Everything, under God's blessing, depends upon our ministry. This, which is important to every denomination, is especially so to ours. We go forth, not only unsupported by the wealth and the power of the Established Church, but without the aid of that elaborately organized combination which is to be found in some sections that separate from it. Our ministers, so to speak, do not contend in regiments and in rank and file, but single-handed, and should therefore be all picked men, each possessed of courage and of skill. Let us only take care to send none but such into the field, and we may hope for a still more abundant measure of prosperity than we at present enjoy. There is room enough for all denominations in the vast wilderness of our neglected and unchristianized population, and we have no need to look at each other's labors with jealousy and envy. Satan is ruining souls faster than all of us united can save them. It is a mark of deep malignity of heart, and a proof that it is the distempered zeal of bigotry that moves us, and not a pure love to God and souls, when we see with uneasiness the success of other denominations of evangelical Christians, and rejoice over their failure. To seize with avidity any acknowledgements of, and lamentations over, a want of usefulness, and then tearing them from their connection and exaggerating their statements, to hold them up exultingly to the world, and tauntingly to the denomination from which in frankness and in sorrow they have come, may suit well with the strategy of polemical warfare, and serve the cause of a party, but ill accords with the spirit of divine charity, and promotes but little the cause of our common Christianity.

In how many places of worship connected with the Establishment, and even where the gospel is preached, but preached with feebleness, do we find small congregations, and few souls converted to God. Do we rejoice over this? On the contrary, it is for a grief and a lamentation. And is there a heart so envenomed with the gall of bigotry, as to rejoice in the confession that is now made, that many of *our* congregations are withering away under the effete ministrations of incompetent men? Such a withering is indeed going on in many places. The fact cannot be concealed, it is notorious. We have been incautious in the admission, not of bad men, for few of these ever find their way into our pulpits—not of heretical men, for we take care not to receive such—but of incompetent men; not always incompetent in intellect, but in talents for public speaking, and the active duties of the pastorate. From this cause, combined with the increased energy and activity of the Church of England, our congregations are diminishing in some places, though multiplying and increasing in others. With the freedom of action we possess, unrestricted by parochial limits and ecclesiastical laws; with the world all before us, and Providence our guide; with a good feeling towards us on the part of the middle and lower classes, we have every ground to hope for success, if we can obtain an adequate number of energetic and earnest preachers: but we have not taken sufficient care to find out and educate this right sort of men, and in some places are certainly losing ground. Considerable towns might be mentioned, where congregations once numerous and flourishing are reduced down to mere skeletons under the dull and deadening influence of heartless men, and yet perhaps good men too. It is more easy to settle an incompetent minister over a church than to remove him. It is true, we have advantages for such removal not possessed by the Church of England. The pastorate is not in our churches a freehold; yet it must be confessed that even with us the difficulty of getting rid of a pastor, except for immorality or heresy, and only on the ground of inefficiency, is not small. That a minister should wish to stay when he has preached away nearly all his congregation, breeds a suspicion of the purity of his motives, and is a reflection upon the integrity of his character. To reduce a congregation and scatter a church, first by inefficiency, and then by obstinacy in retaining his post in opposition to the wishes of his flock and the advice of his friends, is a serious matter to account for to God. Some such men talk of waiting for the leadings of Providence. One is at a loss to find out what rule of interpretation for ascertaining the will of God they have adopted: to everybody else but themselves, deserted pews and a dissatisfied as well as a reduced church, are a sufficient indication of the leadings of Providence for their removal. In such a case one should suppose there needed no voice from heaven to say to the minister, "Arise, and go hence;" nor any finger to come forth, and in flaming characters write "Ichabod" on the walls. It is sometimes said, in reference to such men and their flocks, that the people must suffer the consequences of a hasty choice: and so far as *they* are concerned, they deserve it; but then they suffer not alone, for the denomination in its strength, and character, and efficiency, suffers with them. The work of conversion, not only in our own denomination, but in the Church of England, and among the Methodists, goes on but slowly, and the spirituality of the great bulk of professors is too low. This is confessed and lamented by the Evangelical clergy, and by the Wesleyan ministers, as well as by ourselves. The Spirit's influence seems in some way and from some cause obstructed, and in the absence of this, our denomination is more likely to feel and manifest the visible results of it than almost any other; and such a consideration should lead us to more serious thoughtfulness and earnest prayer for a revived and intensely devoted ministry.

CHAPTER X.

MEANS TO BE USED FOR OBTAINING AN EARNEST MINISTRY.

This is a most important part of our subject; for however desirable the blessing may be, yet if it cannot be obtained, or if there are no means by which *we* can obtain it, the discussion and contemplation of it are quite useless, and even worse than this, being calculated only to excite a fruitless wish, or what is most injurious of all, a disposition to neglect the means we have, in the hopeless desire after what we have not. But we are not to entertain so desponding a view. Such men there have been, and, blessed be God, such men there are, and that in no small number, in every section of the Christian church; men laboring with intelligence and zeal, and success, both in the metropolis and in the provinces; men of whom their age need not be ashamed, and over whom any age would have rejoiced. Still there are too many of an opposite character; far too many to render the question impertinent and out of season, "How shall such a ministry be obtained?"

I. It is imperative, first of all, to have the truth deeply engraven upon all hearts, that *the church is the conservator of the Christian ministry*, and that it is her business, and almost her first and most important business, to see that she discharge well her duty in this momentous affair. She has not only to provide for her own edification at the present time, but also to secure, by all possible vigilance and care, the administrative transmission of our holy religion through every age, pure, and undefiled, and unimpaired in its capacity to confer essential and eternal benefits upon the children of men. But then it is obvious that for such a function the church must be regarded as a purely spiritual body. And it should be deemed a question of no small moment bearing upon the controversy about church government, what system of polity has the most direct tendency and the greatest power to call out, to secure, and to perpetuate, an evangelical and effective ministry. An ecclesiastical system which of itself has no effectual provision for this, cannot surely be of divine origin, and that of which the tendency to this is most obvious and direct, is most in accordance with the word of God. A church *without* such a conservative principle cannot be the church of the New Testament, much less that which includes various and ever-active influences *against* it. Nothing but a spiritual church can provide a spiritual ministry, and whatever spiritual ministry a worldly church may have, cannot be so much the result of the system itself, as of something extraneous to it: and even in spiritual churches, if discipline be relaxed, and worldly-minded persons be admitted, the conservative principle, which in fact consists of the vital piety of the members, is impaired; and if, at the same time, there be neglect of discipline, it will be altogether lost, and heretical men come in to fill the places of those who were the preachers of the truth as it is in Jesus. It is well, therefore, for all our churches to bear in constant recollection, this their high and sacred function as conservators of an evangelical ministry, and to maintain the power of vital godliness, and the exercise of a salutary discipline, as that in which this power of conservation resides. Let the churches consider their high, their glorious commission; let them remember they must be of such character, and such order, that Christian truth as to its essential doctrines and holy practice, and at the same time the calling out and supporting such men to uphold and preach it, may be safely trusted to their vigilance and care. But let them forget this, and corrupt their fellowship by the admission of worldly-minded professors, "the mounds are gone, the fence is broken up, and wolves may enter in, not sparing the flock. Preserve this spiritual condition of the church, and it is, what it was intended it should be, an undying torch, which, while it is the light of the present age, shall safely light successive ages along the only way which leads to happiness and heaven."

II. *Let the subject be thoroughly considered, and universally admitted, that this is the ministry we want, and must have.*

In an age, like the present, when so much is said about knowledge, and such high value is attached to it, there is a danger of our being seduced from every other qualification, and taken up with this. The establishment of the London University, and the incorporation of our Colleges with it, have given access for our students to the fount of academic degrees and honors; and there is some danger, in the new condition of our literary institutions, lest our young men should have their minds in some measure drawn away from much more important matters, by the hope of having their names graced by a Bachelor's or a Master's degree. It is a foolish clamor that has been raised against *all* attention to such matters, and a vain and barbarous precaution, that would fortify the ministerial devotedness of our students by restraining them altogether from such scholastic distinctions. The studies necessary to enable them to attain the object of their ambition, are a part of their professional education; while the vanity likely to be engendered by success, will soon be annihilated by the commonness of the acquisition. Pride and vanity are founded on conscious distinction, and when these academic University degrees are so common that almost all ministers possess them, they will no longer be a snare to the humility of their possessors. Besides, like every other object of human desire, when once they are possessed, much of the charm that dazzles the eye of hope has vanished. HENRY MARTIN, when he came from the Senate-house at Cambridge, where he had been declared Senior Wrangler foı his year, and had thus won the richest prize the University had to confer, was struck with the vanity of human wishes, and expressed his surprise at the comparative worthlessness of the bauble he had gained, and the shadow he had grasped. No, it is not by closing the door against such distinctions that we can hope to raise the tone of devotedness in our ministry, but by fostering in the minds of our young men at College, and equally in the minds of our congregations, and ministers in general, the conviction that earnestness is just that one thing, to which all other things must be, and can be, made subservient, and without which all other things are as nothing, whatever else education can impart.

Our congregations need perhaps a little instruction on this subject. I am afraid the taste is not quite so pure, correct, and elevated on this matter as it should be. There is, it is true, a demand, and it is well there is, for a vivacious and animated manner of preaching; and provided there be what is intellectual, there is a decided preference for what is evangelical in association with it; but there is reason to fear that in some cases a small modicum of evangelical truth would do, provided there was an abundance of talent. Earnestness is demanded, but with some, it is rather the earnestness of the head than of the heart; the labored and eloquent effusion of the scholar, the philosopher, or the poet, rather than the gush of hallowed feeling of him who watcheth for souls, as one that must give account. Dullness, however learned or profound, will not do, but the heartless declamations of the pulpit orator will do for some, though it have little tendency to do anything more than please the intellect or captivate the imagination. There is an idolatry of talent in this day which runs through society; and this man-worship has crept also into the church, and corrupted its members. It is painful to perceive how far this is carried in many circles, and to see what homage is paid, what incense is burnt to some popular favorites. It is not religion or holiness that is thus elevated, but genius and knowledge: it is not moral beauty, but intellectual strength, that is lauded to the skies: the loftiest models of human goodness receive but few devotees and scanty offerings at their shrine, compared with the gods of the understanding. There can be no surer mark of a moral apostacy, a lapse from man's primeval innocence when he came perfect from the hands of his Maker, bearing the moral image of his Creator, than this disposition to exalt genius above piety. What an inversion is this of the right order of things, since it must be allowed that man's intellectual nature is inferior and subordinate to his moral being. It is by this latter that he is removed to the greatest distance from the brute creation, is placed in most direct opposition to fallen spirits, makes his nearest approach to the angels of God, and bears the most correct resemblance to the Holy and Eternal One. The God of the Bible is not merely a Divine intellect, though it be true that his understanding is infinite: nor is Omniscience his only attribute, though this is one of his glorious perfections;—but God is Love; and when the seraphim select for the subject of their anthem that view of his nature which calls forth their loftiest praise, they contemplate him as the Holy, Holy, Holy, Lord God Almighty. Infinite goodness, and not merely infinite greatness, is the Deity we are called by the inspired writers to worship, and all the most sublime speculations or descriptions of God that are not founded upon true goodness, are but the mere inventions of men's minds, and no true copies of God's representations of his own nature. The prevailing disposition, therefore, to do such homage to talent, rather than to moral excellence, is only another species of idolatry that exists in our world, more refined and subtle than the worship of stocks and stones, but still scarcely less guilty.

That some respect must be paid to talent, even in the ministry of the word, is admitted; such a disposition is inseparable from human nature, and is a part of the design of God in creating our race, and forming man with varied powers of the understanding: a fine intellect is to be admired as well as an elegant form or beautiful flower; and so much the more as that which is mental is superior to what is corporeal. But when the Christian public shall be so enamored of talent as to admire that more than the message which it is employed to set forth; when no preacher can be heard with pleasure or endurance, however sound his doctrine, or clear his statements, or impressive his manner, or earnest his address, unless his discourse is radiant with the light of genius, or fragrant with the flowers of rhetoric; when truth itself is unpalatable unless it be sweetened with the honey of human eloquence, and even error *so* sweetened can be swallowed for the sake of the luscious accompaniment; when the hearer of a sermon can turn from it with disgust, because it fails to regale his fancy by the brilliancy of its images, or to lull his ear by the smoothness and harmony of its periods; when this is the state of the public taste; and it is to be feared that to a great extent it is the state of it; surely, surely, it is time to call the attention of our congregations to something higher and better than such matters as these.

No one who is attentive to the features of the age, can doubt that there is much now going on which has an obvious tendency, though of course not a design, to corrupt in some degree the simplicity of the public taste with reference to preachers and their sermons. The pulpit has some reason to be jealous of the platform, and the sermon of the speech. If the modern practice of endless speechifying had only done something to break down the stiffness and formality of sermonic speaking, and to introduce a more easy, fluent, and energetic method of address on the part of the preacher, and a corresponding taste for a more vivacious method of instruction on the part of the people, it would have conferred a substantial benefit; but with this has come, perhaps, the opposite evil of making the preacher too oratorical and the people too fastidious, and of destroying somewhat of the solemnity and spirituality of both. No doubt some degree of earnestness will come in with this, but it may be it is the earnestness which is anxious to please, rather than that which is desirous to convert, which aims to gratify the fancy rather than to save the soul.

It is in vain then to hope for such a ministry as that which it is the object of this work to describe and to recommend, till our congregations are brought to see its vast importance, and to demand that it shall be given them. In this case, as in every other, both the demand will bring the supply as well as the supply create the demand. When the churches shall be brought up to that state of piety, that deep solicitude about salvation, that intenseness of pursuit of eternal life, which shall make them anxious for ministers who will aid them in this momentous business; and when they shall say to the tutors and committees of our colleges, "You must not only send us learned men, but earnest men," then will the minds of our excellent professors be still more fixed on the most essential qualifications of the Christian ministry, and still more anxiously endeavor to meet this demand. And when our destitute congregations shall let it be distinctly known that it is not merely a Master of Arts, nor a merely eloquent speaker, nor even a good divine, that they want, but one who shall watch for their souls, and feed the flock of God, the attention of our young ministers will be still more turned upon the end of their ministry and the necessary qualifications for the just discharge of its functions. Let the church therefore only be rightly instructed on this subject, and fix properly its standard; let it be brought up to this conviction, that nothing less and nothing else than such men as are intently fixed upon saving souls, will be likely to be useful; and such men will come at its bidding; especially if—

III. *There be much earnest prayer presented to God for such a blessing.* It must never be forgotten that ministers are called, qualified, and blessed by the Lord, the Spirit. Hence the promise of God to the Jews, "I will give you pastors according to mine heart, which shall feed you with knowledge and with understanding;" and also the language of the apostle, "He gave some pastors and teachers, for the perfecting of the saints, for the work of the ministry, for the edifying of the body of Christ." It was a special injunction of Christ to his disciples, and intended to apply to his people in every age, to pray to the Lord of the harvest to send forth laborers into the field. From these passages, as well as from the general principle that every good gift is from the Lord, we learn that a faithful ministry is one of God's gifts, and a precious one t is; and were the church in a high spiritual state, this would constitute one of its chief subjects of prayer. Perhaps we are not brought to feel with sufficient depth of conviction our dependence upon God for this great blessing, for there is little doubt that the church's possessions and the church's prayers would bear in this particular some tolerable proportion to each other. We cannot conceive of any case in which the promise "Ask, and ye shall receive," would be so abundantly fulfilled, as in reference to this. It has not been enough considered what kind of men are wanted at all times, and especially in these, for the ministry of reconciliation; that in fact we need men formed exactly and in all respects, except inspiration and the power to work miracles, upon the apostolical model. Much the same work is now to be done as was done by them, and we must have men as full of the power of God, and the graces of the Holy Spirit, to do it. Let it be seen what ministers have to contend with in this day of their vocation; not indeed the spirit of persecution, not sanguinary laws, not the amphitheatre, the axe, or the stake; but obstacles almost as formidable as these things, and in some respects more so; for such impediments, if they lessened the number of professors, raised those that stood firm into the devotion of seraphs, the courage of heroes, and the constancy of martyrs;—but our obstacles are the emasculating influence of ease and prosperity; the insidious snares of wealth, knowledge, and fashion; the engrossing power of trade, politics, and secular ambition; and then let any one consider what kind of preachers and pastors we want for such an age. If we had nothing more to do, and were contented to do this and no more, than to keep religion up to the low level which it now maintains, then ministers of common stamp might suffice; but to keep in check all the enemies of vital godliness which threaten the devastation of the church; to resist by the potency of personal example and the energy of the pulpit, the worldly spirit which threatens to eat out the very core of vital piety; to keep up the evangelizing zeal which is awakened, and to blend with it a sanctity and a spirituality, which shall make it as effective as it is busy; to do battle with all the forms of error by which our common faith is likely to be assailed; and to do this not only by the force of intellect, but by being strong in the Lord, and in the power of his might—to achieve this, we want men of the same spirit as those who, under the direct commission of Christ, preached the word of salvation, with the Holy Ghost sent down from heaven. Have we many such men in the field? If not, why not? Must not the church of God blame herself, for has she sought such men by all the wrestling power of believing prayer? Had she felt the need of such men, and had lifted up not her hands, or her voice merely, but all the energies of her renewed nature, in beseeching supplication to Him who is ascended to bestow this very gift upon men, she would have obtained all she asked or wanted. Let the church only set her heart upon such a blessing as this, let her faith be equal to the expectation of it, and her prayer be as her faith, and she will have it. And why should she not expect it? What is there in the nature of the boon that forbids her to look for it? Does it contradict a single promise, or contravene a single arrangement of her Divine Head? Does it compromise his honor, or require his miraculous interposition? Does it involve any stepping out of his ordinary course of action? Why then should it be thought incredible that she should obtain a more, a far more devoted and successful ministry than she now possesses? Does the gospel of God's grace, either at home or abroad, prevail as could be wished and might be expected? Does the work of conversion go forward, and Christ's kingdom make those encroachments on the empire of darkness which might be looked for? Who will venture to answer in the affirmative? Whose love to Christ and souls beats with so feeble a pulsation as to be satisfied with what is doing, and to be contented that things should go on as they do? Is there nothing to be done, no way to accelerate the work of redeeming mercy, no method to pour the principles of spiritual fertility more rapidly and more diffusively through the moral wilderness of our barren world? One is yet open, and that is for Zion to awake and bestir herself, and lay hold of God's strength, saying, "Send us more laborers into the field." We have forgotten to pray for ministers of a right stamp. The subject has never occupied the place in our private, family, and social devotions, which its importance demands. It has been only occasionally and coldly alluded to, but has not been lifted up to heaven with all the importunity of men who felt that they could not do without it.

"Truly, if ever there was a period when the whole Christian world should be down upon their faces before the throne of mercy, imploring with all the importunity, and boldness, and perseverance of faith, a race of ministers, each full of the Holy Ghost, as was Barnabas or Paul, that period is passing over us. Not from one place or another, but from all quarters of the earth, testimony multiplies daily that amidst the greatest possible facilities for converting the world, a greatly increased and more devoted ministry is indispensable. This testimony comes to us, not indeed as the Macedonian cry came to the apostle in a supernatural vision, but in a manner not less affecting or decisive as to its purport. It is a real sound, which flies round the land and rings in our ears all the day long; 'Send us preachers,' is the universal, ceaseless demand, at home and abroad. It comes from more than a thousand of our destitute churches; it comes from the cities, from the wilderness, from the islands, from the uttermost parts of the sea, from tracts until lately unknown to civilized man. This cry, which sounds so loudly and so complainingly in our ears, should, by general consent, be turned into prayer and sent up to heaven. And shall we longer forbear to do this? Shall we stand and hear that unusual cry, and feel no inclination to direct it to the ear of him from whom help alone can come? Is it not a mysterious species of infatuation to forbear to lift up our cry to the Lord of the harvest? Why do we not, if this be the case, abjure the very religion of Jesus, and abandon ourselves, as well as the heathen, and the whole race of man, to despair? Why should not a reform forthwith commence, and the place of prayer have more attractions than the eloquence of any mortal, or any angel's tongue? Why then will not every true Christian make a covenant with himself to change his life in this particular, and from henceforth make it one of his chief subjects of wrestling supplication, that God would give us a more faithful, earnest, and laborious ministry? Why will we not call to mind how Abraham, and Moses, and Elias, and Daniel, and Paul, and above all, how the blessed Jesus *labored in prayer*, and resolve in God's strength to pray in the same manner? Oh what an amount of beneficient power would such prayers exert upon the external destinies of our world! What wonders of grace would be witnessed in our churches; what accessions would be made to the sacred ministry; what an impulse would be given to the cause of missions; what brightness would be shed on all the prospects of the church!"*

I echo these beautiful sentiments, and earnestly implore for them the attention they demand. They touch us at the right point, and they speak to us at the proper season. We have multiplied and extended of late our collegiate institutions, and greatly improved our systems of ministerial education. We can speak of colleges whose architecture would not disgrace either Cambridge or Oxford, and of professors whose attainments in biblical literature would not be surpassed by many of the teachers in our national seats of learning; but, as if to teach us our dependence upon God, few of them are at the present moment filled with students, and of those who are coming forth from them, how much fewer are the eminent and earnest men we would wish to see them. The same remark will apply to the evangelical men of the Church of England, and of all other denominations. I would be the last man to speak lightly of education, but I would be the first to caution the church of Christ against the sin and the folly of making this our supreme dependence. Tutors can give Latin, Greek, and philosophy, but God alone can bestow those physical and spiritual gifts which constitute the chief qualifications for the work of the ministry. It is a fact which must have struck every attentive observer, that of those who are employed in the ministry of the word, whether in the Established Church or out of it, very few are eminent in any way. The brightest flowers of humanity are not in great numbers laid upon the altar of the Lord. Many of those

* Religion of the Bible. Select Discourses, by Dr. SKINNER, of New York.

who are engaged are of a common order of intellect, while, as in the firmament of heaven, only here and there a star of unusual brilliancy meets the eye and attracts the attention by its magnitude and brightness. Let it not be said that God chooses the weak things of the world to confound the mighty. This appertained to apostles, who, as they were clothed with the power of God by their gifts and miracles, could dispense with all other potency; but this is not the case with us, who, without appropriate qualifications of native talent and education, can scarcely expect the blessing of God.

IV. *A revived state of the church* would produce a ministry such as that which has been described in the foregoing pages. In the natural order of things it would seem that the church cannot be revived without a previous revival of the ministry, and yet, as the ministry are the children of the church, they can hardly be expected to rise above the level of the community out of which they spring. There is a kind of average piety of almost every age and every church, and our young men rarely come with more than this to our colleges; and, therefore, although we do not dispute the fact that little expectation can be indulged of an increased piety in the churches without an augmentation of ministerial devotedness, yet, at the same time, the latter can almost as little be looked for without the former. Revivals have sometimes begun with the people, who have drawn the ministry up to their own level. A lively church could not long endure a dull and lukewarm pastor, who, if he partook not of the prevailing excitement, would feel himself soon obliged to leave his situation. If, therefore, the ministry cannot revive themselves and each other, it were unspeakable mercy if they should receive an impulse from the people.

As we have already seen, there are many things in the present age which are of a most auspicious character, and which give it a lofty pre-eminence above some others that have preceded it. Who can witness its busy activity, its generous liberality, its exhaustless ingenuity, for the conversion of the world, without admiration and gratitude? But, as we have before remarked, these are not *all* the elements of true piety, and it may be apprehended that in innumerable cases, these things are only the substitutes for the essential work of regeneration and sanctification. It may be feared that Satan is taking advantage of these matters to blind the judgment, and to delude the souls of many. Men of keen observation, who can penetrate the surface, and see what lies below, are of opinion that underneath this external covering of liberality and zeal there lies a want of vital godliness; that much of what we see in our multiplied public institutions, is but as the flowers which bloom in a shallow and sandy soil. They who are best acquainted with the state of our churches, express a doubt whether there is not a deplorable lack of that separation from the world, in its spirit and customs, which the Christian profession implies. While this is the case, the ministers who come out from such a state of things are likely to rise no higher than the source. Hence does it become our churches to consider the urgent necessity of their being elevated to a higher tone of piety, and of joining heartily in any efforts that are made to bring about so desirable a state of things. Even they who have themselves drank deepest into the spirit of the world, will sometimes lament the want of intenseness on the part of their ministers; but do they not remember that their own worldly-mindedness is exerting an influence over their pastor, and producing that very state of mind in him which is the subject of their remark and censure? He was perhaps a more holy and heavenly man when, young and flexible, he came to them from college, and was at first surprised and grieved to witness the prevalence of lukewarmness, but after striving in vain to produce a better state of things among the members of his church, he was gradually drawn down to that low level from which he found it impracticable to raise them. Thus while we admit there is little hope of a revived church which does not rest on the previous revival of the ministry, we are tempted almost to argue in a circle, and to say there is little hope of a revival of the ministry which does not rest on the previous revival of the church.

Let us then, both ministers and churches, set about in good earnest the revival of religion. We act and reäct upon each other. We help or hinder one another. We both want more religion; let the ministry seek it for the sake of the people, and the people for the sake of the ministry. If the ministers will not lead the people, let the people lead the ministers. If the blessing cannot descend from the pulpit to the pew, let it ascend from the pew to the pulpit. Let the church of the living God arise, put or her robe of righteousness, her garment of salvation, shake off the dust from her apparel, and shine forth in the beauties of holiness. We want a better church to make a better world; and a better church *would* most assuredly make a better world: and we also want a better ministry to make a better church; but if we cannot have this order may we have the other, and find that a better church is making a better ministry. If the rain of heaven collect not upon the hills to pour down its streams upon the valleys, may the dew of the valleys rise to revive and refresh the tops of the hills.

V. *We should as pastors of the churches look round our*

respective flocks, and see what devoted youths of ardent piety and competent abilities, we have in our circle, who are likely to be useful as ministers of Christ, and should call them out to the work, without waiting for the first impulse to come from themselves. A radical mistake has been committed through our whole denomination, in supposing it is necessary in all cases for the desire after the sacred office to rise up first of all, and spontaneously, in the breast of the aspirant. In consequence of this, many have thrust themselves forward who were altogether unfit for the work; while many, as eminently qualified for it, have been kept back by modesty. Does it not seem to be the work of the pastors and the churches to call out from among themselves the most gifted and pious of their members for this object? Is not this the working out of the principle we have already considered, that the church is the conservator of an effective ministry? Are not they the best judges of talent and other prerequisites? Should this matter be left to the inflations of self-conceit, the promptings of vanity, or the impulses, it may be, of a sincere, but at the same time of an unenlightened zeal? Nothing can be more erroneous than that this call of the church would be an officious intermeddling with the work of the Spirit in calling the ministry; for it may surely be conceived to be quite as rational a notion to suppose that the Spirit calls a person through the medium of the church and its pastor, as to imagine that the commission from above comes direct to the heart of the individual, especially as the church and the pastor, or at any rate the latter is usually applied to, as a judge of the candidate's fitness for the work; and thus, after all, the power and the right of pronouncing a judgment upon the alleged call of this Divine Agent, are vested with the pastor and the church. To affirm that an individual cannot be supposed to have a very great fitness for the office unless his love of souls has been strong enough to prompt him to desire the work of the ministry, and that he is not likely to be very earnest in it, if he be thus sent, instead of his going of his own accord, is assuming too much; for in the plan here recommended, it is supposed that the individual who attracts the attention of the pastor is one who, in addition to true piety and competent abilities, has manifested an active zeal in the way of doing good. It is only on such a one that his eye would light, or to whom he would venture to make the suggestion. In all the official appointments recorded in the New Testament, from an apostle down to a deacon, the people were requested to *look out for suitable men*, and not to wait till they presented themselves. Let us then give our serious attention to this subject, and look out for the most pious, the most intelligent, and the most ardent of our young men, not forgetting at the same time to ascertain their physical qualifications of voice and energy. It is not studious youths only that will do for this work, mere book-worms who will devour knowledge and make no return; but such as will unite a thirst for knowledge with an intense desire to employ every acquisition for saving souls. We must be inquisitive after such; and if they are youths in the more respectable classes of society, young men that have known something of good society, and have acquired the manners and habits of gentlemen, that have had something to do with business, and have acquired such a proper degree of self-confidence as shall give them weight and influence of character, all the better. Low men, with coarse, vulgar manners, may by the power of great talents rise above their origin, and be of value, as diamonds uncut and unpolished; yet how much would the value of these spiritual diamonds be increased by the lapidary's art: but when vulgarity is associated with slender talents, it is only as flint set in lead. There is nothing in gentlemanly manners that deteriorates piety; though much, very much, that adds not only to the gracefulness, but to the usefulness, of the ministerial character. The graces, when baptized at the font of evangelical piety, arrayed in the robe of righteousness, and wearing the ornament of a meek and quiet spirit, are useful handmaids to the Christian pastor, and procure favor for him in the solemn duties of his office. If we may judge from the specimens left on record in the Acts of the Apostles, Paul united the manners of a courtier with the fidelity of a prophet, and threw over the stern courage of a martyr the mantle of a gentle courteousness. What could be more polished, yet what more faithful, than his address to Festus and Agrippa? and we can imagine that even his denunciation against the high priest, who had commanded him to be smitten on the mouth, was all the more terrible because of the dignified severity with which it was uttered. Earnestness, then, is not incompatible with refinement, but is rendered more effective by it, and hence the importance of our sending our *patrician* youths to the sacred office.

Occasionally we may find in our churches, some who are possessed of extraordinary talents for speaking and for active duty, who are too far advanced in manhood to go through a college curriculum, but who, notwithstanding, would make admirable preachers, and attain to considerable usefulness, as well as respectability. A man of natural genius, of strong intelligence, of eminent piety, and of pulpit power, is not to be rejected because he has not passed through the schools. Those who remember WILLIAM THORP, and especially that giant in theological literature ANDREW FULLER, will not deny that he who called his apostles, not from the philosophers of Greece, nor from the orators of Rome, nor the rabbis of Jerusalem, but from the fishermen of Galilee, may sometimes select a servant, even in our day, from those classes which have been debarred the privilege of a classical or a philosophical education. Among the prophets of antiquity was Amos, the herdsman of Tekoa. These, however, are the exceptions, but not the rule. Even the bishops of our ecclesiastical establishment are lowering their standard of qualifications as necessary in *all* cases for the ministerial functions, and are accommodating their system to the wants of the people by ordaining men to the sacred office whom their predecessors, an age or two back, would have unquestionably refused. We must not pretend to more fastidiousness than they, nor be horror-struck at the idea of introducing to the pastorate men who, though they are neither scholars nor philosophers, are likely to be powerful and useful preachers of the gospel. A collegiate education must be our general rule, which it may be hoped we shall never abandon; but it is a rule from which we must make exceptions in the case of those strong-minded, warm-hearted, earnest men, whose tough broad-sword, and their strength in wielding it, may do more execution than many a weapon whose blade has received the highest polish that art can give it, and whose hilt sparkles with the richest diamonds.

VI. This is a subject which demands *the close and serious attention of the ministry themselves.* The whole present generation of our preachers, from the oldest to the youngest, must give their attention to this matter. We have known men of a past age, whose names are dear, and whose memory is fragrant, who to the last retained the ardor of their zeal, and whose labors, like the flame of the volcano rising from beneath the snow-covered surface of the mountain-top, were carried on in association with their hoary hairs; and some such, though they are very few, still linger amongst us. Even they, and we who come next to them, and are verging on old age, must all do something more and something better than we have done for Christ and souls. Our sun is declining and our shadows lengthen on the plain, but the day's work is not done; and instead of relaxing our diligence, we must work the harder because the time of working is nearly over. As long as we have strength to grasp the sickle, or light to bind a sheaf, let us work on. Harvest-home will soon be here, and it is time enough for enjoyment when that arrives, and we shall meet the Master, and our fellow-servants. To us comes with solemn emphasis the admonition, "Whatsoever thy hand findeth to do, do it with thy might: for there is no work, nor device, nor knowledge, in the grave whither thou goest." For the sake of our younger brothers let us be diligent. They look upon us as patterns, and let us therefore set them an example which shall come to them with the correctness of a good model, and the power of an ardent inspiration. Let there be no running from our post as if we were weary of our service, and panting for the *otium cum dignitate*. Let it be seen as if the earnestness of our minds imparted vigor to our bodies, kept off the infirmities of our declining years, and enabled us to renew our youth like the eagle's. It is a spectacle which the admirer of military glory loves to witness, to behold the veteran soldier, on whose countenance the suns of innumerable campaigns, and the swords of his foes, have left their visible marks, outstripping in courage, in feats of arms, and in swiftness of foot, all the younger warriors that fight at his side, and to see him rallying their fainting hearts by the strength of his own. Veterans in the hosts of Emmanuel, see then your duty! On you it devolves to train the young recruits, and form their character: let them feel that they are by the side of heroes, and catch the inspiration of your heroism. Cast over them your shadow while you live, and they will then be anxious to find your mantle when your spirit has dropped it in her flight to the skies. Let them see you intent upon the conversion of sinners, given up to your work of saving souls; and hear in your conversation how much your heart is set upon this work. Show them, by the manner in which you are finishing your course, how they ought to begin and carry forward theirs. Correct their mistakes, elevate their aims, and inflame their zeal. Do all you can, by your private intercourse with them, to form their character aright for the service of the Lord. Talk to them modestly of your own success in the ministry, and how you succeeded in this high and glorious achievement. What manner of men ought ye to be, by whom the ardor of others will be kindled or extinguished? May God's grace be sufficient for you.

But of what momentous consequence is it that our *younger* ministers and *students* should give to this subject its due attention. You have advantages which some who have gone before you never enjoyed, and which at times make them almost envy your privileges; but if this be all you seek, if it be the best and the highest object you aspire to, you have mistaken your way in going to the pulpit, and had better, whatever of literature you may acquire, have drudged out life in one of the darkest of its recesses, or the humblest of its occupations, than to have entered the Christian ministry. Oh, what scenes attract your attention, and ought to engage your energies. There around you are immortal souls perishing in their sins, each one of more value than the whole material universe, each capable of being saved by your ministrations, or sure to acquire by them a deeper guilt and a heavier condemnation—there, in sight of your faith, is the Son of God, bleeding upon the cross for their redemption—there beneath you is the pit of hell, opening wide its mouth to receive them, if they die in unbelief—there above you is heaven, throwing back its everlasting portals to receive them, if they are saved—there before you is the bar of judgment, at which you must soon meet them, to account for your ministry in reference to them—and there, beyond all, is eternity with its ever-rolling ages, which are to be spent by them and you in rapture or in woe. Is this true? Is it fiction or is it fact? If these things are not so, you are found false witnesses for Christ, for they are the common topics and the first principles of your discourses; but if they are all realities, then with what state of mind and heart should they be handled? Begin your ministry, beloved young brothers, with a clear understanding of its nature, and a deep impression of its importance. Do you covet usefulness? Earnestness is essential to it. You cannot do good, at least in any extensive degree, without it. Listen to those who have gone before you; their testimony is founded both upon experience and observation. All, all will unite in this exhortation, "Be in earnest;" as well the very men who have had least, as those who have exhibited most, of this quality of character, and mode of action. Without this you cannot even be popular, to say nothing of usefulness. The public will hear an earnest minister, and will not hear any other. You may call this, if you will, bad taste, and wonder they will not listen to your highly intellectual and philosophical discourses, and be ready in resentment to withdraw the elaborate preparations they so little value, and retire from the pulpit. No matter whether they or you are wrong, this is the fact. He is an unwise tradesman, who, because he thinks the public taste is vicious, and ought to be corrected, will exhibit in his window, and place upon his shelves, no other goods than those the public will not buy. In this case the taste of the public may be wrong, and that of the tradesman right; but in the case of preaching, if the people demand an earnest exhibition of gospel truth, and the ministry instead of this will give them nothing but dull, dry, abstract sermons, it is they who are right, and he is wrong; they, better than he does, know not only what they want, but what he was appointed by God to furnish them. Do not then mistake, and determine to try to be useful in some other way than that which the God of nature and of grace has determined upon. Do not resolve to try the experiment of opening a new road to usefulness for yourself; another way than that which apostles, martyrs, and reformers have trod, and which the ministers and missionaries of every age and every country have found to be the power of God unto salvation, even the doctrine of the cross; a way which you may deem more befitting the talents of a scholar, and an age of philosophy. You will inevitably go wrong if you do, and close your career lamenting your folly, and confessing that your ministerial life has been a lost adventure; a melancholy confession, and one that is not unfrequently made. God gives to no man in any department of action more than one life, and affords to none an opportunity to live through another term of existence, and to profit by his own experience; but he gives abundant opportunity to avail ourselves of the knowledge gained by trial, as it goes on, and by extensive observation. You have known enough, and seen enough already of what will do, and what will not do, to answer the ends of your office, and save souls. You have only to look back, and to look around, to find evidence to guide you. You cannot mistake your means easily, if you do not mistake your object. Settle with yourselves what is the latter—that it is to save sinners by leading them to repent of sin, to believe on Christ, and to lead a holy life; and then you can scarcely fail to perceive that this never has been accomplished, and ordinarily never can be, but by beseeching them and praying them, in Christ's stead, to be reconciled to God.

We who are growing gray in the service of Christ, feel somewhat anxious about those who are to succeed us. We see with gratitude and wonder what God has wrought by us; and we know how, as instruments, we have done this thing. We see how souls have been converted, churches have risen up, and believers have lived and died in the faith, and know full well that it was under the testimony of the gospel, plainly but energetically stated. In looking back we often feel regret that the activities of the age have taken from us the opportunity to make greater attainments in elegant literature and general knowledge, but none that we have made the great theme of Christ crucified the subject of our ministry, and the salvation of souls the object of our lives. We feel amidst the gathering shadows of evening, a calm and sweet satisfaction that in this we have made a right choice; mingled at the same time with a profound humiliation that we have not followed it with more intensity of devotion. We see many things in the review of the past that we would alter, but we would make no alteration in these matters; much that we could improve, but only in the manner by which we could more successfully accomplish this object: and if it *were* permitted us to live over again our existence, or, to speak more correctly, to spend another term, and set out afresh, it would be our high resolve to get more of what the men of science and literature admire, but only to enable us to preach with greater power the doctrine of the cross, and to be better qualified to seek with more ardor, and better hopes of success, the end of our ministry. The love of applause, and we have all too much of it, is, we hope, dying in our hearts, or at any rate appears to be more and more worthless in its object, and the approval of the great Master more and more intensely desired. Whether we look back upon the past, or consider the complexion of our feelings for the present, or look at the prospects and anticipate the disclosures of the future, we know of no arguments cogent enough, no language sufficiently expressive, by which to enforce upon our younger brethren in the ministry, and in reference to the purpose of their lives, the important admonition, BE IN EARNEST.

VII. *Considerable care and caution are requisite, much more than has been exercised hitherto, in the introduction and reception of young men to our colleges.* Incompetent ministers are the burden, as inconsistent ones have been the dishonor, of every section of the church, and the hindrance of the progress of the gospel in the world. In hearing many of them, one is ready to wonder how it ever entered into their hearts to conceive they had been called of God to a work for which they seemed to possess scarcely a single qualification beyond their piety; and the wonder is doubled to account for it that any minister could recommend them, or any committee receive them: without intellect, without heart, and equally without voice, they seem sent into the ministry only to keep out others more competent for the work. How many have been permitted to escape from the pursuits of business, in which they might have done well, to endure the greatest privations, and submit to the most humiliating mortifications, in an office for the functions of which they were deplorably unfit. How many of them have passed through life in the misery of being amidst a discontented people, or in wandering from place to place without remaining with any church long. Such cases have been found in every age and in every denomination, but they were never so numerous as they are now. A spirit of fastidiousness has crept over the churches, and of unsettledness over their pastors. How great then is the responsibility of recommending a young man to enter the ministry. It is an act drawing after it consequences of a most momentous nature, and should never be done without the utmost care and caution. It would be well if ministers would call in others to bear the burden with them, and to share the responsibility. It may in some cases expose a pastor to some risk of giving offence, if in the exercise of his fidelity he should discourage the aspirations of an unsuitable candidate; an evil from which he would be sheltered, at least in part, by referring the case to the consideration of two or three of the brethren in the vicinity. It is not, however, the pastor only who should be cautioned about recommending candidates, but the committees of our colleges should be no less careful about receiving them. It is extremely difficult by a first examination, or even by a probationary term, to judge of eligibility and fitness: as great excellence in some cases lies hidden under a very uncouth and unpromising exterior, and in others is very slow to develop itself; while, on the contrary, in a different class, a showy exterior, over a shallow substratum, is so deceptive, that not only months, but even years must roll on, before the necessary qualifications can be determined upon. A false delicacy, however, has sometimes led all our committees to retain young men in the college of whose unfitness there remained no question, rather than put them and their friends to the pain of recommending them to discontinue their studies and return to trade. It should be recollected, that to carry on the education of those of whom there is no rational probability that they will ever attain to usefulness of any kind, either as authors, tutors, or preachers, is on the part of the committee a betrayal of their trust, and a malversation of the funds intrusted to their care. Let there be then a far greater degree of care and discrimination exercised in the initiative by our pastors than there has been: ten earnest men are better, and will do more for us, than a hundred incompetent ones. It would be better that many of the churches should remain longer without a pastor, than gain an unsuitable one; just as it is a far more endurable evil for a man who wishes for connubial felicity to endure the privations of celibacy any length of time, than to hurry from those into the miseries of an unhappy marriage. We *must* be more careful in the selection, the reception, and the retention of our students, than we have been. Since it is so difficult to find an egress for those who are once in, it is highly incumbent upon us to watch with greater vigilance the door of entrance.

VIII. *There is no class of men to whom we can look so naturally or with so much entreaty for their aid in furnishing us with devoted ministers, as our tutors.* If the college be the mould in which the preacher and pastor are cast, the tutor is the man who shapes the mould, and pours into it the metal. How much then depends upon these beloved and honored brethren. What a trust is reposed with them, how solemn, how awful, how responsible! If it be a momentous thing for a pastor to have the care of a single church, how much more so, for a tutor to have the care of twenty or thirty youthful minds, each of which is looking forward to the pastorate; and to have these replaced by others every five years! Such an occupation is enough to make the stoutest heart to tremble under an oppressive sense of its responsibilities. The strength of our churches lies in our ministry; of our ministry in our colleges; and of our colleges in our tutors. There is nothing about which we ought to be more anxious than about this part of our system. Happily, to whatever department of ministerial education we look, whether to the philological, mathematical, or philosophical; whether to hermeneutical or dogmatical theology, we find in our various academic institutions, professors of whom we need not be, and are not ashamed. If we need improvement anywhere, it is in the homiletical and pastoral. We can scarcely wonder that, in such an age as this, our professors should be anxious to push forward their alumni as far as possible into the regions of literature and science; or that they should feel a solicitude, now that the London University gives an opportunity to Nonconformists for obtaining academic degrees and honors, to give full proof of their official assiduity in the distinctions won by their students in these laudable contests for scholastic fame; but at the same time it is well for them to remember that while these things are not neglected, one popular, earnest, and successful preacher will bring more real credit to their college, and give it more favor with the public, than a dozen Bachelors of Arts, and half-a-dozen Masters to boot. The occasional exhibition, and it can be but occasional, of the titular letters affixed to a man's name, will not often excite the inquiry, "Where was he educated?" but the constant exhibition and effect of his preaching powers will be a public and permanent recommendation of the institution where such a character was formed. It is true that natural preaching talents will grow in almost any soil, and under almost any culture; but it may still be carried to a higher degree of perfection in one place, and by one hand, than another. There is also such a thing as colleges gaining an identifying character, one for turning out better scholars, a second for giving more philosophy, and a third for carrying on a better theological training; but that in the long run will be the most useful, and deservedly the most popular, which succeeds in sending forth the greatest number of earnest and successful preachers.

All earnestness has a tinge of enthusiasm about it, and as no man can kindle enthusiasm in the soul of another who has none of this mental fire in himself, our tutors should have some fire, though with judgment enough to keep it in its proper place, and to do its proper work: and however enthusiastic they may be for classical, scientific, and philosophical studies, let them concentrate their energies, their aims, and their hopes in the formation of the popular, powerful, and useful preacher. They who know how much there is to do with many young men that enter our seats of learning, and how much of necessity the time and attention must be divided among the various objects of study, will confess that it is no easy matter to give that prominence to homiletics which their supreme importance demands. But, notwithstanding this, opportunities will continually present themselves to an anxious and observant professor for inculcating upon his students that all he is teaching them will be useless, if they do not make it subservient to their great business in preaching the gospel and converting sinners. But it is of especial importance that our tutors should be much upon the alert when the students begin to preach, that these young men in their first pulpit labors should select the true subject of all preaching, pursue it by the right course, and seek it with due vigor.

What a student is in his first essays at pulpit effect, that he is likely to be through life; and if there be no earnestness then, there is likely to be little afterwards. It happens that as all excellencies rarely combine in one man, many of our professors, though so highly gifted as regards talent and acquirement, are not all of them distinguished as preachers, and therefore can present in themselves no living models of what pulpit power, as to manner, really is. Still, they who cannot illustrate it by example, can teach it by precept. May they see the importance of the subject, and labor to the utmost to inculcate it upon the youth that are looking up to them for instruction, and labor to the utmost to kindle in their breast the ardor of a pulpit enthusiasm!

We can easily imagine with what delight they must sometimes witness the advance in extensive and accurate scholarship, in analytical power, in logical acuteness, in metaphysical subtlety; and in some rare cases may felicitate themselves on such results of their labor, though they can foresee they will never be associated with pulpit efficiency—but, as a general rule, nothing should gratify, much less satisfy them, with reference to their students, short of adaptation for popular effect. The demand preferred by our country upon the military schools is, "Give us soldiers;" upon our medical colleges, "Give us skilful surgeons and physicians;" upon our Inns of Court, "Give us lawyers." The cry sent up to our colleges is, "Give us powerful preachers, devoted pastors,"—nor will it do to meet *this* demand, any more than it would the others, by replying, "We will send you Bachelors and Masters of Arts." Much less will it do to send men who will feed the churches with the dry and sapless verbal exegesis of German theology, instead of the sweet and succulent expositions of our Scotts, our Henrys, our Wardlaws, and our BARNESES. Ministers may study the profoundest criticisms for their own improvement, and carry on a course of exegetic exposition in the pulpit; but it must be of a character that shall combine impression with instruction; and let our tutors aim to train preachers, who shall make their sermons expository, their expositions sermonic, and both instinct with life, and essentially popular. Let them with the men they send into our churches, give us as much as they can of everything which can polish the taste, inform or even adorn the intellect, and give weight and influence to the character in general society—the more of all this the better; but let them never forget that what is always wanted for the momentous subject of religion, and what is especially wanted in these times of intense earnestness, is a race of ministers as earnest as the times in which they live. May God help them to train such ministers for us!

IX. If it be the duty of the churches to call out a ministry, *it must of course be no less their duty to provide the means for the education of those who compose it.* Among all the objects of Christian benevolence, there is not one which has a prior or a stronger claim than our collegiate institutions, and yet it is too true that they are the last whose demands are properly regarded. Among Protestant Dissenters especially, the main pivot of their whole system is their ministry; upon this everything, under God, must turn. As this is strong, everything else amongst us will be strong; and as this is weak, everything else will be weak. The springs which supply the reservoirs of our evangelizing societies, both at home and abroad, are to be traced back to our colleges; and yet, the churches do not yet seem, if we may judge from their conduct, to be duly aware of this fact. They are not however to be considered as eleemosynary institutions, where a race of literary paupers are sustained by the alms of the affluent; for it is becoming increasingly the practice for our students to pay for their own board; but beyond this, we have the invaluable services of our professors to reward, and many other expenses to defray. This must be borne by the churches, in all cases where there is no vested property, or where it is not adequate to the support of the institution. How can property be better applied? What expenditure produces a quicker or more abundant return? A good education for our ministry is cheaply obtained at any price; and every shilling we expend in this way tells at once, and before our eyes, upon the object for which it is intended. And yet, strange to say, there is no object for which we find it more difficult to obtain a regular and adequate supply of means. Foreign and home missions have an annual collection from almost every church in our denomination, and yet how few are there of these churches who grant an annual collection for any college, and what multitudes who never grant a collection at all! The platform is the stage of modern activity, but our colleges can make no exhibition there; we can employ no succession of orators to advocate our cause by speeches in support of resolutions; can exhibit no foreigners; can produce no excitement by tales of horror, of pathos, or of adventure; yet where would be the platform, but for the pulpit, and what is the pulpit without the college? We ought not, it is true, to do less for our other organizations, but we ought to do far more for our educational system. We must bestir ourselves, and not allow this, on which everything depends, to fall into the rear and to pass into the shadow of one or two deservedly popular societies. If a larger part of the zeal manifested in arguing for our voluntary principle were employed in a more liberal support of our denominational institutions, they would be in a far better state than they now are. With all our ardor in the cause of Nonconformity, it is easier to raise large funds for other objects of benevolence than for this. The London Missionary Society, which is chiefly supported by the Congregational body, has an income of nearly eighty thousand pounds a year, while that same body does not raise, by voluntary contributions, more, perhaps, than eight or nine thousand for our seats of learning; and even this is not so economically expended as it might be by a consolidation of our colleges. It is high time this whole system were looked into.

It is, however, somewhat cheering to know that this subject is *beginning* to be understood by our churches, and a more just appreciation to be made by the intelligence of the age of the value of an educated ministry; and as a natural consequence there is springing up a more general disposition to support the expense which it incurs. Many instances have occurred of late of the owners of property apportioning a large share of it either in the way of founding colleges or establishing scholarships for the education of young men for the ministry. An individual who founds one of these scholarships may, if he give his property at at the age of thirty-five, and should live to be seventy, have six or seven ministers preaching the gospel at the same time, who were educated by his means; and when he has reached his heavenly home, may welcome to glory through a long succession of ages the souls that were saved by the labors of those ministers for whose education he had set apart his property. How laudable and how noble an object of honorable ambition does such a proposal present to those who have at once the wish and the means to do good. Let the churches collectively, and their wealthy members individually, well consider, then, the obligation, which is laid upon them to provide all that may be necessary to insure the education of a ministry adapted to the circumstances of this extraordinary age.

CHAPTER XI.

ON THE NECESSITY OF DIVINE INFLUENCE FOR AN EFFICIENT MINISTRY.

THIS work would be essentially defective in the estimation both of its author and its readers, if, after so much has been advanced about instrumentality, nothing were to be said about the agency which is necessary to render it effectual for the accomplishment of its object. In all Divine operations, whether in the world of nature or of grace, God employs a chain of dependent means for the working out of his purposes and plans; but though dependent, they are appropriate. In acknowledging, as we must do, the adaptation of these means to the production of the intended result, we do homage to his wisdom; while in confessing their dependence for efficiency upon his blessing, we do no less homage to his power and grace. There is no analogy which we can borrow from the world of nature that can satisfactorily illustrate the operation of Divine grace on the human mind. We know very well that second causes in the material universe depend for their efficiency upon Divine influence; but it is an influence of a totally different kind, and exerted altogether in a different manner from that of which we now write; and we are very little aided in our perceptions of the nature of the

Spirit's operation upon the human mind, by anything we observe in the world of vegetable or animal life. There are two aspects in which man is to be viewed in relation to the means employed for his salvation, as both a rational and a sinful creature; or as a rational creature whose reason is under the dominion of sin: consequently, whatever method be adopted for his salvation, he must be dealt with in both these views of his condition. His fallen state as a sinner has not bereft him of his reason, will, and responsibility; but his reason and will alone will never lift him out of his condition as a fallen sinner. He cannot be dealt with otherwise than he is, and as a rational creature he must be treated as such, and not as a brute or a block. His intellect must be appealed to by argument, and his heart by motives. Now it will be seen that in the means of grace, and especially in preaching, there is a provision for all this. Here is truth to be presented to the intellect, truth which represents the whole state of the case between God and the sinner, the nature and obligations of the moral law, the exceeding sinfulness of sin, the weight of the tremendous penalty of the violated precept, the wonderful love of God in the provision he has made for the salvation of the sinner, with the eternal results of misery or bliss which follow upon faith and unbelief. In all this, there is something in its own nature adapted to engage the attention and to interest the heart of the sinner. It is not only the truth, but just the truth that suits his condition. In addition to this, there is in preaching the adaptation of the manner as well as the matter to his circumstances, the tendency of the living voice, and ministerial solicitude, and earnest elocution, to engage the intellect and impress the heart. It will follow, of course, that earnestness is a part of this well-adapted system of means, and the more earnest a man is, the more likely, so far as means go, is he to do good; for if it be the *matter* which God blesses to change the heart, it is also the *manner* which he blesses to fix the attention preparatory to this change: there is as obvious an adaptation in the latter as in the former. How comes it to pass that there is greater efficiency usually attendant upon hearing the word, than there is upon reading it? Just because there is a greater adaptation to fix attention and to impress the heart; and by the same rule we argue there is more adaptation to do this in one man's manner, than in that of another. Hence we see that those preachers are the most successful, whom, independently of a Divine power, we might expect to be so. This does not disprove the necessity of a Divine influence, but only shows what order of instrumentality it is that the Divine Spirit usually employs, and consequently what instrumentality we should select. As God does not usually bless ignorance, or dullness, or obscurity, or feebleness, we should avoid these; and to look for great results from them, is to expect not only what God has not promised, but what he very rarely bestows without having promised it. Thus God deals with us as rational creatures, by presenting to us that truth, and requiring us to understand and believe it, the reception of which into the heart changes the whole character and conduct.

But then there is in the heart of man, not only an indifference, but an opposition to this truth; both a disrelish for, and a dislike to it. "The carnal mind is enmity against God, and is not subject to the law of God, neither indeed can be." The heart so blinds the judgment, that "the natural man discerneth not the things of the Spirit of God, neither indeed can he know them, because they are spiritually discerned." Therefore, however the attention may be gained by the manner, and gained it must be in order to conversion, yet the heart is still opposed to the truth; hence the need of the Spirit's influence to subdue this resistance of the heart to truth itself. Now here it will be perceived is the concurrence of the truth and the Spirit in conversion—conversion is the sinner being brought to know and love the objects presented in the truth—therefore the truth must be presented to the intellect in order that it might be thus known and loved; but then it never will be so loved, however theoretically understood. till the Spirit takes away the disrelish for it which is in the heart. Without the truth, there is nothing to engage the attention and employ the intellect of man, as a rational being; without the Spirit, there is no inclination of the heart, when the truth is so presented. If a certain quality of an object be the ground of dislike to it, an increasing knowledge of the object and of this quality cannot in the nature of things subdue our hostility; the taste must be changed ere the object can be relished. It is precisely thus with the sinner and the truth; he dislikes the gospel for its holiness, and no increase of light will vanquish enmity. Consequently, whatever be the earnestness of the preacher's manner, or whatever be the clearness of his matter, no saving result will follow, unless the Spirit give his blessing. Yet preaching is as necessary as if all were done by this alone, without the Spirit, because it is by this order of means that the Spirit works in the conversion of sinners. And since it is by appropriate means that he accomplishes his purposes, there is nothing in this doctrine to discourage exertion. There are means which carry in themselves the rational hope, if not promise, of success. God will not accept the lame for sacrifice, nor send down the signs of his approval on the service which involves no real effort of heart or mind in his cause. No: the influence of the Holy Spirit comes not as a bounty upon indolence, but as a stimulus to exertion. Its office is not to give the human faculties a license to slumber, but to supply them with motives to watchfulness. Its descent upon the church is not as the creeping torpor which betokens disease, but as an element of activity bespeaking moral and spiritual health. This blessed influence is unquestionably sovereign in the dispensation of it. God giveth it in such measures, on such occasions, and to such instruments, as it seemeth good unto him. He that directeth the course of the clouds, and causeth them to drop their treasures where and when he pleaseth, makes the dew of his grace, and the rain of his Spirit, to fall according to the counsel of his own will. There is no such necessary connection between the exhibition of the truth and the conversion of the soul as there is between the application of fire and the combustion of inflammable matter. The apostle says, "Who then is Paul, and who is Apollos, but ministers by whom ye believed, even as the Lord gave to every man? I have planted, Apollos watered, but God gave the increase. So then neither is he that planteth anything, neither he that watereth; but God that giveth the increase." 1 Cor. iii. 5, 7. One should think it impossible to mistake the meaning of this language, or to doubt whether special Divine influence be necessary for the conversion of the soul, or whether the communication of it be a prerogative of Divine sovereignty.

Still there is every ground to expect the influence we need. It is our privilege to live under the dispensation of the Spirit, as well as under that of the Messiah. The former of these follows the latter: or perhaps, more correctly speaking, they are identical; the covenant established in Christ's blood *is* the economy of the Spirit. The ministry of reconciliation *is* the ministry of the Spirit. We do not mean to assert that this Divine influence is confined to the Christian economy, for since the beginning of time hath no soul been converted or sanctified but by this heavenly power; but the communications before the coming of Christ were limited, partial, and scanty, compared with what they have been since: they constituted not the shower, but only the drops which precede it. Hence the language of the evangelist, "This spake ye of the Spirit, which they that believe on him should receive: for the Holy Ghost was not yet given; because that Jesus was not yet glorified." John vii. 39. This idea, that we are under the Spirit's economy, should enlarge our expectation of the richest communication of this invaluable and essential blessing. The view we have given of Divine sovereignty is not intended, nor, when rightly understood, is it even calculated, to discourage hope, but simply to teach dependence. While God reserves to himself the right of bestowment, and acts upon his own rules of communication, he warrants and invites the most expansive requests, and the largest anticipations. Since he has promised to give the boon in answer to the prayer of faith, it would seem to be our own fault that we have it not in more abounding measure. The very recollection of our privilege, as placed under such an economy, might seem to be enough to call forth our prayers, and to awaken our expectations. Instead of being surprised that we receive so much of this Divine power on our ministry at any time, even the most successful periods of our history, we should be surprised that we receive so little, and inquire after the cause of obstruction. In a country like Egypt, where rain seldom falls, the shower is the exception, and a dry atmosphere the general rule; but in our variable climate, the long drought is the rarity, and the frequent shower is the common occurrence. The husbandman ploughs and sows in this land, with his expectant eyes upon the heavens, and feels disappointed if the fertilizing rain is withheld. So should it be with us, in reference to the shower of God's grace. We are not under the dry and arid atmosphere of the Levitical economy, but we enjoy the privilege of the cloud-dropping, rain-falling dispensation of the Spirit; and with us the question should be, Why have we not more of this Divine influence? what has provoked the Lord to withhold from us the genial influences of his grace? Instead of being at any time astonished that our ministry is so much blessed, we should inquire why it is not always so. When we consider what is said, that God "willeth not the death of a sinner, but would rather that he should repent and turn from his wickedness and live;" when we recollect what he has done for the salvation of sinners; when we add to this, that the gospel is his own truth, and preaching his own institution; we are sometimes ready to wonder that he does not pour out that influence which is necessary to give effect to the purposes of his own benevolence, and almost to inquire, "What does the Lord now wait for?" In answer to this it might be replied, "He waits for the earnest labors of his ministers, the faith of his church, and the believing prayers of both."

It is quite perceptible that the necessity of Divine influence is rather a dogma of faith than a principle of practice, both with ministers and their flocks. Did the people really believe it, were it matter of inwrought conviction, and were there the least seriousness of spirit in their religion, how much less dependence would there be upon men, how much less said about talent, how much less homage paid to genius and eloquence, and how much more looking up to God by intense and persevering supplication. Recollecting that God works by means, and by means adapted to promote the end, there would be no danger of sinking into an enthusiastic and irrational neglect of these, while on the contrary there would be more constant and serious attendance upon them. The knowledge that preaching, and especially earnest preaching, is the Spirit's instrumentality, would lead men to seek that very instrumentality, in order that they might have the blessing. How highly would it exalt the minister to consider him as the Spirit's instrument, and how important would it make the sermon to view it as God's means to bless the soul. It is immeasurably to sink both, to view them apart from God's agency; it is to cease to view the preacher as an ambassador for Christ, and instead of this, to listen to him only as the lecturer on religion. With what sacred awe would he be heard, and with what fervent prayer, too, by those who viewed him as the appointed medium of that influence, which, if it be received, would illuminate, renew, and sanctify the soul?

But if it be incumbent on the people to remember the dependence of means upon the Divine blessing, how much more is it the duty of ministers themselves. It is an article of our creed, it is often the subject of our sermons, and it is acknowledged in our prayers; but after all, is our conviction of dependence upon the Spirit so deep, so practical, and so constant, as to prevent us from attempting anything in our own strength, and to impel us to be strong only in the Lord, and in the power of his might? Do we conduct the pursuits of the study, as well as regulate the prayers of the closet, by this conviction? Do we with childlike simplicity, and in the very spirit we inculcate upon our hearers in reference to their own personal salvation, habitually give ourselves up to the guidance and blessing of this Divine agent? Do we look up for wisdom to guide us in the selection of our texts and the composition of our sermons? Do the eye and the heart go up to heaven, as we think and write for the people? Do we go to our pulpit in a praying frame, as well as in a preaching frame—praying even while we preach, for our people as well as for ourselves? Do we thus clothe ourselves with Omnipotence, and go forth as with the Lord ever before us. Do we recollect that from all that crowd of immortal souls before us, we shall gather nothing but human praise or censure, except the Lord be with us; that not one dark mind will be illumined, not one hard heart softened, not one inquiring soul directed, not one wounded spirit healed, not one uneasy conscience appeased, unless God the Spirit do it? Do we really want to accomplish these objects, or merely to deliver a sermon that shall please the people, and gratify our own vanity? If the former, how entire, how confident, how believing, should be our sense of dependence upon something far higher than the best and most appropriate instrumentality! Such a feeling of dependence would cramp none of the energies of our soul, would stunt none of our powers, quench none of our fire, repress none of our intensity of manner. So far from this, we should derive from it unspeakable advantage in addressing our hearers; a seriousness, tenderness, and majesty would pervade our discourses, beyond what the greatest unassisted talent could command; a something superhuman would rest upon us, a Divine glory would irradiate us, and we should speak in power and demonstration of the Spirit. "Possessed of this celestial unction, we should be under no temptation to neglect a plain gospel, in quest of amusing speculations and unprofitable novelties; the most ordinary topics would open themselves with a freshness and interest, as though we had never considered them before; and the things of the Spirit would display their inexhaustible variety and depth. We shall pierce the invisible world, we shall look, so to speak, into eternity, and present the very essence of religion, while too many preachers, for want of spiritual discernment, rest satisfied with the surface and the shell. We shall not allow ourselves to throw one grain of incense on the altar of vanity, and shall forget ourselves so completely as to convince our hearers we do so; and, displacing everything else from the attention, leave nothing to be felt or thought of but the majesty of truth and the realities of eternity."* The preacher who cherishes such a frame of mind will appear with a radiance not less dazzling perhaps than that of genius, but far more sacred, heavenly, and divine; and when carried to his highest pitch of earnestness and dependence, seems almost to reach that sublime symbol of the Apocalypse, of the angel standing in the sun.

"But this kind goeth not forth but by fasting and prayer." A deep, practical conviction of the need of the Spirit, would make us men of prayer, would send us much to our closets, and keep us there. Here perhaps is the cause why we have not more success in our ministry, and are not more frequently and more heartily gladdened by the conversion of souls to God: we seek to be men of the pulpit merely, and are not sufficiently men of the closet. It is a mystery in God's moral government that he should make the commu-

* Mr. HALL on the Discouragements and Support of the Christian Ministry.

nication of his grace for the salvation of sinners dependent in any degree upon the prayers of others: yet he does so, and we know it: and yet knowing it, how little have we been affected by it and stirred up to prayer on this account. We have uttered our complaints of the fruitlessness of our ministry long enough before one another; but, as the BISHOP of CALCUTTA says in his introduction to the "Reformed Pastor," "One day spent in fasting and prayer to God is worth a thousand days of complaint and lamentation before men." The author of this work can assure his brethren that it is not with any disposition to accuse them, and exalt or exculpate himself, that he writes thus. He takes his full share of blame in the deficiency of a spirit of fervent prayer, and his full share of humiliation too, on that account. The activities of the age, which require us to be so much in public, may furnish some mitigation of blame, if not an excuse, for the too little time spent in the fervor of private prayer. Devotion is damped by business. Still, even with this palliation, we are verily guilty, for we do not pray as if we believed we were sent to save souls from death and could not be successful in a single instance without the grace of God. Who of us can read the diaries of such men as DODDRIDGE, and BRAINERD, and PAYSON, and MARTYN, and very many others, and not stand reproved for our lamentable deficiency in the exercise of prayer? Perhaps in modern times there was never so much of social prayer, and never less of private. We introduce all our business transactions with prayer, and too often in a kind of business spirit, and with a sad want of sincerity, seriousness, and deep devotion; so that the very frequency and want of reverence with which we engage in these exercises of devotion, tend to diminish the spirit of prayer. Nothing is more to be dreaded than a depression of the spirit of devotion, and nothing more intensely to be desired, than its elevation. A praying ministry must be an earnest one, and an earnest ministry a praying one. Let us then feel ourselves called upon by all the circumstances of the times, to abound more and more in fervent supplications. Let us, if we can in no other way command more time for prayer, take it from study or from sleep. We have neither right nor reason to expect the Spirit, if we do not ask for his gracious influence, and without him we can do nothing. Let us take care lest a bustling activity, and the endless multiplication of societies, should supplant, instead of calling forth, as they ought to do, a feeling of intense devotion. We never more needed prayer, we were never in more danger of neglecting it. There is plausibility in the excuse that we had better abridge the time of praying than the time of acting. But it will be found in the end that doings carried on at the sacrifice of prayer, will end in confusion and vanity. A public spirit, even in the cause of religion, however prevalent or energetic, if it be not maintained in a feeling of dependence upon God, will be regarded by him as the image of jealousy in the temple, which maketh jealous. Our sermons are the power of men, or perhaps we might say, their weakness; but our prayers are in a modified sense the power of God. Let us not slacken in preaching, but let us quicken in devotion; let us not quench a ray of intellect, but let us add to it the warmth of devotion; let us labor as if the salvation of souls depended upon our own unaided energies, and then let us feel as did the apostle when he said, "though I be nothing." The eternal destinies of our hearers hang not only upon our sermons, but upon our prayers; we carry out the purposes of our mission, not only in the pulpit, but in the closet; and may never expect to be successful ministers of the New Covenant, but by this two-fold importunity of first beseeching sinners to be reconciled to God, and then beseeching God to pour out his Spirit upon them: thus we honor his wisdom in the use of the means he has appointed, and then his power by confessing our dependence upon his grace.

BAXTER concludes his "Reformed Pastor," with an expression of his confidence in the usefulness of the book he had written, which it would be unwarrantable and ridiculous vanity in me to adopt in reference to mine, at least in any other way than that of hope and prayer, and in this spirit I borrow the language of that great and holy man, and say, "I have now, brethren, done with my advice, and leave you to the practice. Though the proud receive it with scorn, and the selfish and slothful with distaste, or even with indignation, I doubt not but God will use it, in despite of the opposition of sin and Satan, to the awakening of many of his servants to their duty, and to the promotion of a work of right reformation; and that his blessing will accompany the present undertaking for the saving of many souls, the peace of you that understand and perform it, the exciting of his servants throughout the nation to second you, and the increase of the purity and unity of his churches. Amen."

THE END.

www.ingramcontent.com/pod-product-compliance
Lightning Source LLC
LaVergne TN
LVHW010218110826
845151LV00004B/1130

* 9 7 8 1 4 2 5 5 2 7 0 7 5 *